Ghost Tracks
What history, science, and fifty years of field research have revealed about ghosts, evil, and life after death

by

Cheryl A. Wicks
with Ed & Lorraine Warren

1663 Liberty Drive, Suite 200
Bloomington, Indiana 47403
(800) 839-8640
www.AuthorHouse.com

© 2004 Cheryl A. Wicks
All Rights Reserved.

No part of this book may be reproduced, stored in a retrieval system, or transmitted by any means without the written permission of the author.

First published by AuthorHouse 10/05/04

ISBN: 1-4184-6767-7 (sc)

Printed in the United States of America
Bloomington, Indiana

This book is printed on acid-free paper.

Table of Contents

An Introduction vii

SECTION I
Meet the Warrens

Who Are the Warrens? 1
How the Warrens Became Psychic Researchers 9
What Makes the Warrens Unique? 12
The Warrens Now 16
The Life of a Demonologist 24

SECTION II
Ghosts: Fact or Fiction? Harmless or Harmful?

Case Study #1 The Commander's Ghostly
                     Caretaker 46
Case Study #2 A Murdered Boy's Unrest 65
Case Study #3 A Ghostly Interview 86
Case Study #4 Water Poltergeist 100

SECTION III
Evil: Beast or Behavior?

Case Study #5 Amityville: Hoax or Horror 152
Case Study #6 Haunted by Evil 193
Case Study #7 Like Someone Possessed 207

SECTION IV

The Unexplained: Real or Ridiculous?

Case Study #8 Bigfoot in Tennessee 228
Case Study #9 Scottish Spirits 253

SECTION V

Paranormal Research: Snake Oil or Science?

Historic Summary 294
Psychic Research Observations 304

GLOSSARY 313

Endnotes 316

An Introduction

For more than fifty years, Ed and Lorraine Warren have been tracking ghosts and other paranormal phenomena around the world. Their popular interviews and lectures have provided thousands of people with insight into the unusual. The Warrens' credible work has also been the basis of two movies and now ten books.

Ghost Tracks pulls together five decades of field research experience, along with a historic, scientific, and religious perspective, to reveal that even the paranormal has predictable patterns of behavior. These patterns determine how the Warrens conduct a psychic investigation to discern what is happening and why.

The introductory summaries and real case studies that follow demonstrate what it is like to experience and research mysterious phenomena. This material is organized into five sections.

In Section I, The Warrens introduce themselves and explain how they became psychic investigators. Ed tells us what it means to be a **demonologist**.

Section II discusses **ghosts** and presents four case studies to illustrate this type of phenomenon. We see how an investigation with a valid psychic may be the only way to resolve mysterious manifestations that defy any other scientific explanation.

Section III explores **evil** infestations and presents demonic encounters through the words of the victims themselves—including an update from the former homeowners of the famous Amityville case, with corresponding pictures.

Section IV reviews the reality of unexplained **mysteries** that span many cultures as well as centuries. This incorporates reported sightings of Bigfoot and the challenge of identifying fraud during a psychic investigation.

Section V looks at what modern **science** says about the paranormal. This might be the most surprising revelation of all.

Come join us in seeking the supernatural and tracking ghosts to better understand what triggers the things that go bump in the night.

SECTION I

Meet the Warrens

Who Are the Warrens?

"Ed and I have been married for almost sixty years," Lorraine tells us as of this writing. "We have one daughter and a terrific son-in-law, and we are also grandparents and great-grandparents!"

Ed and Lorraine Warren reside in a modest, cottage-like house nestled among the mature trees and shrubs they planted decades before. They share their New England home with rescued pets and have a wild raccoon, turkey, and possum that show up regularly looking for the treats they have come to expect. Inside, the house is cozy with cluttered collections of knick-knacks covering every flat surface. Angels and crucifixes of all shapes, sizes, and designs are plentiful and prominent. In the basement, Ed and Lorraine each have an office separated by their Occult Museum.

Lorraine's office files bulge with contracts from lectures, book deals, thousands of speaking engagements, hundreds of television and radio guest spots, and numerous periodical articles featuring their work. Videos from television appearances, their own psychic investigations, and their cable show pack the small space. The room is brightened by three small windows and softened by a diverse assortment of pictures, pillows, and cute ceramic creatures. A lifetime collection of *New England Society for*

Cheryl A. Wicks

Psychic Research (NESPR) Journals is stacked in a corner. Correspondence via fax, printed e-mail, and post from around the world accumulate in unruly piles. Each piece details phenomena ranging from psychic photographs to ghostly hauntings and evil infestations.

Outside Lorraine's office door, and at the bottom of their cellar stairs, is a dimly-lit room with no windows. Large tables form a "T." An eclectic group of chairs surrounds the tables and room. The area is decorated in "spooky Halloween." Artifacts reflect the Warrens' humor as well as their work. It is here that many of the curious have been introduced to the Warrens' work, warned of its dangers, and enlightened by fascinating insights garnered from over fifty years of psychic investigation.

Those more inquisitive than nervous will venture through a long corridor lined with Ed's dramatic oil paintings of haunted houses. At the opposite end of this tunnel hunkers the Warrens' Occult Museum.

"This is said to be one of the most haunted places in the world," Ed tells his guests. "Most of the museum's collection has been used for the diabolical with dire effects ... leaving people maimed, insane, or dead. Some of these artifacts are still dangerous."

The L-shaped room is filled from floor to ceiling. Items range from skulls, horrific masks, disturbing sculptures, and a coffin to benign-looking trinkets, an organ, and a not-so-innocent Raggedy Ann doll confined to a glass case. It is near the outside door of this room that Ed has his office.

Inside Ed's office is a large desk, enveloped by shelves supporting books referencing the archaic lore of demonology. Photographs of Ed with monks and stone-faced exorcists dot the small wall space over his desk.

Audiotapes from thousands of interviews, taken from psychic investigations around the world are crammed in every available nook and cranny. An old chapel clock keeps time with loud ticks and periodic deep bongs that reverberate in both Ed's office and the museum just outside of it.

Yet, this is not a gloomy place. It is here that Ed has written some of his most peaceful and inspiring thoughts. It is here that Ed would strive to help as many people as he could and struggled to discern between those clients who are sincere and those who are unstable or simply seeking attention. With a steaming cup of coffee in front of him, he would lean back in his chair and listen to tapes over and over. It is also here that Ed would pray for guidance and support.

Ed is a barrel-chested, clean-shaven man with thinning gray hair and merry green eyes. His deep voice commands the attention of pets, grandchildren, and associate researchers. His sense of humor triggers both groans and smiles. His knowledge of the occult is exceptional, and not just from reading. His comprehension comes from studying and experiencing the consequences of such practices. He'll also tell you that much of his information seems to come from beyond his human experience. The most learned scholars will admit Ed has an uncanny awareness and understanding of evil phenomena.

Lorraine, meanwhile, is a lady in both manner and appearance. Her hair is always pulled back in a flattering, soft bun. She seems to have an endless supply of scarves and jewelry to complement her well-matched outfits. She is comfortable in skirts, stockings, and heels, even while exploring haunted ruins in England and Scotland. She favors Irish and Scottish tartans and carries them off well on her tall, slender frame. Her voice is always cheerful—her memory phenomenal. She enjoys meeting people and has always been described as outgoing. She practices genuine empathy towards people, wildlife, and pets. Lorraine is sensitive. Her feelings are easily hurt ...and she sees dead people.

"I was born Lorraine Moran in 1927 in Bridgeport, Connecticut, to a loving Irish family committed to fun, education, and religion," Lorraine explains. "My psychic abilities date back to the age of nine. It was while I attended Laurelton Hall (a prestigious private school in Milford, Connecticut) that I discovered that not everyone shared my ability to see auras and ghosts," she adds with a laugh. "My teachers—the nuns—expressed horror and dismay when I described the colored lights I saw outlining people's bodies. This was my first experience with the misunderstanding, fear, and alienation I am apt to encounter due to my clairvoyant abilities."

Fortunately, while Lorraine might have been shunned, she was not burned at the stake. Since the late 1800s, clairvoyant phenomena, telepathy, and ESP (extrasensory perception) have warranted the serious study of at least a portion of the scientific community—work that continues to this day.

In 1976, Lorraine learned about a Russian-designed Kirlian camera at UCLA that could see and photograph auras. She was intrigued about this instrument that could discern the same colored lights around people that she had seen since childhood. She flew out to this California university that year, immediately following their "Bigfoot in Tennessee" case.

While Lorraine was curious about the camera, Dr. Thelma Moss, a psychologist at the UCLA School of

Medicine, was curious about Lorraine's clairvoyant skills. Lorraine was tested, her skills verified, and her abilities identified as that of a "light trance medium." Unlike a "deep trance medium," Lorraine doesn't allow bodiless spirits to speak through her using her voice box.

Ed depends on his more mundane human senses to observe the paranormal. He was born in 1926—just four months before Lorraine. His family lived in the top story of a two-family home, across from a church in Bridgeport, Connecticut. Ed's beloved mother spent most of her life battling alcoholism. It didn't help that Ed's childhood home was haunted.

"Between the ages five and twelve, I was convinced I heard footsteps, along with pounding and rapping sounds when no one else was home. At night I would see the face of an unfriendly old woman in the darkness of my bedroom closet," Ed clarified.

"My older brother was never around while I was growing up. He always stayed overnight with friends instead of at home. It wasn't until we were both grown men that my brother admitted to being too afraid as a child to stay in a house full of unexplained sights and sounds that no adult would acknowledge.

"One night, my twin sister and I heard halting footsteps along with the tap of a cane, as if our grandfather was climbing up the stairs for his Sunday breakfast. However, it wasn't Sunday morning ... and our grandfather was dead! The scary footsteps and tap stopped with our mother's reassuring bedside visit. It wasn't until later, however, that we learned that our mother had been out of the house all evening to check on our grandmother, who died later that night. We then believed we had seen an angel in my mother's form."

While these experiences certainly seemed supernatural to Ed and his sister, his policeman father insisted there was a logical explanation. Yet, no plausible cause was offered or uncovered. Instead, his parents attributed these strange events to childhood imagination. Nonetheless, Ed's father was an extremely religious man who went to church every day, and encouraged Ed to trust in God based on faith. However, at the same time, Ed was discouraged from believing what his own ears and eyes were telling him. Ed's solution was to believe in both.

Lorraine and Ed met at the Colonial Movie Theater on Boston Avenue in Bridgeport, Connecticut. Ed was working as an usher there when Lorraine went with other girls from the St. Charles Christian Youth Group. Ed and Lorraine were only sixteen years old at the time.

While everyone was in the theater, there was an air raid, forcing them to leave. Ed offered to take Lorraine and her friends to a place called Rich's, where the floor and tabletops were marble, making it safe in case of another air raid. Lorraine's friends ordered five-cent Cokes, but Lorraine ordered an ice cream soda. Ed called her a "gold digger." Despite that, Lorraine was impressed with how neat, clean, and polite this young man was.

Later, they all walked home together; lurching with one foot on the curb while the other was on the road. They reached Ed's house first. As this boy ran up his front steps two at a time, Lorraine had a vision of Ed as a grown man. That evening, she wrote in her diary, "I just met Ed. I will spend the rest of my life with him."

When the relationship seemed to be growing serious, Ed's father extended only one bit of advice: "See how she treats her parents, and that is how she'll treat you." Lorraine and her parents were very close, with a relationship based on mutual respect as well as love—a relationship she would mimic in her marriage.

The tough kid and lady from Bridgeport fell in love and got engaged just as Ed turned seventeen and enlisted in the navy. Ed served with the U.S. Navy armed guard aboard a Merchant Marine ship during World War II. On February 5, 1945, Ed's ship came under enemy attack and caught fire while cruising the North Sea. Just before Ed jumped off the ship's bow, someone called his name and threw him a lifejacket. While Ed struggled to stay afloat in the icy waters, another sailor from Texas climbed on his back.

"We fought our way to another boat that also caught fire," Ed remembers. "Meanwhile, we were both in danger of becoming completely engulfed in flames in that oil-fueled water. I called on the protection of the Blessed Virgin Mary, and suddenly the fires miraculously parted around us. A PT boat was able to approach and rescue the man from my back. However, our rescuers feared the second ship was ready to explode, and I heard them say, 'Leave him.' The man I had saved insisted they save me, and I felt myself pulled up by my arm."

Lorraine interjects, "Stateside, I was frantic. Only sixty-nine men out of two ships survived the ordeal, and most of them were severely burned. For twenty-four hours, Ed was not listed among the survivors. Later I learned Ed was sent to the marine hospital in Staten Island, New York for treatment of a head injury. I was just recovering from surgery myself from a burst appendix. I had the doctor tape me up so I could visit Ed."

While Ed was on survivor leave, the Warrens got married in 1945. Ed returned to the Pacific Theater shortly thereafter. He received word of the birth of his only child, a daughter, while he was in Nagora, Japan after Hiroshima.

When Ed returned home from the service, he was still thin enough to hide behind a fencepost. Years rounded out his shape, but they never diminished his sense of humor, warm smile, direct approach, and curiosity about his unusual childhood and miraculous military experience. He has also remained devoted to the Blessed Mother Mary and convinced of the power of prayer.

The Warrens complement each other, with Ed's strength of character and tough street smarts balancing Lorraine's sophisticated graciousness and sensitivity. Together they share a firm sense of purpose and morality. They also enjoy a comfortable friendship in their long marriage. Their constant bantering entertains everyone who comes into contact with them.

Ed and Lorraine remain devoted Roman Catholics, feeling their work and discoveries have only enhanced their religious beliefs. Their research also gives them a sincere respect and reverence for all religions that encourage unconditional love. Their only objection to atheists and agnostics is their potential vulnerability to evil forces.

"If they unintentionally invite or encounter an evil infestation, they have no defenses," Ed explains. "In fact, evil will specifically target them for this reason." He adds, "It is said that there are no atheists in foxholes. Lorraine and I can tell you there are not many atheists in haunted houses either."

How the Warrens Became Psychic Researchers

"After I was discharged from the navy, I took art courses and painted country landscapes in oil," Ed begins. "Lorraine taught art at a local school. Despite the distractions of raising a child and making a living, we remained curious about our respective paranormal experiences. While touring the New England coastline harbors during summer tourist season to sell my paintings, Lorraine and I also sought out haunted sites."

The Warrens traveled the East Coast, year after year, in their cherished, 1933 black Chevy Eagle, purchased for just $15—a car they named Daisy. The vehicle still resides at their home, sitting outside their Occult Museum like a hearse from a different era.

One of the first detours the Warrens made to explore the mysterious was to the "Ocean-born Mary's" house in Henniker, New Hampshire. It was here that the ghost of Mary Wallace was said to return in a phantom coach drawn by six horses. It was also rumored that the pirate who built the house and invited Mary to live there, had hidden treasure under the hearthstone. Ed and Lorraine were only twenty-one and twenty years old respectively when they made this early visit.

Ed tells this story: "When the friend we were with refused to go up to the imposing house in the dark to see if we could be invited inside, I did the next logical thing. I threw Lorraine out of the car and locked the doors! I knew if anybody could get us in, it would be Lorraine. No one could refuse her Irish charm and persistence. My friend and I watched from our parked car as she made her way up the gloomy path to the front door. She knocked, and we saw a light in a window high above. The light traveled to the lower level and finally the door opened. Soon, we saw Lorraine motioning for us to join her."

Once inside, the Warrens discussed the house's reputation with the current owner, and reviewed the strange occurrences that had taken place since the owner took up residence. It was during this conversation that Lorraine had her first out-of-body experience. Since that first "investigation," Lorraine's psychic abilities have grown, along with her confidence in them. She quickly learned that more than the living were troubled and in need of help in haunted houses. During a subsequent visit to the same house, she and others present saw the apparition of "Ocean-born Mary," drifting down the steps.

What began as curiosity and a need for validation grew into an opportunity to help others resolve their own concerns and sense of sanity. To gain entrance to other reputed haunted places—without resorting to locking Lorraine out of the car—Ed painted eerie pictures of each house they wanted to investigate. Lorraine would subsequently offer the painting to the homeowners for free ... providing they were willing to share the ghost stories linked to the house.

Invariably, the residents were relieved and comforted to learn they were not alone in their strange experiences. After several interviews, the Warrens began to notice distinct similarities and patterns to the strange reported events. They also came to realize that while much of the phenomenon was benign in nature, some seemed deliberately destructive and malicious. Their information gathering took on a different objective—to truly understand so they could do more than commiserate with the people troubled by the phenomena.

Lorraine explains, "We began our investigations in the mid-1940s. We founded the New England Society for Psychic Research in 1950. However, it wasn't until the late sixties that our work became public. Our parish church was holding a fundraiser and they asked Ed to offer a painting or two for auction. Ed invited the planners over to choose the paintings, and found himself explaining the stories behind his collection of haunted house portraits. His guests were so intrigued that they asked Ed and I to offer those paintings, and share our stories."

At the time, the Warrens hesitated, reluctant to be labeled crackpots or sacrilegious. Also, as a painter, Ed had no public speaking experience and was uncomfortable with being the focus of attention. What finally motivated them to speak about the pictures they would present for auction was what has always motivated them. Perhaps someone could benefit from the experience and information they had accumulated.

Ed chuckles, "It turned out to be the most successful fundraiser the church ever had. Word spread and a line formed around the block of people who wanted to hear what we had to say."

Ed and Lorraine's matter-of-fact tone, dry humor, and genuine concern lent credibility to their experiences and observations. The crowds treated their tales with respect as well as curiosity, and listeners offered credible stories of their own. The Warrens have since followed this same format and kept their unassuming style through thousands of interviews and lectures at fundraisers and colleges around the globe.

The Warrens developed into frequent and popular guests on television and radio talk shows, and had their own local cable TV program entitled *Seekers of the*

Supernatural. They founded the New England Society for Psychic Research (NESPR) to give a name to their work and encourage the safe and professional research and documentation of the paranormal. They still generate the quarterly *NESPR Journal* with actual experiences gathered throughout the world. They offer historical perspectives, along with advice and possible explanations based on science as well as the Warrens' expertise.

Their income comes from lectures and books. To remain completely objective, the Warrens have never accepted a grant from the many institutions that offered one. Clients are expected to pay the Warrens' expenses, as much to weed out the frauds as anything. Yet, the Warrens are willing to help those unable to pay travel costs, if there is cause for legitimate concern.

What Makes the Warrens Unique?

For over fifty years, the Warrens have talked to thousands of credible witnesses from all walks of life, cultures, and religions about the paranormal. To date, no other single researcher or research pair has ever done this to such an extent before. The Warrens' offices overflow with more than 3,000 case files. They have conducted over 7,000 interviews with people connected to those cases and personally witnessed or arranged almost 700 exorcisms with well-regarded and respected religious leaders.

Their unprecedented fifty years of psychic investigations have taken the Warrens to Australia, Japan, most of Europe, and all over the continental United States—at the request of government officials, the church, or tormented people who seek help with what makes no sense in physical terms. Whether it is working with the Church of England or Buddhists in Japan ... exploring haunted pubs, abbeys, or tunnels ... the Warrens have consistently noted reliable patterns that defy dismissal in the serious study of paranormal events.

Lorraine's UCLA-validated clairvoyant skills bring a perspective that many other researchers—lay and scientific—don't have. Ed has had his own paranormal experiences, but he has also developed a unique body of knowledge about the occult and demonology that is sought and respected by law enforcement and religious leaders alike.

Ed points out, "Today, science is beginning to more accurately test, validate, and measure clairvoyant abilities and also recognize patterns in unusual phenomenon. Parapsychology, once a fringe science, is gradually moving to mainstream as the more modern, acceptable, and intellectual areas of quantum physics and mechanics join in the serious exploration of the metaphysical. Many of today's most brilliant minds agree that there is a lot more to our world than meets the eye ... or can be perceived by man's most sophisticated technology."

Meanwhile, any one who has had a premonition, "bad feeling," felt the power of prayer, or encountered something either miraculous or unnaturally disturbing also believes there is more to our world than meets the physical eye. Because of the Warrens' credible reputation and style, they continue to attract accounts of such phenomena through their Occult Museum tours, annual Halloween party, quarterly journal, and Web site. Many of the stories gathered come from lawyers, surgeons, scientists, the police, and other well-educated professionals. These are people who respect the Warrens as professionals as well. If they didn't, they would keep their strange stories to themselves.

Ed adds, "It was us that Channel 5 TV called to help investigate the strange tale of terrifying supernatural events in a house in Amityville. Lorraine and I were the only psychic researchers the Lutzes allowed into their home after they had fled. We led the only investigative team that was in the house almost immediately after the reported events occurred—giving us a unique perspective of this controversial case."

While Amityville triggered its own book and movie, the Warrens' work has been the subject of ten books and two movies to date. Although out of print, there is still such a demand for their books that *The Demonologist*—originally published in 1980 and authored by Gerald Brittle—was recently reprinted and quickly became a bestseller. The movies, *The Devil in Connecticut* and *The Haunting* are still popular enough to be replayed on late-night TV ... always triggering hundreds of requests for copies and for the Warrens' books.

The Warrens' credibility and unique body of work have also had an impact on modern law. In 1990, a terrified and frightened woman contacted the Warrens for help. This nurse and single mother had rented a Victorian home in Rockville, Connecticut, with the option to buy. However, from the very first night, her son was afraid to stay alone in his room. She was comforting him that inaugural evening when they both heard strange sounds coming from the first floor. However, no one else was in the house.

Lorraine explains, "For six months, she and her son were tormented every day by loud pounding noises, items flying about, and hanging plants swinging and lifting off their brackets. The kitchen phone was pulled off the wall by an invisible force in front of their eyes. And, they entered the kitchen one day to find a large knife still reverberating after being stabbed into the floor. On the second floor, they were terrified listening to the sound of footsteps and something heavy being dropped, as an invisible someone crept up the stairs."

The Warrens themselves observed much of these bizarre phenomena and captured some of it on film and audio recordings. They verified that something unconscionable was happening in that house due to an earlier tragic event. When the woman's landlord refused to let her break her lease, the Warrens testified in court on the woman's behalf. The woman won her case and a national precedent was established.

As a result, Connecticut and many other states have laws requiring property owners—if asked, to disclose any unexplained sounds or activity. Even if all is quiet, but a dead body was found in your cellar, someone hanged himself in your attic, or a family was murdered before you acquired the house at a bargain price, you are legally obligated to disclose these events to potential buyers or renters. Failure to disclose can void realty sales and rental contracts.

Over the years, the Warrens have increasingly come to use the science of infrared photography, and modern film, video, and audio technology in their investigations to capture some startling images and sounds. Yet, Ed and Lorraine have never ignored observed evidence simply because it couldn't be seen or measured with man-made instruments.

Throughout the inevitable controversy and criticism surrounding their work, the Warrens stand by their observations—which only match the experience of countless others.

The Warrens Now

In their seventies, the Warrens were still traveling around the world and from coast to coast to lecture and investigate cases. Weekly, they held training classes for aspiring psychic researchers and hosted a local cable television show. Once a year, they still throw an annual Halloween party that attracts hundreds of people from all over the country and sometimes the world.

Also, every spring the Warrens would lead a group of investigators on a haunted tour of Scotland. This trip allowed Ed and Lorraine to visit one of their favorite places on earth—the Isle of Skye. At their Connecticut home, the Warrens continue to offer guided tours through their private Occult Museum for hundreds of groups. Worldwide, the Warrens remain in demand for talk shows, magazine and newspaper articles, movies, and books. Meanwhile, and up until recently, Ed still painted and sold his art.

On the morning of March 26, 2001, at age 74, Ed Warren collapsed at home while calling the cat named Coon inside. Despite medical consensus to the contrary, he survived the night and remained in a coma for five months. Doctors recommended to the family that all life support be discontinued. Lorraine refused. Despite all odds, Ed came out of his coma and began rehabilitation. He spent over a year in and out of hospitals and rehab centers. Lorraine prepared their house to accommodate his wheelchair, and he finally returned home to the care of his wife and a host of professional caregivers.

Meanwhile, Ed was barely out of his coma and at a rehabilitation facility when he grabbed the necklace of a young nurse's aid and bellowed: "Get out!" Later, Lorraine apologized to the girl and looked at the necklace that had triggered Ed's outburst. It was a pentagram pendant—a symbol of dark witchcraft. Although Ed could barely function at the time, he was still on the job as one of the world's only lay demonologists.

Lorraine adds, "On September 10th while at his urologist's office, Ed suddenly grabbed a news magazine and refused to let it go. I was forced to ask if we could take the periodical home with us. Once we got home, I set the magazine aside and forgot about it. The next morning, I heard the tragic news about the terrorist attacks while I was getting Ed ready for the day. Later, when I looked at the magazine Ed had grabbed, I saw that the New York Twin Towers were on the cover."

Meanwhile, months before Ed's collapse and the September 11th terrorist attacks, Ed compiled an audiotape with soothing music and these words:

> "Remember what St. Teresa of Avila told us: 'Let nothing disturb you ... nothing frighten you. All things are passing. God never changes. Patience and faith overcomes all things. He who possesses God lacks nothing. God alone is sufficient.'"

Lorraine is quick to assure people that caring for Ed around the clock is the best job she has ever had. Yet, this work requires a lot of her time and attention. She still gives phone interviews and counsels clients regarding the many cases that continue to come her way. With the help of her

Cheryl A. Wicks

daughter, son-in-law, and many dedicated volunteers, she still maintains a Web site, generates the quarterly *NESPR Journal*, hosts an annual Halloween party, schedules Occult Museum tours, and does some lecturing at sites that are no more than a day's drive from her home.

The Warrens' unshakable love and support of one another mirrors the integrity they display in everything they do. Ed and Lorraine's unexpected life's work has always been about seeking the truth regardless of how bizarre it may seem. Despite their growing fame and reputation, they have remained dedicated to helping others achieve peace of mind ... understanding the strange things that might be happening to them ... and learning what can be done to minimize or prevent the more frightening supernatural events.

Ed Warren: Lay Demonologist

Ed Warren tells us in his own words how he became one of only seven demonologists in the United States and one of the few "lay demonologists" in the world.

Some people fear "demonologists," thinking we like to hang around demons or—even worse, encourage and worship them. Nothing could be further from the truth. Demonologists study demons to discourage the practice of the occult and help those who find themselves victims of such practices.

Few people call the police if they think they have "Casper" in their closet or the comforting presence of a favorite, but dead, relative lurking about the family room. They call the police when invisible forces that have become so violent and threatening they have nowhere else to turn. The police are experts on crime, but that doesn't make them criminals. I have become an expert on invisible dark forces, but that doesn't make me a devil worshiper.

Most demonologists are "religious" in that they are priests, ministers, and other pious organized-religion leaders who commit their lives to their religion. No one would mistake me for a priest. Therefore, I am considered a "lay demonologist." However, at the risk of confusing you, I also consider myself a religious demonologist… because I strongly believe God is the only power over evil forces.

A demonologist is not the same thing as an exorcist. Only an extremely pious religious person, carefully trained, can perform this function. This is a very dangerous work. Yet, there are many claiming they can exorcise, just as there are many who claim they can tell your future. As one priest said, "The devil is no damn fool, but he is a damned angel, and he can make a damn fool out of you." He can do worse than that. He can kill you and take over your soul. An exorcism is not a responsibility to be given to amateurs. Your first clue to level of expertise is if a so-called exorcist hands you a price list for services.

Nonetheless, when people see some of our horrific cases, the subject of so many television and magazine interviews, books, and even some movies, they have the mistaken idea this work is the secret to fame and fortune. Again, this could not be further from the truth. Yet many, many times, people have come up to me after a lecture and asked, "What do I have to do to become a demonologist? I want to be a demonologist just like you."

Well, the truth of the matter is this. I never *became* a demonologist. I was *born* a demonologist. What does this mean? This is not a career I planned or chose. It chose me. While a lot can be learned from books and experience, everyone has an affinity for some things more than others do. The circumstances where someone is found and the opportunities that come his or her way contribute to the interests, skills, and opportunities that develop.

Looking back, I feel I was born with a certain awareness and placed in a position to gather more knowledge in that area. When I didn't have the knowledge I needed, it always seemed to come to me… maybe in the form of an insight, another person, or a book, but it would always come to me when I needed it.

I did not wake up one day and say, "I want to be a demonologist." Yet, I became a respected expert in this field without degrees in theology or psychology or courses in parapsychology. And after twenty-five to thirty years of psychic research, many different clergy and leaders in all kinds of religions discovered that I somehow understood and knew more about the preternatural than even their learned scholars.

John 15: 16-17: *"You did not choose Me, but I chose you, and appointed you, that you should go and bear fruit, and that your fruit should remain, that whatever you ask of the Father in My name, He may give to you."*

Attracted to the exciting public life it looks like we are having, many believe all they have to do is visit haunted places to become just as renowned as Lorraine and I are. It took us over fifty years—fifty long years of our life dedicated to exhaustive traveling over many hundreds of thousands of miles, and tirelessly staying up many nights while working on investigations in strange places. There are also physical and emotional risks.

Fortunately, Lorraine and I are well grounded in our religion and unshakable in our faith. Our motives have always been to understand and to help—not to become rich (we still aren't) or famous (only as long as today's sound bite). Humility is critical in our ability to recognize and respect powers greater than we are… and to call on the divine powers we regularly need. We also recognize the benefit of a good sense of humor. This *is* a strange business.

Lifelong Training

From a very young age, I was interested in ghost stories. "Nothing unusual there," you might say. However, when most boys would be interested in baseball or football, I played sports only to a certain degree. My interests ran more to anthropology, history, geography, and the science of the supernatural... the unexplained.

I wasn't what you would call a good student. In fact, I was probably one of the bad students—always in the back of the class throwing spitballs, causing trouble. But, I also knew what trouble was about. I knew what the dark side of life was all about, even at an early age, because I was born into that life.

2 Corinthians 1:4: *"He helps us in all our troubles, so that we are able to help others who have all kinds of troubles, using the same help that we ourselves have received from God."*

My mother was an alcoholic. Yet, I wouldn't trade her for any other mother. There were some embarrassing times for me as a young boy when I didn't understand why my mother drank as she did. Yet, I always loved and respected her.

I was always very proud of my father—a man amongst men. My dad was a tough, rough guy... a police officer, boxer, served in the navy and fought in World War I. I wanted to be just like my father. My dad never smoked and he never drank. I never did any of those things either. Although I had plenty of opportunity and sometimes wanted to do these things, I consciously choose *not* to do them. I'm grateful to both my mother and father for teaching me I had a choice. It has served me well as a demonologist.

"Free will" is one of the most precious gifts we have. To give it over to peer-pressure, psychics, or a dependency on drugs and alcohol is dangerous and an incredible waste. As a war veteran, husband, father, and demonologist, I believe that the struggle in this world is for control. There are those who protect their free will and respect it in others. Then there are others who look to control others through manipulation, lies, and threats. Fanatics and despots, as well as demons, fall into this latter category. They want absolute control… at any cost.

Lorraine has been very important and instrumental in my life. We have been married almost sixty years. Her childhood experience was with a healthy, loving family. She taught me the finer things of life that I hadn't seen or understood before I met her.

The neighborhood where I grew up was extremely tough. I had to be just as tough to survive. As if that wasn't scary enough, from age five to twelve, I lived in a haunted house. Very frightening things occurred to me there. My twin sister and I would see images in the closet. Together we heard footsteps accompanied by a thump from a cane coming up the stairs. And we even had a close encounter of a miraculous kind when we thought our mother was comforting us. Later, we learned our mother had been out of the house at the time.

These spooky experiences were as necessary to my becoming a demonologist as were a strong father, suffering mother, tough neighborhood, and a loving, psychic wife. By the time I was eighteen or nineteen years old, I knew what haunting phenomenon was like because I had lived with it. When Lorraine and I began investigating haunted houses, I knew how frightened these people actually were … and how "real" these experiences could be.

I knew how frightened people could become from just a small sound in a dark room in a home that was haunted. I understood how frightening it was to think you had to go into that house alone and perhaps sleep there alone at night. I understood that, because I had lived it. There's an old saying: "You can read about doing a thing, but until you actually do it, you don't know what it's really like."

I was motivated to understand the scary things that happened to me as a boy… and to help others who were also frightened by these things. My childhood experiences and circumstances raised questions that no one seemed to be able to answer. However, the same experiences and circumstances gave me the strength and faith to face these terrifying things. Lorraine understood my curiosity and concern because as a child, she had discovered she had clairvoyant skills—abilities that were misunderstood by others.

Whether your calling is as an athlete, artist, businessperson, or in law enforcement, "good instincts" come from someplace else other than education. And they often make the difference between success and failure. I believe "instinct" is no more than a subtle awareness to both the spiritual and physical clues we are all given. Over the decades, I have come to trust these instincts more and more. This has certainly helped in my authenticating demonic cases.

The Life of a Demonologist

Being a demonologist is not an easy life. Sometimes you are loved. Many times you are damned, praised, and insulted. And this is only by people. Devils are worse—much worse. The way people react to my work depends on their opinion and what they know about my work and me. There are many who will try to strike me down, who will try to belittle me, who will insult me, who will lie about me.

Like most abusive behavior, this criticism is based on fear, ignorance, and the need for control. People fear the unknown, mistake my work for devil worship, and don't want to know that science does not give them complete control over their world. Demonology is not a subject that all people accept. They have their opinions, and I respect those opinions.

John 15: 18-19: *"If the world hates you, you know that it has hated Me before it hated you. If you were of the world, they would love its own; but because you are not of the world, but I chose you out of the world, therefore the world hates you."*

They say there are no atheists in foxholes, and I can tell you there are no skeptics under demonic attack. Regardless of what you believed or didn't believe beforehand, there is nothing like a life-threatening, soul-wrenching mysterious violent event to raise some doubts. If I can help, I will. Meanwhile, devils, demons, and evil spirits will try every dirty trick in the book to discredit or get back at me. Sometimes I say to myself, "Why am I doing this? I don't need it. I could have made a comfortable living focusing on my art. I didn't have to go around looking for trouble."

That's what a demonologist does. He or she looks for trouble, for culprits of an inhuman nature that are causing trouble for others. Demonologists are like police of the supernatural, bringing the inhuman, unnatural evil culprits to an exorcist instead of a judge.

Remember how I wanted to be like my father? As a policeman, he didn't want to break up fights, deal with bad people, or see people in pain, but it was his job. I break up fights over "free will," and I have to deal with evil and people in pain to do it. Instead of getting lawyers involved, I involve pious religious leaders of all faiths.

For those who are interested in doing what I do, I warn, "If you want to get in with the tough guys, you better be just as tough as they are." They will not hesitate for one moment to bring you down. When they fight dirty, you'd better be prepared to fight dirty. Rather than turn the other cheek… if someone slaps me, I'll slap him back. If someone kicks me, I will kick him twice. Sometimes a good policeman has to use his gun to hurt or even kill someone. Sometimes it is to keep others from being hurt. Sometimes it is to keep from being killed.

To an untrained eye, the exorcism itself may seem worse than letting evil keep control or looking the other way. However, the victim's pain evident during an exorcism is only an example of what the individual was already suffering within his or her body and behind closed doors for an extended period of time. No one human touches the possessed person during an exorcism. The torment inflicted comes only from the inhuman one being asked to leave. This entity is forced to reveal its ugly, cruel, vile self in the process. Pretending it doesn't exist won't make it so.

If you are squeamish about blood, you shouldn't be a surgeon. If you are squeamish about pain, you shouldn't be a doctor who resets bones. If you are afraid to confront the devil with all the power you can call upon and face the consequences, you should not be a demonologist.

This is why I say, "When the demonic and evil spirits fight dirty, you have to be prepared to do the very same thing." What you are dealing with as a demonologist is not human. He isn't a human enemy you are asked to forgive. He isn't a neighbor you are expected to love. Reason and mercy are useless avenues. Imagine the most terrible, ruthless, cold, cunning psychotic killer, and realize that pure evil is still worse.

I don't believe "the weak and the meek will inherit the earth." I believe those strong enough to protect their free will and the free will of others are the ones who will endure. I believe you have to be strong in mind, faith, and spirit to stand up to terrorists—both human and inhuman.

Remain Humble

When I go to bed every night, I thank God for everything God has ever given me—and *will* give me. I ask God to protect my loved ones and myself from the evil that Lorraine and I are always fighting. Despite my toughness, I know *only* God; the angels and the saints can protect us from evil.

No human being can go up against the devil or a demon alone. As Catholics, Lorraine and I call on St. Michael the Archangel, Jesus Christ, the saints and the martyrs. We need all that is holy to protect us and bring victory over any evil spirit. Never be foolish enough to think that you have powers that can conquer evil. You may have the knowledge; but regardless of your religious beliefs, the *power* comes from the divine. Never, ever forget that!

Ephesians 6:11: *"Put on the full armor of God, that you may be able to stand firm against the schemes of the devil."*

So if God is so powerful, why does He allow devils and demons to possess people? Well to begin with, human beings have free will, and it is they who open the door to evil infestation and possession. But to a certain extent, God does allow it; because through exorcism, God reminds us He is always more powerful than any evil spirit.

Another important thing to always remember in this work is that *there is one God*. We may call that God by many different names, and we may worship Him in many different ways and religions, but there is only one God. No matter how we pray, or what religious beliefs we have—as long as they are founded and based on a solid foundation of love of that God and love of your fellow man—it's a good religion. We are always willing to work with a Moslem domo, Shinto priest, a Baptist minister, Evangelical minister, Buddhist monk, or clergy of *any* faith… including rabbis.

People ask, "Rabbis? Rabbis don't believe in devils and demons."

The greatest exorcist who ever walked the earth was a rabbi. You remember his name? Jesus. And there are rabbis today that do exorcise evil spirits from people. They don't do it the same way as a Catholic priest. They are just as effective, however, because they are calling on the same God that a Catholic priest does.

Lorraine and I do not believe God is all-powerful because Jesus said it. Instead we believe Jesus—and the prophets and martyrs throughout the ages—said it because it is true. Anyone else who believes this can call on God's help when confronted with the unknown. This is why I work with people of all faiths and levels of worship. The devil does not discriminate, and neither do I.

So, You Want to Be a Demonologist?

I sometimes have to smile when people say to me after just six months of psychic research classes that they are determined to be demonologists. Yet, I always encourage them because maybe they, too, have this destiny. Only time will tell. Only you know what inspires you—what drives you on. No one else can know what's in your heart—except the devil and God.

Make sure you are not vulnerable. Look back on your life and see when it was that you decided to do this work. When you were very young, did you have similar interests and experiences as I did? As you became older, did you learn lessons in life that made you strong but humble and grateful enough to ask for help when you tried to help others? Look back at the steps in your life. What guided you here tonight? What is it that you want out of this work?

Is it glory? Do you want to be famous? Do you want to be rich? If these are your goals, they are the wrong ones. There is compensation for being in this work, but most of it is not financial. There will be many people who cannot in any way pay you for your services. When these people come to you, help them. There will be others who will compensate for them. That's the way God works.

Matthew 16:24-25: *"Then Jesus said to His disciples, 'If anyone wishes to come after Me, let him deny himself and take up his cross, and follow Me. For whoever wishes to save his life shall lose it; but whoever loses his life for My sake shall find it.'"*

If you know they can afford to pay your expenses, ask them for it. If they wish to donate something towards your work, take it gladly and gratefully. Some people may criticize you for taking any compensation. That's because they're not in this work. That's because they get a paycheck every week. That's because they have a grant, or they're supported by regular collections.

Remember that you don't have to be a demonologist to help others who are affected by evil in some way. Teach others to avoid self-destructive habits and activities that attract and invite evil. Help child, parent, or spousal abuse victims, those with addictions or other handicaps overcome obstacles and regain control of their life. Encourage people to take responsibility for their happiness, their behavior, and their choices. Set a good example and maintain a low tolerance of abusive behavior. Don't look the other way.

The Scariest Thing?

What is the scariest thing about what I do? The power and intelligence of evil and how it can impact on so many is what scares me most. Its real strength, however, is our ignorance. It uses this to disguise itself and create fear and confusion.

It is like a serial killer who pretends to be your friend. By the time you realize what is happening, it is too late to protect yourself. He has already isolated you and possibly your family.

My biggest challenge as a demonologist is to educate people without alarming them. Protect your free will. Don't put your happiness, life, or future in tarot cards and fortunetellers. Don't let others tell you what you should be doing with your life. Don't tolerate bigotry because you happen to have the right color, culture, religion, or bank account.

Lock your spiritual door to strangers. Don't dabble in the occult, play with Ouija boards, or participate in seances. Avoid people who do.

Know how to protect yourself when exploring cemeteries, haunted houses, or sites of terror and violence. Ask for help. Bad things can happen to good people and strange disturbances may not be your imagination.

The normal resources for people—their friends, family, law officers, and religious leaders—often turn away from what they don't understand. Even if they do believe, they don't know how to help. I hope through education, trouble can be avoided.

I also hope that more professionals like psychiatrists, social workers, and crime fighters will be able to discern between a disturbed mind and an oppressed or possessed soul... between evil influences and social influences. Further, I hope more legitimate demonologists and pious clergy of all faiths can be properly trained, more easily found, and more willing to help those who are desperate for the help only these experts can give.

Ephesians 6:12: *"For our struggle is not against flesh and blood, but against the rulers, against the powers, against the world forces of this darkness, against the spiritual forces of wickedness in the heavenly places."*

While my work as a demonologist has not been easy, it has never been boring, to say the least. But as Lorraine and I get older, we get a little more tired each day. One day we woke up, found we were seventy years old, and became concerned about what will happen to all the knowledge we have acquired... as well as the "awareness" we apparently brought with us into this world. If we are successful in making people question and give some thought to evil phenomena and avoid it, this is good. If we can realistically encourage someone to be a dedicated demonologist, that is good, too.

> **"The only thing necessary for the triumph of evil is for good men to do nothing."**
> Edmund Burke

SECTION II

Ghosts: Fact or Fiction? Harmless or Harmful?

Ed and Lorraine Warren sat down among their psychic research students to begin the evening's lecture. The subject was ghosts. Most of the people in the room had had a supernatural experience of some kind. Their ages ranged from the early twenties to sixties, both men and women. Occupations included college students, full-time mothers, shopkeepers, business executives, medical doctors, and other professionals with doctorates. There were also police officers and detectives in the group. Out in the parking lot were beat-up pickup trucks and well-used economy cars alongside top-of-the line luxury vehicles.

Lorraine Warren introduced herself to the newest members of the group. "We are not theologians, scientists, or philosophers. We are just two people who trust our senses—all six of them. My clairvoyant skills have been validated at UCLA. Ed is a respected demonologist. For over fifty years, we have explored paranormal phenomena all over the world and uncovered certain paranormal behavior patterns that defy dismissal."

Ed introduced the subject. "Ghosts are truly lost souls. They are often denied and not recognized by both the religious and scientific communities. While religions might encourage a belief in life after death, they do not envision their followers spending eternity as a ghost, haunting stairways. The physical sciences historically dismissed the idea of spirits all together.

"Yet, since Einstein, modern scientists have found the basis of our existence to be more ethereal than real. Quantum mechanics now theorize that energy and matter are all expressions of some deeper reality where particles, energy fields, and even time blend. It has taken 2,350 years, but today's physics has finally abandoned the materialist Greek philosophy that says if you cannot touch or see it, it isn't there.

"Meanwhile, ancient biblical interpretation says there are two sides to the equation of existence. One side deals with the material world, the other with the spiritual. Plato likened our perception of life to viewing shadows on a wall while unaware of the far grander reality that produced the shadows.[1]

"Still, many people may agree with Ebenezer Scrooge who first thought ghosts were 'more of gravy than grave.'[2] But in the end, even Scrooge believed there was more to ghosts than one's indigestion. From the earliest spoken and written word, humankind has been reporting ghostly encounters. This continues to this day, despite widespread education, the reduction of superstition, and the fluctuating popularity of organized religion. Too many consistent reports span all cultures and walks of life throughout the ages to be ignored."

Ed stood up and walked around the room as he continued. "There is also a growing scientific certainty that dimensions and forces exist beyond our physical human senses and the capabilities of our modern instruments. In labs around the world, telepathy, telekinesis, clairvoyance, and psychometry are now studied. Science also knows 'something' holds the particles of an atom together, but it cannot yet see or isolate these forces. Science already knows there is more energy than matter in all physical things—including us. Today we can photograph auras ... and ghosts."

Lorraine stood up to say, "Ed and I laugh when after every college lecture, someone invariably comes forward and asks, 'Do you really believe in ghosts?' Yes, but belief has little to do with it!"

"Ghosts are real people, too," Ed says with a chuckle. "However, not all so-called ghosts are true ghosts. And, not all haunted houses have ghosts. They may have something more mundane, or they may have something worse—much worse.

"What Lorraine and I are going to try to do tonight is teach you how to interpret ghostly phenomena. We'll tell you what we look for and how we can tell one type of manifestation from another. You will learn why it is as unlikely to see a penguin in the tropics as it is to see a true ghost follow you on vacation. There is also a big difference between aspiring psychics and a legitimate clairvoyant who can describe an image so clearly that a sketch artist can match the picture to an historic photograph. Speaking of which, I'll now turn over the lecture to Lorraine."

Ed sat down and Lorraine began to walk around the room as she addressed the group. "Very few reported ghost sightings actually involve ghosts. Parapsychologists and we agree on this. Outside of fraud, the most frequently observed occurrence is more apt to be the result of a 'psychic impression.' This is an emotional imprint left behind by a once-living entity—both human and animal.

"Imprints are likely to be left where there was a lot of strong emotions. This includes suffering, fear, rage, depression, and even joy and love. Battlefields, prisons, and hospitals are frequent places for such phenomena. Places where a murder, suicide, or tragic accident occurred may also trigger a psychic reenactment. In some cases, psychic impressions are the result of redundant or frequent human behavior such as walking to a well, working in a garden, children playing, or even the routine of hanging up one's hat upon coming home.

"Given the right circumstances, a redundant or strong emotional experience is replayed like a psychic recording. Like a photograph, these impressions need the right conditions to be developed. Yet, this type of psychic event presents itself to the most people. While it occurs to different people at different times, it is always in the same place and of the same image or event."

Lorraine stopped to ask for water, and then continued. "Next we have our truly disembodied human spirits. Ed and I and other professionals in this field differentiate between ghosts and apparitions. A true 'ghost' is a disembodied spirit that is not recognized. An 'apparition' is a spirit of someone familiar. The most frequent encounters with true ghosts are with what we call 'transition apparitions'. These entities are often seeking out loved ones to let them know they are dead and that life continues beyond one's physical demise."

Ed interjected, "What makes these apparitions 'scary' is that usually the loved one doesn't find out the person is dead until sometime after the paranormal event. Also, these apparitions usually appear as they were at the time of their death, which could have been from a car accident, murder, or in a battle. Therefore, these manifestations are always unexpected and sometimes horrible to see. This is what gives 'ghosts' their bad reputation."

Lorraine nodded in agreement, sipped her water, and resumed. "The next frequently reported true ghost sighting is of what we call a 'crisis apparition.' Usually in these cases, a deceased loved one comes back to comfort or guide the one they visit. Sometimes they come back to share in a family celebration or to welcome a new baby. A disturbance to something the apparition valued and loved in life could also trigger a visitation. Either way, the entity comes from the 'crossed-over side.'

"These apparitions are less startling and are generally comforting. Their death is not a surprise and they always appear in images of good health or sometimes younger than the age they died. Both transition and crisis apparitions can appear anywhere at any time, but they seldom appear to others and are less likely to reappear once the crisis has passed."

From the opposite side of the room, Ed said, "There is another type of crisis spirit, and they are often called angels." Ed continued: "Lorraine and I consider any manifestation of an entity that had not been human before to be a spirit. There are good spirits and there are bad ones. There have been many accounts of good spirits—often appearing in solid human form—showing up at accident sites, in hospitals, or at deathbeds. These comforting or life-saving individuals are later revealed to be unknown to anyone either before or after the event."

"True," Lorraine said. "Ed and I have been blessed with a few such encounters throughout our lives. Meanwhile, when most people think of ghosts, they think of an invisible or ethereal being that has been haunting someplace for ages. This type of true ghost is the rarest but the most likely to star in the best ghost stories. Earthbound ghosts don't travel, can exist for centuries, and often remain dormant for long periods. Triggers for their manifestation are becoming easier to predict, and often make sense upon careful psychic investigation.

"The most common reason these spirits remain bound to our world is they really don't know they are dead. This could be the result of an accident or murder where death was completely unexpected. Earthbound ghosts may stay where the spirit left the body, go to stay somewhere familiar, or hang around where either the body was prepared or buried."

Ed added, "This is why one is apt to encounter a ghost in a place where a murder or tragic accident took place. Other common sites are hospitals where people are sick and die, or funeral parlors where a lot of bodies are taken. Also, if a relative died in an accident elsewhere, their confused ghost may very well end up back home, because that is where they were headed at the time of their death."

Lorraine continued, "There are other reasons ghosts remain earthbound. Some feel they have unfinished business on earth and cannot rest until it is completed. Others simply refuse to cross over, feeling they don't deserve what is promised. Some are just stubborn, determined never to leave their homes or someplace else."

Ed offered, "Interestingly, we have never encountered a ghost that sought revenge or to right an injustice. Many are trying to understand what happened to them and why. Some are actually seeking to communicate forgiveness to their killer. In those cases, it is the killer's guilt that won't let these spirits rest."

Ed continued. "Ghosts themselves have been attributed to superstition, but to complicate things, ghostly phenomena stimulate yet more superstition in every culture. European folklore, for example, assumes ghosts can only be seen at night, reside primarily in graveyards, and cannot cross running water.

"Ghosts are seen day and night. However, the ethereal is more visible at night. Also, people are more likely to notice phenomena in the evening, when they are less distracted. While graveyards are reliable sites for paranormal activity, ghostly encounters can occur virtually anywhere. Transition and crisis apparitions and all non-human spirits—both good and bad—can and do travel, including across water. Some human ghosts actually reside on water, where they might have died.

"Also, in order for these non-physical entities to manifest into something we can see, feel, hear, or sense, energy is often taken from our environment. Resources include thunderstorms—like that famous 'dark and stormy night', electronics and electricity, plant life, or even body heat. If our body heat is used, a room will feel cold to us, even though there is no actual change in room temperature.

"Many assume all ghosts are transparent. Yet, some sightings involve solid manifestations. For example, a transformer blew one winter evening in 1992 outside a graveyard in Monroe, Connecticut. A fire truck rushing to the site couldn't avoid the woman who seemed to materialize from nowhere. Witnesses from the truck and the car behind it claim to have seen "a lady in white" just before the truck hit her. Despite these credible witnesses and the significant damage to the truck, no lady was ever found."[3]

Lorraine added, "Earthbound ghosts are also more apt to be 'seen' by young children, animals, and clairvoyants.

Cheryl A. Wicks

As depicted in the movie *The Sixth Sense*, most clairvoyants are just as confused and frightened by what they 'see' with their mind's eye, as anyone else would be if they saw it with their two eyes. Very young children and clairvoyants often take such sightings for granted ... at first. But when they realize others don't see the same things and are afraid of what is revealed, those with this gift become just as frightened."

"Lorraine, as a child, terrorized a few nuns with her visions," Ed remarked, causing the students to laugh. "Just as in *The Sixth Sense* movie, sometimes voices can be heard on tape and images captured on film that are not audible or visible to our ears and eyes. Lorraine has been able to describe images that later appeared in the photos that were taken at the time. Yet, no one else in the same room at the same time saw these figures. This is why every good psychic investigator should take a good psychic with them. I found one who also keeps me well fed."

Once again everyone laughed. "Seriously," Ed interrupted, "ghosts are usually frightened and confused themselves. These entities maintain self-awareness, but they usually are not aware of their own physical death. They have no physical pain, but their capacity for emotional pain remains. Ironically, it is these emotional, non-physical issues that seem to keep them bound to our physical world. They also have a different concept of time. One hundred years ago seems like yesterday to them."

Lorraine resumed, "When it comes to paranormal phenomena, rarer still is the 'poltergeist'—a noisy or mischievous ghost. Poltergeist disturbances date back to ancient Roman times and appear in medieval records found in Germany, China, and Wales. Documented cases included rock and dirt throwing, flying objects, dancing furniture, raps, loud noises and shrieks ...and all the way to biting, spitting, pinching, punching, and sexual molestations. Prior to the nineteenth century, it was believed that invisible demons, devils, former witches, or restless ghosts of the deceased were the cause of such activity.

"Studies in the 1920s and '30s theorized that the phenomena were caused by sexual conflicts and tension found in puberty. In the 1940s and '50s, scientists theorized that repressed hostility and anger unconsciously produced thought processes capable of creating this activity. Telekinesis—the mind's ability to move matter—had already been proven in labs at this point.

"In his 1972 book, *The Poltergeist*, William G. Roll summarized his personal observations after studying forty-seven cases that occurred before 1958. He found there was often a stressful situation in the household and an apparent agent for this activity. The agent was usually a child or a teenager who either harbored anger or was in poor mental or physical health. Individual psychologists would find anxiety, hysteria, phobias, mania, obsessions, dissociation, or schizophrenia.[4] In many cases, psychotherapy would eliminate the strange phenomenon.

"However, Roll observed that there were some cases where the 'agent' was stable in both physical and mental health, as well as environment. In these cases, psychotherapy did not work. Even when a psychosis seemed to be present, psychotherapy didn't help in all cases.

"A little later, British researchers Alan Gauld and A.D. Cornell did a computer analysis of five hundred of the world's poltergeist cases reported between 1800 and the late 1970s and observed that 64% involved the movement of small objects. Another 36% involved the movement of large furniture. They found that 58% were most active at night, 48% involved rapping noises, and 24% lasted longer than a year. Only 12% involved the opening and shutting of doors and windows.[5]

"Gauld and Cornell also concluded that 16% of the poltergeist cases involved some sort of communication between an invisible entity and a human 'agent' (usually female and under age twenty). Of the total, 9% were eventually linked to earthbound ghosts. Only 7% were linked to the practice of witchcraft, and 2% were considered caused by intelligent, malevolent spirits or demons.[6]

"Psychiatrist and parapsychologist Ian Stevenson later concurred with these findings. He felt there were two different types of poltergeist activity—human and inhuman. The events unintentionally triggered by living people involved meaningless raps, the random movement of light objects, short and simple trajectories, and much breakage. These things happened around someone under twenty, and psychotherapy provided relief.[7]

"Stevenson observed, however, that other poltergeist cases involved a purposeful movement of large heavy objects, complicated and long trajectories, little breakage, meaningful raps in answer to questions, and only sometimes focused on a person. Relief would come only from intercession, exorcism, or placation."

Ed spoke up. "Our fifty years of field research spanning the 1950s through the '90s and into the next millennium has led us to the same conclusions. We witnessed many cases where the so-called human catalysts were nowhere around when the poltergeist activity was occurring. We agree that children and teenagers often inadvertently provide the extra energy needed for this physical activity, but they are not always the direct cause. After ruling out psychological disorders and their influence, Lorraine would investigate to discern the involvement of other forces. Many times they were restless but harmless earthbound ghosts. But sometimes the demonic was involved."

"The dark shadows are Ed's area of expertise," Lorraine interjected. "I let him discern those. The rarest paranormal event, but the most newsworthy, is what is considered demonic infestation and possession. It will be the sole topic of another night's lecture. This type of phenomenon continues to be surrounded by the most doubt and controversy. Except for some psychiatrists and criminal experts, science dismisses the concept of evil as an entity altogether. Even today's religions tend to deny its existence or try to sweep it under a carpet. We wish we could do the same.

"However, many religious beliefs do involve a sense of 'soul.' Beliefs vary as to what happens to the soul after someone dies. This 'afterlife' can be in the underworld, under water, across the ocean, above the sky, or west where the sun sets. Tribal Melanesians believed that after death, the soul divided into two ghosts—one the bad part, the other the good part. Many of these islanders felt the bad part eventually died, while the good part enjoyed eternal life.[8]

"The Chinese also believe in superior and inferior parts of the soul, along with a possible third part that is the ancestral link throughout generations. Egyptians believed in BA and KA—individual soul and group consciousness respectively.[9] In the Christian West, the soul is expected to depart after death for heaven, hell, or purgatory. Virtually all religions profess some sort of afterlife or continuance."

Ed added, looking directly at Lorraine with a grin, "Not so long ago, clairvoyants were burned as witches. Since the mid 1900s, however, scientific experiments have proven the more benign existence of these psychic capabilities. Meanwhile, Einstein theorized—and experiments have since proved—the bizarre and totally illogical reality that every bit of existence is composed of or comes from energy. Instead of matter giving off energy, energy actually creates matter. Celtic wisdom has always maintained that the spirit houses the body, rather than the other way around. This ancient wisdom could very well explain auras, telepathy ...and the existence of ghosts.

"Today, physicists and quantum mechanics are now telling us 'the mind may be our only link to the reality of the metaphysical'—the mysterious forces that create life, develop it, and hold it together.[10] In other words, both science and religion now agree that there is more to our existence than meets the eye, ear, nose, hand ... and instrument."

Lorraine wrapped up the evening's lecture. "Paranormal phenomena are seldom straightforward, but they do have patterns and leave clues or 'ghost tracks' for us to follow. We have selected four cases to illustrate how we investigate and discern what may be happening in houses considered haunted."

- **Case Study #1:** <u>The Commander's Ghostly Caretaker</u>

A naval commander and his family appear to have an invisible houseguest. Clairvoyant research reveals the reason for this haunting, and an uncovered skull further resolves the mystery.

- **Case Study #2:** <u>A Murdered Soul's Unrest</u>

    The gruesome murder of a young boy takes place outside an apartment complex. The police who solved the murder ask the Warrens to investigate subsequent hauntings to bring peace to the community ... and the child's restless spirit.

- **Case Study #3:** <u>A Ghostly Interview</u>

    A man's misinterpretation of an apparition causes him anguish both in life and death. A deep-trance medium is used to help this ghost overcome more than a century of hostility and fear.

- **Case Study #4:** <u>Water Poltergeist</u>

    The difficulty in determining whether or not a mischievous ghost is demonic is illustrated in this unusual case. Three separate homes and generations are simultaneously tormented by the strange manifestation of water. The solution surprises.

Cheryl A. Wicks

<u>Case Study #1</u>
The Commander's Ghostly Caretaker

All names and places in this true story have been changed or modified to protect the privacy of clients. Ed Warren describes the case.

Getting Started

As Lorraine and I were rushing out for breakfast one morning, we received a call from a submarine commander by the name of Carroll. He apparently had heard about our paranormal research work and us from a recent story in the Associated Press. The Commander explained he and his family had been witnessing some strange activity in their home. He was concerned about leaving his wife and three children alone in the house when he was sent out to sea for several months.

What he told me next certainly caught my attention. Things have been knocked over or seen moving with no visible means by him and his wife, strange things kept happening in one of the bedrooms, and their son had seen a ghost. I could appreciate his concern. We agreed to an investigation, set a date, and took directions.

I scared up some researchers, and a week later, we all piled in my car to explore the Commander's mystery. It was a cold, crisp, bright day in February as we drove up the Connecticut coast towards New London. Being a former navy man, I always welcomed the opportunity to visit this part of the state.

New London and Groton lie opposite each other on the Thames River. Here, seafaring is not just part of the past, but also the present. The U.S. Coast Guard Academy has a riverside campus in New London. The U.S. Navy has an active submarine base in Groton. There is more ferry service here than any other place in Connecticut—to Long Island, Fishers Island, and Block Island. The first lighthouse on the Connecticut shore was built in New London in 1760 to handle the large maritime traffic.

The Electric Boat Company is still a major Groton employer. This company manufactured and launched seventy-five submarines in WW II. In 1954, they launched the first nuclear submarine—the *Nautilus*. The *Nautilus* now resides at Groton's Submarine Force Museum—the only submarine museum operated by the navy. It has the world's finest collection of submarine artifacts, documents, and photographs. Its research library boasts five thousand volumes on U.S. submarine history alone.

In the mid-nineteenth century, New London was second only to New Bedford, Massachusetts in the size of its whaling industry. The square-rigger *Morgan* is berthed at nearby Mystic Seaport on the banks of the Mystic River. Built in 1840, the *Morgan* is the last surviving wooden whaling ship built in America. The seaport itself recreated a nineteenth century whaling village. Its accumulation of historic buildings, workshops, and vintage watercraft make it the country's leading maritime museum.

With this much history in the area, I wasn't surprised there were a few ghosts. In the car with me were three people who knew all about ghosts. Like Lorraine, Mary and Steve were light-trance mediums. This meant they could see and communicate with spirits trapped on this side. Mary was a short, thin, middle-aged woman with a thick mop of dark hair and the uncommon ability to be able to match Lorraine word for word. Steve was a tall, lanky, young fellow, with sandy hair and a long face. If he could get a word in edgewise, it was usually thoughtful. We had all worked on other cases together, and we enjoyed some early-morning banter as we drove north. As long as they contained their comments about my girth behind the steering wheel, my outlook was as sunny as the weather.

The Commander's careful directions led us to a neighborhood of modest homes near the shore, outside of New London. Our destination was a small, two-story, blue house, crowded between others much like it. There were no trees and not much privacy, but the beautiful Long Island Sound sparkled beyond the frozen back yards. The Commander's house was in good repair and its property was neat. While I could hardly expect less from a naval officer, appearances tell Lorraine and me a lot about the kind of phenomena that are attracted to a place.

I parked the car on the street, and we all clambered out. After stretching reluctant muscles and my stubborn knee, we began to gather our paraphernalia. This included purses, recorders, tapes, and Steve's photographic equipment. We approached the tiny house like an invasion. As usual, Lorraine was up front.

Getting Acquainted

Before anyone could knock, the door opened. A towering, slim, athletic man with a military haircut filled the doorway. "I'm Commander Carroll. Please come in," he announced.

I squeezed through the door with my equipment and wondered how someone barely out of diapers could be a naval commander. Had I ever been that skinny or young? Lorraine had pictures to prove it; but that was not why I was here. I introduced our crew and Commander Carroll introduced his.

"This is my wife, Lucy and my son, Donald," he said, indicating a pretty, petite brunette standing next to an alert boy, who was about ten years old, with big brown eyes. "Our baby is asleep and our daughter Grace is playing at a friend's house," he explained.

We exchanged greetings and then Commander Carroll got down to business. "How does this work? What would you like to do first?" he asked.

"What I would like to do," I answered, standing a little straighter, "is move into the kitchen where you, your wife, and son and I can sit around the recorder. While I'm interviewing all of you, our psychic investigators—Lorraine, Mary, and Steve—would like permission to explore the rest of the house, without disturbing your baby. It is important that they do their work without being influenced by anything you might tell us. Does this sound okay?"

"Fine," our host said. "The kitchen is through here, the den is over there, and the bedrooms and bath are upstairs." I followed the Carrolls into their cluttered but clean kitchen, while everyone else started up the stairs.

I sat down in one of the wooden chairs and set up my tape recorder. The Commander, his wife and son took three more chairs around the rectangular table. I asked their permission to tape our interview and use any information garnered. They agreed.

The Interview

"What prompted you to call us when you saw the press release about our work?"

"I guess the thing that made us really believe we had something here," the Commander said, "was when my son saw something when he was on the stairs. This was only last month, in January. We just didn't know if we should be worried or not... especially with the children."

"I can appreciate that, Commander," I said. "For the record, can someone recount that particular event for me?"

"I will," Lucy Carroll volunteered. "One night in the first part of January of this year, I was in the den, reading. It was about ten o'clock. Donald was supposed to be in bed. He called out to see if he could please come down and get something he really had to have, and then he would go back upstairs and to sleep. I said, 'All right.'

"I heard him stomp halfway down the stairs and then complete silence. A few minutes later, he dashed into the den with his eyes as big as saucers. He said, 'I saw a man in the hall.'

"I was terrified, thinking we had a prowler. 'What do you mean you saw a man in the hall?' I asked. Donald said he was coming down the steps when he saw the top half of a man with a brown suit and gray hair standing in the hall. They looked at each other for about a minute, and then the man disappeared."

"This is quite remarkable," I said as I turned to the boy. "Donald, could you tell me what happened, in your own words? Don't be nervous, just tell me what you told your mother."

With encouraging nods from his parents, Donald began. "I wasn't really used to him, 'cause I never saw him before."

"What did he look like?" I asked.

"He had one of those funny black bow ties and brown suit and gray hair. I only saw the top half, and then I bent down so he couldn't see me any more."

"Was he looking right at you, Donald?"

"Yes."

"Did he look pleasant or did he look mad?"

Donald brightened and exclaimed: "He looked pleasant! And friendly."

"Very good, Donald. Just one more thing, was he solid like I am?"

"I couldn't really tell you that… you could see halfway through him, like a dirty window or glass or something."

"Thank you, Donald."

What Donald described was most likely an earthbound ghost. These entities belong to the place rather than to specific people. However, specific people and circumstances are apt to trigger the ghost's appearance or other manifestations. The children themselves could be the attraction or trigger for such phenomena. They tend to be more open-minded and sensitive. Like people, ghosts get lonely or want attention. The ghosts want to be seen by those they know can see them. Donald's obvious and spontaneous eagerness to describe who or what he saw as friendly was a good sign this haunting was not harmful. However, there were some disturbing aspects to this case.

"Actually, the most frightening thing that happened was the first thing," Lucy offered. "About two months after we moved in, my sister and her husband and children spent the weekend with us. One of the children was downstairs in the den, watching TV. The rest were scattered. The adults were in the living room talking.

"We heard a terrible crash. We dashed into the den and found the television on the floor upside down. The back of the stand was broken although the stand itself is very sturdy. The television is quite heavy. It took two of us to lift it back on the stand again.

"Nothing was wrong with the television. It worked beautifully. The child said she had been nowhere near the television when it fell. She said it lifted off the stand and turned upside down by itself. She could not have pushed it over because it was against the wall. Despite the awful crash, the television worked fine and was not damaged in any way."

What Lucy described was classic poltergeist activity. The "terrible crash" she heard, despite nothing being broken, was probably because the sound was telepathic. A spirit with enough energy to physically materialize could move objects. It gets its energy off the abundance children seem to have, particularly at puberty. To confirm my theory, I asked, "How old was the child in the room when this happened?"

"My niece was ten or eleven then," Lucy admitted.

The Commander slowly leaned forward and said: "One of the most disturbing things that happened here involved our Siamese cat, Jake."

Lucy nodded in assent and began the next story. "One night, I was sitting on the couch, when out of the corner of my eye, I was conscious of something being thrown down the steps. I heard a thump and turned to see the poor cat getting up off his haunch and shaking his head before wandering away. The children had been downstairs, so I rationalized that somehow the cat must have fallen.

"Several weeks after that, however, I was fixing dinner when my daughter Grace says to me: 'You should have seen what Jake did!' She said she had watched Jake leave the top of the stairs, do a somersault in midair, and land on his back."

"What was interesting," the Commander inserted, "is we had two cats at the time. The other cat never had a problem. That tabby would go up and down the stairs with impunity to use the litter box in the bathroom upstairs. Poor Jake, however, would sit and look up those steps with his tail twitching. He'd wait until nature wouldn't allow him to wait anymore. Then he'd run up the steps, skid into the bathroom, and come back down the stairs as fast as he could. We were afraid our ghost was doing something to our Siamese cat."

"Do you still have Jake?" I asked.

"No. Last winter he stayed outside too long and froze to death. Siamese cats don't have the vital capacity to withstand cold for long," the Commander explained.

Apparently, the poor creature was too afraid to be in the house as well as upstairs, which, of course, led to its death. Changing the subject, I fumbled through my notes from our first phone conversation and I asked: "Wasn't there also a problem with a bedroom in the house?"

"Yes," Lucy said. "It was the room we used as a guest room before the baby arrived. When we first moved into the house, I tried to get one of our children to use it as their room, but they didn't want it for some reason.

"After we got settled, one of them would decide they might like to try it, but they never lasted the night. They were always frightened. Our daughter Grace would have a friend sleep over, and I would make the two beds in there. The two girls would go to bed, but within an hour they were out of there. They said they would hear doors opening and creaks and things."

Barely stopping for breath, Lucy continued. "Another time, my sister was here with her son, who was seven years old. She told him to sleep in the bed closest to the wall. He wanted to sleep near the door. Finally, she gave in and let him sleep in the bed by the door. He fell out of bed every night. He had never fallen out of his single bed at home. The only night he didn't fall out of bed here, however, is when he slept in the bed by the wall—where she first told him to sleep.

"He insisted something was frightening him in there at night. He asked my daughter, who was nine years old at the time, to go in the room to see a cloud. She said they both saw a cloud in there. They were terrified."

I found it significant that both children said they saw the same thing. Also, psychic orbs and energy wisps are apt to be described as "clouds" by youngsters. Usually, these images are seldom seen by adult eyes and only picked up by cameras.

Lucy continued. "Another child about nine or ten who stayed with us was mature for his age. Yet, he wouldn't sleep in that room without a nightlight. For some reason, children don't want to be in that room… except for the baby. The baby is fine.

"One day, Donald and his friend Sam were playing in that room, when I heard them yelling. I ran upstairs to tell them to be quiet. They said they couldn't get the door open and were starting to panic. I opened it easily from the outside. I tried it again from both sides without any trouble. But for some reason, they apparently couldn't get the door open just moments before.

"Yet another incident involved my sister's earring. My sister and her husband stayed overnight. When she entered the guestroom to go to sleep, she felt one of her earrings drop off, but didn't hear it hit the floor. Then something said to her: 'You ought to have your ears pierced.' She said it was almost as though a separate voice inside her head was saying this. She said, 'All right, if it's a ghost that has my earring, I want it back by tomorrow morning'. She undressed and went to bed.

"The next morning she asked her husband to be careful when he got up, because she thought she had dropped her earring the night before. They both got up and stared in disbelief. Her earring was resting on top of her clothes, on top of the crib."

"This is indeed interesting," I agreed. "Are there any other strange things that have happened here since you moved into this house three years ago?"

"I remember something," the Commander said. "One early evening I was sitting in the living room when Lucy said: 'Hey look at this!' The candelabra sitting on the dining room table was making circular motions. I stood up and stopped it and joked, 'It's probably the poltergeist.' I went back to the living room to read. A few minutes later, I looked over and saw it was doing it again. By that time, I was getting interested.

"The baby was asleep and the other children were out of the house. No one else was around to shake the floors. The windows were closed and the dry corn hanging nearby was not moving at all. I got up and stopped the candelabra again. A few moments later, it started again. When I put some felt underneath it, it stopped and hasn't done it again."

Lucy wanted to add one more story. "Several weeks after the event with the television, I woke up in the middle of the night to a noise I couldn't place. I got up to look around. When I turned on the dining room light, I saw that a good-size hunting print had come off the wall and was resting against the chair rail. The picture wasn't broken. I assumed the nail had come out of the wall, and went to bed.

"The next day, I found the nail was still firmly in the wall and the wire on the back of the picture was intact. I hung it right back, and it's still hanging there today."

Sometimes ghosts disturb specific things for a reason. When I asked Mrs. Carroll about the picture that fell, she described it as a picture of a horse with hunting dogs—an old English hunting print bought by her grandfather.

Psychic Impressions

I could hear our psychic researchers chattering outside the kitchen, so I invited them into the room. They had just come downstairs and hadn't heard any of what the Carrolls and I had discussed. I encouraged everyone to settle down. Mary was a valid clairvoyant, but had not been quite as many cases as Lorraine. Steve was also a gifted, but less experienced clairvoyant who specialized

Ghost Tracks

in capturing ghostly manifestations on film. They were both excited about what they had apparently uncovered. Lorraine let Mary take the floor.

"I psychically saw something completely unexpected," Mary exclaimed before I barely had a new tape in my recorder. "I expected something related to former owners of the house, but this was like a guest. Yet, he wasn't family or a family friend. He had been an English sailor. I knew he was English because he tried to trick me with his language using the words 'bloody' and 'ruddy,' but I wouldn't let him get away with that."

Ghosts sometimes deliberately make themselves hard to understand, trying to get Mary back on track, I asked, "What was this man's relationship to this house?"

"He was a man who worked for the captain who owned this house. There was something wrong with the man's left arm. It was injured in some way, and he could no longer sail. The captain made him his family's caretaker while the captain was away at sea."

"What did this man look like?" I asked.

"He was an old-fashioned man. He dressed in a brown suit and a silly bow tie. He gave me the impression that boys grew into men, but girls were always girls. He liked horses and dogs. He thought all cats were nuisances, especially a cat that didn't look like a cat, like a Siamese. He might have accepted a cat that looked like a cat. But a Siamese didn't look like a cat. It looked like a little rat or something. Slanty eyes… that was a foreign type of cat to him."

In this short burst of information, Mary addressed a few of the mysteries that have plagued the Carrolls. First of all, she described the same ghost that the boy had seen at the base of the stairs. He apparently was English and had an affinity for horses and dogs. I thought of the hunting print that had been removed from the wall. Also, without the cat currently in residence, Mary had described the ghost's confusion and animosity towards the Carrolls' Siamese feline.

Lorraine tells me that psychic information tends to come in a rush like that. It is almost as if ghosts have so much to tell, they cannot communicate it fast enough when they find someone who can listen. I asked Steve what his psychic abilities observed.

"The man was about forty-five years old with gray hair. This man seemed to be wandering about lost. There were walls or something that was not in the same place. Things were not exactly the way they had been. When I asked him: 'What are you doing here?' he got a little irate at that and said: 'Naturally, I'm looking after the place, what else?'...Or something to that effect. When Mary asked him his name, she got, 'William Rogers.'"

"That name could be reversed, 'Roger Williams' like the famous Baptist minister," Mary suggested. "It sounded familiar. I was afraid I was subconsciously dragging that name up. I kept rejecting it and turning it around. The name 'Bristol' kept coming up as well. I don't know if that is where he was from or the name of his captain's ship.

"My general impression was that this man was under the command of the captain, and because he was a valuable man that no longer could work at sea, he was put in charge of the care of the captain's house whenever the captain was away. He is back because he has not finished his job here. He is looking for something."

Steve asked, "What was the square metal container with the cylinders sticking out?"

"I don't know," Mary said. It looked like a square metal box with a lot of little round sticks on end sticking up. Also, was the back of the house different? Was there a room with many small glass windows? Was there ever a greenhouse out back?"

The Commander admitted, "The back of the house was different at one time, but I don't know anything about small glass windows or a greenhouse."

"It was different," Mary said with authority. "The place where the floor is brick used to be the porch, and the room by the three outside stairs used to be the tack room. Is that correct?"

"Yes," Commander Carroll agreed, "that is all true based on the original floor plans we've seen."

"Good!" said Mary. "He knows where he is anyway. Where the porch used to be is where he would get into and out of the house."

Lorraine added that the man's quarters had been what is now the baby's room—the same room the other children didn't like. Mary suggested that perhaps this caretaker came out of ghostly retirement because of the "new" naval commander and his family in the house.

House and Family History

"From the beginning, this house always seemed to have a definite personality," claimed the Commander. "Lucy and I both felt it when we came to look at it for the first time. It was warm and cheerful and welcoming. When Lucy began telling me about all the odd things that happened, I wasn't surprised. And for some reason,

I always felt there was a protective male presence in the house."

"That's right, he did," Lucy confirmed. "That's why we weren't surprised when what Donald saw was the figure of a man. But it was a little disconcerting just the same, especially with a heavy TV overturning and the cat being thrown down the stairs."

"Commander," Lorraine said, "do you feel you are clairvoyant to any extent?"

The tall, stern man chuckled. "Well, actually... I experienced at lot of déjà vu when I was a kid. I still get them every once in a while. I think as you get older, you are not as sensitive to these things."

"That's true," Lorraine said, nodding in agreement.

"I still get lots of feelings about things," the Commander added. "I get feelings about ships, machinery, people, cars, and things like that. It is almost as if things have souls or personalities."

"Commander," said Mary, "how do you feel about the male presence in your house? Do you think he is prim and proper?"

The Commander laughed again. "No, definitely not... definitely not. He must have been a tough, horny old sailor."

Mary smiled in accord and the rest of us laughed.

"Mrs. Carroll?" I asked. "Have you ever felt frightened when you were alone here in the house? Did you ever feel as if you were being watched?"

"No," she said, "no fear whatsoever. I have always felt very, very safe. Even Donald was more surprised than scared by the man's image. He said the man looked very, very friendly."

"That's good," I said. "It looks like your ghost feels a responsibility to protect you. He may be simply calling attention to himself or expressing his opinion when it comes to television, cats, earrings, children listening to their mothers as far as what bed to sleep in, and keeping the candelabra from scratching the table. He was probably teasing the boys in the bedroom when they couldn't open the door. All this seems to fit his protective yet tough 'personality.'"

"But why is he here? Why hasn't he crossed over?" asked Lucy.

"The history of the house could shed some light on those questions and this character," Lorraine suggested.

Lucy agreed. "I don't know if it will help, but we did some research when all these things started happening. The house was built in 1745. It was built by a William Wadsworth for his daughter, who married a Douglas. It stayed in the Douglas family until 1938."

"No information on a sea captain?" asked Mary.

"Nothing that popped up," answered Lucy. "Nor was there any mention of a 'Williams' or 'Rogers'. But I was not looking for anything in particular, just some general information. I don't know what Wadsworth or Douglas did for a living."

"Was there anyone named 'Rogers' or 'Williams' in your families?" asked Mary.

"No," the Carrolls said in unison, shaking their heads.

"Lucy's family was in the shipping business, however," pointed out the Commander. "Her ancestors were ship captains and she had great uncles, many times removed, who were lost at sea. Could this ghost person be one of her ancestors or someone attracted to her background?"

"A relative that has crossed over has the ability to go anywhere at any time. However, these entities are not likely to stick around and turn over televisions or tease children. They are more apt to appear to you in a crisis situation and then be gone. But tell me a little bit about your family, Lucy."

"They owned a line of clippers," she said. "They built clippers and packets after migrating here from the Virgin Islands in 1848."

"That would have been some time after the man died in 1842, if my psychic impression of that date is right," Mary offered. "The year I got when this man died was 1842. That would have been 97 years after the house was built."

Lorraine and Steve concurred with this additional information. "At least now, we have some specific names, dates, and ideas to research," I offered as I began to gather my things. It had been several hours since my donut stop on the way to the Commander's house. A person could starve while discussing historic possibilities.

"We'll look into it," the Commander agreed. "Thank you very much. We appreciate your coming out here to help us sort this thing out."

"It's nice to know we're not crazy," Lucy added, "and reassuring that the children are safe."

"You're not crazy," I confirmed. "Lorraine and I have seen this phenomenon probably thousands of times. But you were right to call us to verify it was harmless. Now only further research will answer our final questions."

We said our good-byes, grabbed all our belongings, and trooped out to the car while still discussing the case. The car seats were cold, and I started the motor to begin warming up the engine. As the windows began to defrost, the only mystery left in my mind was when and where we were going to eat next.

Subsequent Discoveries

True to their word, the Carrolls did more research and called us eagerly one weekend with the information.

A former seaman, originally from Bristol, England, named Chester Hubbard had served under the captain who owned the house. He was made the family's caretaker when a debilitating injury made him useless as ship's crew. Despondent over not being able to return to sea, he blew himself up in 1842 using three sticks of dynamite tied to his body. They never found the man's head.

The name "William Rogers" or "Roger Williams" never came up. This means it very well may have come from Mary's subconscious, just as she first thought. However, the "mysterious metal box with sticks on their ends inside" was probably the box that held the dynamite Chester used. And there was one more thing. The ship Chester sailed aboard in the early 1800s was named *Polaris*—the same name as the type of submarine Commander Carroll was serving aboard.

Yet, this wasn't all. Almost two years later, we heard from the Commander again. Apparently his son Donald and some friends were playing in the back yard when they uncovered a human skull. The police and forensic specialists said the skull was from about the mid 1800s.

"Could this be what our ghost was searching for?" the Commander asked.

"It's possible," I agreed. "Throughout history—particularly in England—there have been tales of screams and other disturbances at the site where a skull was not properly interred. This phenomenon might have been what kept your particular ghost earthbound."

The Commander laughed and admitted, "All the pieces fit together. It's hard to believe we're dealing with something so ... so intangible."

"Ghosts make perfect sense," Lorraine said from the other phone extension, "…once you understand them. It can be very frustrating for both sides as we try to find out what they need and what they are trying to tell us."

"What do you recommend we do now?" asked the Commander.

"You should try to put this poor man to rest. Have the skull buried in consecrated ground or have it cremated and 'buried at sea.' Either way, have a few words said over it…commending it and its ghost to eternal peace."

"Yes, I see where that would help, and we'll arrange all that," the Commander agreed. "But ..." he said, "I think we're going to miss the raunchy old fellow."

"He can always come back as a guiding spirit," said Lorraine, "but at least he can finally leave behind his old life on earth."

"Yes, yes, I understand. We will take proper care of Mr. Hubbard's skull," the Commander promised. "Thank you for all your help."

After a few more pleasantries, we finally said goodbye to the Commander, his family…and their ghostly caretaker.

Case Study #2
A Murdered Boy's Unrest

All names and places in this true story have been changed or modified to protect the privacy of clients. Ed Warren describes the case.

A Call for Help

Lorraine and I had just sat down to relax with the newspaper after dinner one evening when the phone rang. It was Officer David from a police department in Massachusetts. His captain had referred him to us.

Occasionally, Lorraine and I have been asked to help the police solve a murder or interpret what may be a crime based on the occult. These cases are not fun or pleasant, but if we can help the overworked police bring closure to a victim's family, we are willing to assist. We only help, however, at the request of authorities. Lorraine and I don't need fame and there is certainly no fortune in it.

Officer David wasn't a "believer" in the supernatural, but he was genuinely concerned about the families in one particular apartment complex on his beat. Over the years, he had developed a rapport with the tenants there—first the kids and then their parents. These people were being harassed by something the police officer felt helpless to handle.

This policeman had explained his concerns and frustration to his captain, who had worked with us before. When Officer David expressed his doubts about our work, the captain laughed and said he used to have doubts, too. Then the seasoned man reassured the young officer, "If it is mass hysteria or some sort of hoax, the Warrens will tell you that. If it's not, they'll tell you that, too. They'll also tell you what to do about it. And when it works, you and your doubts will just have to reconcile themselves to the facts."

On the phone, Lorraine's Irish charm probably won the officer over more than the captain's words. I took the more direct approach. My father had been a policeman, and I knew it wasn't an easy job. "You say these tenants seem to be experiencing a haunting phenomenon. Did something violent ever happen at this site?" I asked.

"Yes," Officer David admitted. "About a year ago a young boy was found murdered behind these buildings. It was a particularly brutal murder done by other kids. These kids were caught and convicted and are currently serving time."

"And how soon after the boy was murdered did the tenants start experiencing problems?" I asked.

"I'd say a month or two later," answered the officer. "I parked my patrol car in the parking lot at that complex and the kids come to hang around. First they started telling about some weird stuff that was happening. Then the adults started to tell me the same things."

"What sort of things?" I asked.

"They'd say they saw the specter of an eight- to ten-year-old boy on the complex steps or in a hall, and that all kinds of crazy things would happen. At first, I thought they were putting me on, but they seem really frightened. These people are tough. They don't scare easily, but one lady in particular is terrified. She just moved there and didn't even know about the murder, until…"

"Until what?" I coaxed.

"Well, I know this all sounds hokey, but," Officer David continued, "she said she found out about the murder from a Ouija board, and she thinks the dead kid is haunting her apartment."

"Unfortunately, it doesn't sound hokey to us," I said. "And if a Ouija board is involved, she may have a good reason to be frightened. How soon can we get together and meet this woman?"

We agreed to meet early in the evening in two days. We refreshed our directions and hung up the phone. Lorraine and I exchanged concerned looks. There could be more than a human spirit haunting this apartment complex. The phone call and the evening news could be depressing, but a piece of pie might cheer me up. "What's for dessert?" I asked.

Mean Streets

It was dusk when we arrived at Officer David's precinct two days later on a dreary October day. The captain, we knew, had already left for the day. I don't blame him. It was in a tough neighborhood. I was glad we were leaving our car at the police station, but even then, I had my doubts about ever seeing it again.

The desk sergeant referred us to this freckled, open-faced, redheaded youngster of thirty-seven who looked like he should be walking a beat in fictional Mayberry. Patrolman David was taller and a few years away from showing the donuts and fast food he probably lived on while on the job. He offered each of us a large hand, and proceeded to share his plan for the evening.

"I'd like to give you a brief tour of the neighborhood." he said. "This will give you the feel you said you wanted of the place and for the people who live here. Then I will take you to the project complex where the murder took place... and where all these strange things are said to be happening. There you will meet Juanita. She is the one who is convinced this murdered kid spoke to her through a Ouija board and is haunting her apartment."

"Sounds like a plan," I said, "but don't tell us anything more about the boy's background, murder, or what the people in these buildings are experiencing." I explained how we didn't want to taint what Lorraine might be able to discern from what we knew. It was hard enough to interpret psychic data without introducing outside information. Also, it was much more credible if Lorraine could come up with it on her own.

"Okay, no problem," the policeman agreed. "I can tell you as much as you want to know later. Let's hit the road."

While he still had his doubts about what was happening and how we could help, he probably expected us "Ghostbusters" to look more like kooks than grandparents. We followed him to his patrol car, slid behind the wire barrier into the back seat, settled down in the worn indentations, and let our "uniformed chauffeur" take us into the darkening night.

The sun had set and the harvest moon was hidden behind thick heavy clouds. The pavement was still wet from a recent shower. There was more litter than leaves in the seedy streets we traveled. When we were by a dumpy diner in a dilapidated strip mall, Lorraine asked Officer David to pull over. "It was here," she said. "It was here where the boys had an altercation that led to that one boy's death."

"An 'altercation'?" asked Officer David, a little cynically as he pulled right and stopped the car against the curb.

"It was here," Lorraine repeated. "This boy was not a hundred percent in the head. He was mentally handicapped in some way. The other boy was from a different apartment complex. The murdered boy insulted the other boy's mother. He called her a drunk and a whore, which she was. Weeks later, the insulted boy saw the opportunity to take revenge. He and a friend…" she hesitated. "They killed the boy." Lorraine seemed to physically shake herself out of a nightmare.

I told Officer David "It's okay to go now."

"Whatever you say, boss," the patrolman said over his shoulder as he put the car back in gear.

I was starting to like this guy more and more. Just a few minutes later, we pulled into a rough parking lot with three worn apartment buildings organized into a horseshoe around the cracked asphalt. Trash collected in corners where the wind had blown it, but most of the windows were intact. It was too cold and damp for anyone to be loitering outside.

We parked at the south side of the complex. Lorraine and I crawled out of the back seat as gracefully as possible. I carried my tape recorder. Lorraine clutched her purse. We followed the officer into the shabby doorway and down a dark, musty hallway to a metal apartment door. He knocked and announced us. Seconds later, the door was opened by a young, petite Hispanic woman with bright black eyes that matched the color of her long, straight hair. Behind her was a stocky man in his thirties with deep brown eyes and dark, curly hair cropped tight to his head.

Cheryl A. Wicks

Officer David introduced Lorraine and me to Juanita, and then us to her. She introduced everyone to her husband, Carlos. We walked into a small, crowded two-floor apartment. The living room and kitchen were downstairs, the bath and bedrooms were upstairs. A flowery smell from scented candles filled the air. Religious statues and pictures were present. I was comforted to see that these people were not Satan worshipers.

I explained that we wanted to hear what had been going on, and that I would like to tape the interview. Normally, Lorraine and I separate at this point; but this case was different. Because a Ouija board had been used, we were afraid an unfriendly and potentially harmful entity could be involved. Lorraine didn't want to—and I wouldn't let her—face such a risk alone. Lorraine stayed with me to ascertain what had caused alarm.

Spooky Encounters

Juanita and her husband cleared their kitchen table and sat down with Lorraine and me. I set up the tape recorder in the middle of the Formica table. Officer David stood in the corner, leaning against the refrigerator. Juanita and Carlos gave us permission to use the information learned as a case study for our lectures, books, and talk shows. We were ready to begin.

"All right, Juanita, how many people live in this apartment with you?"

"Six people, including my husband," she said. "It is me and my husband and our four kids. They are with a neighbor next door for now."

Ghost Tracks

"Okay," I said, getting right down to the crux of the matter, "I understand that a Ouija board was used here. What prompted you to use it?"

I was looking for motive. Those with legitimate clairvoyant skills sometimes use tools like the Ouija board, tarot cards, or a crystal ball to focus their attention. Too often, however, people underestimate their own inherent ESP skills, have no directed focus, and become vulnerable to marauding spirits looking to take advantage.

Lorraine and I have discovered that Ouija boards can be particularly dangerous. Many of the most violent cases we have investigated involved the misuse of a Ouija board. For example, the movie and book *The Exorcist* were based on a true case that began with a Ouija board. Unfortunately, malicious spirits often disguise themselves as harmless or as someone you may have known to get you to invite them further into your life. Once you do, they begin to start taking control.

"Yeah, I used the board," Juanita admitted, "to find out what was causing the weird things happening in this house. The cabinets would open by themselves. It felt like someone was following me."

I clarified this: "You used the Ouija board because you thought there might be ghosts in the house, is that right?"

"Yeah. I wanted to find out," she said.

This was encouraging for two reasons. One was that the haunting phenomena were occurring *before* she used the board. This means her using the board didn't trigger them. Second, her intention was to identify and resolve a specific problem. She was not just fooling around to see what would happen. Nor was she dabbling in black magic. She was focused on a positive motive.

Cheryl A. Wicks

However, this is not to say any spirit that could have been causing the disturbances was not already harmful. Nor would her best intentions necessarily prevent "something" with a more malevolent intent to take advantage of the situation. I needed to learn more.

"Besides the cabinets opening and that feeling of being watched, what other things triggered your concern?" I asked.

"I'd hear footsteps following me," said Juanita. "Then, one time, the living room lamp was moving by itself."

"Tell me exactly what happened with the lamp," I coaxed.

"Okay. One day I was sitting on the couch. Then I went upstairs. When I came back down into the living room, the lamp was moving very hard, and without anybody there. The shade was moving back and forth… very hard," she told me.

Human ghosts tend to move light things. According to Juanita, only the shade had been moving…not the whole lamp. Ghosts will sometimes do this to get attention. Yet, malicious spirits are also tricksters and may intentionally start off acting like playful ghosts.

"How long did the shade move by itself?" I asked.

"For a minute or two, I guess," she answered.

"What did you do while this was happening?"

"I sat on the couch. I didn't want to move. I'm telling you, I was very scared."

"Has anything else unusual happened in your living room?" I asked.

"Lots of things," she said. "Once, the lights were on in the room. I went out, and they shut themselves off. But the very bad experience was at three o'clock in the morning. I was sleeping with my husband. The TV came on by itself. I came down to shut off the TV, but it came on again!"

What caught my attention was the time. The hours of 9 p.m. to 6 a.m. are considered the "psychic hours." These hours are usually dark, when it is easier for ghosts and spirits to gather energy in the dark to materialize, move things, or create sounds. The hours between 3 and 6 a.m. are considered the most psychic because they are usually the darkest. Demonic spirits in particular will avoid God's light and consider anything in multiples of three an insult to the Trinity.

"Did your husband also see and hear this happening as well?" I asked.

Carlos, with a serious expression on his face, nodded in agreement. Yet it was Juanita who answered: "Yes, he saw it was three o'clock in the morning. With no one down in the living room, the set just kept coming on and off, on and off. It would come on. We would go shut it off."

"How did you turn the TV off?" I asked.

"With the remote, at first," she told me. "Then Carlos said the remote control wouldn't turn it off. So we put the remote control away… to be sure the problem was not caused by the remote. But the TV just kept turning on by itself."

"How many times did this happen?"

"Five times. And it was a brand new TV."

The activity described could have more playful and annoying than intentionally frightful. Sometimes a new appliance or home improvement may fascinate a human ghost. The television had been brand new at the time. There was still a good chance whatever may be causing these events was disturbing but harmless.

"Anything else happen in the living room?" I asked.

"Yeah, let me tell you," Juanita started. "Remember the movie *Lion King*—the kids' movie? We rented it and everybody—even my baby—were sitting in the living room watching the movie. Then we all heard somebody coming down the stairs. Everyone turned their heads at the same time looking to see who it was. No one was there."

Carlos got to speak for the first time. "It came all the way down to the bottom of the stairs!" he said in a husky voice. "The footsteps were real hard, just like this…" he said while making heavy stomping sounds with his feet on the kitchen floor. "But there was nobody there."

"How many people were in the room when this happened?" I asked.

Carlos answered: "Eight kids, me and my wife, and our neighbors…four adults and their kids."

"When this happened," I asked, "what did you do?"

"I started laughing," Juanita inserted. "Before it happened, everyone was starting to believe I was seeing things. After that happened with everyone there, no one could say it was my imagination. 'This is *not* my imagination!' I said."

Both Juanita and Carlos had seen the event with the television. A roomful of people witnessed the mysterious stomping footsteps on the stairs. These facts lent credibility to both the story and the possibility that it was a human spirit in their home. Demonic spirits tend to isolate their victims. They often show themselves to only one person or they manifest in different ways to each person. This is how they create doubt, fear, and confusion. This is how they gain control.

In this particular case, however, I had reason to believe these events were more representative of a human ghost

Ghost Tracks

trying to get attention. There was a childlike quality to these occurrences. Yet, I had to explore this possibility further.

"Did anything ever happen that truly frightened you, compared to your being surprised or startled?" I asked.

"Oh, in bed, yeah," Juanita began as her eyes became bigger. "Carlos and I were together in bed when it felt like someone was putting something around my throat. I said: 'Stop!' He said: 'I'm not doing anything.' 'You're hurting my throat,' I said. He said, 'I didn't do nothing. I didn't touch you.' I said, 'Oh my God,' and jumped out of bed and ran outside the room. It felt like someone was in the bed."

I asked Carlos, "Do you remember the incident in the bed she just described? If so, could you tell me about the experience in your words?"

Carlos sat up in the chair looking uncomfortable. He looked down as he rubbed his hands together and said, "Yeah. When she started blaming me, I thought she was joking around. Then she showed me she was really scared. When she got up, then…something else. This was totally…it was moving! It was like someone was sitting next to me in bed—moving and stuff."

There was fear in his eyes and concern in his voice as he recounted this event. It obviously disturbed him and Juanita to talk about it. This *was* frightening and upsetting. Had a mischievous ghost gone just a little too far or was something else "at play" here?

I asked Carlos, "Have you yourself witnessed any other strange events in the house?"

He relaxed a little and said, "Yes, once I felt something following me downstairs. I had gone upstairs to get a shirt. As I grabbed the shirt, it felt like someone was looking at me. I took the shirt and started downstairs. I heard footsteps. I looked back, but no one was there. Then I felt someone grab the banister poles behind me. The poles just like shook. I thought someone was following me downstairs or chasing me. I thought all my hair was standing up. Later, Juanita and I talked about it."

"I used to cry," Juanita admitted. "When I was here by myself with my kids, I used to cry."

"You were scared?" I asked as gently as I could.

"Uh huh," she admitted, nodding her head slowly up and down.

It seemed Juanita and her husband trusted me enough now to share their genuine fear. I was still hopeful that what they had was a human ghost either starved for attention or desperate for it. Some of its methods may simply be inappropriate, like a child who doesn't know when enough is enough. Yet I, of course, didn't know this for sure.

I looked at Lorraine—my psychic barometer. We had been married and worked side by side for so many decades and on so many cases that I didn't need her gift of telepathy to understand what she was thinking. Was this a hoax? If not, was it a human ghost or something else? One glance and I knew that Lorraine felt something was here, but that it was something confused and frustrated, not evil. Meanwhile, we both empathized with the terrible fear these people felt.

"Did anything else unusual happen here you want to tell me about?" I asked.

"Well," Juanita began, "we saw grass on the floor. It was in the living room. There were like three or four pieces of grass. The doors and windows were closed. This grass seemed to come from nowhere."

It very well may be true. "Teleportation" dematerializes an object one place and then materializes again someplace else. Crazy? So was space travel not so long ago. If recent scientific theory is correct, than the essence of all particles changes from energy to matter and back again on a continuous basis! All Lorraine and I know is what we ourselves have witnessed. Teleportation happens.

The bigger and heavier the items moved, the more likely something unpleasant is involved. Grass, of course, is extremely light. If, in fact, this grass didn't come in on someone's shoe, it may have been a clue left by the ghost. If so, there was something simple, sad, and lonely about this feeble gesture.

Lorraine asked Juanita, "Are you sensitive? Are you mediumistic?"

"I'm not sure I understand."

"Are you clairvoyant?"

"Not that I know of," Juanita answered.

Carlos interjected, "All these years, she has some sort of way. Everything she says is going to happen, happens. Everything that happens here, happens when she is here."

Again, Lorraine and I were thinking the same thing. A human spirit in distress can sense someone that is more apt to sense it. This person will become its target in its attempt to get attention and help. The movie *The Sixth Sense* does a good job depicting this frustration on the part of ghosts as well as the confusion and fear on the part of reluctant clairvoyants.

Despite all that Juanita and Carlos had already described, something else prompted this woman to call the police. It was time to explore what that was.

Cheryl A. Wicks

Ouija Board Use

"How soon after these strange things began to happen did you consult the Ouija board?" I asked.

"Ah…nine months," answered Juanita.

"Had you ever used a Ouija board before?"

"No, never in my life."

"Did any of the events you just told me about happen after you used the Ouija board?"

"No. They all happened before. After we used the board, I spoke to Officer David, and he brought you to us."

"Who gave you the Ouija board?

"My daughter bought it and brought it to the house.

Lorraine interrupted to ask "Where is the Ouija board now?

"In the closet," said Juanita.

"Don't you think it would be good to get it out of the house?" Lorraine asked out of concern that the children may be tempted to play with it.

"No one is allowed to touch it," Juanita assured us.

"Tell me what happened when you used the Ouija board," I said.

"Okay. The Ouija board told me there was a murder back here, which I didn't know about, because I was new at the time. It gave me the name of the victim," Juanita blurted in a rush of words.

"Who was with you?" I asked.

"My daughter… she's fourteen, and Steve ... he's a Chinese boy about my daughter's age."

"What happened when you began to use the board?"

"The Ouija board told Steve to get out of the house in very bad language," Juanita said.

We needed to know if the language used was demonic filthy or just tough street vernacular. Lorraine coaxed: "Tell us the exact language, dear."

Hesitating, Juanita answered, "It said: 'Get your ass out of the house you ass fucker. I don't like you. Somebody has to get out.' So I said, 'Who and why?' And it spelled out Steve's last name and 'Mother Fucker get out.' That's when we told Steve to go because we want to continue."

It had been a while since I prowled the tough streets of Bridgeport, but those words sounded like street talk to me. "What happened after Steve left?" I asked.

"My daughter and I lit a candle, shut off the lights, and I asked more questions," Juanita told us. "I wanted to know who he was and why he was here. He says he was a boy. He got killed—murdered. I'd say: 'Why? Were you a drug dealer or bad person?' He said: 'No, they murdered me.' I kept asking him why, and he'd say, 'For nothing.'

"I asked him: 'what do you want me to do? Why do you come to me?' He said: 'Because, I want you to do a favor.' I asked: 'Why?' He wouldn't say. So, I say: 'What favor?' And he said: 'Go to the police.' I say: 'Go to the police, why should I?' He said: 'Cause they killed me.' He kept saying: 'Help, help.'"

"Did you know about this murder beforehand?" I asked Juanita.

"No," she answered. "I thought no one else did either, and that was why he was bothering me."

"Did you ask the board if it was the boy's ghost who was causing all the disturbances in your home?" I asked.

"Yes, I did," said Juanita. "He said he did it for attention because when he was here and before he was killed, a lot of people saw him, and nobody did nothing."

"They watched him being attacked and did nothing?" I asked.

"No. Afterwards. They closed their windows and locked their doors. He was screaming loud for help. Every time I used the Ouija board, it kept saying 'Help, help, help!'"

"What did you do after that?"

"I told Officer David about the murder the very next day," Juanita said. "That's when he told me a young boy had been killed behind our buildings. They knew that and had caught and convicted the killers. I said this boy was still upset, and he was upsetting me. The officer probably thought I was crazy, but he said he'd see if he could help. Then he brought you to help."

"Yes, and we will if we can," I assured her while looking over at the patrolman. He was looking a little paler than I remembered. "Has anything happened since?"

"After I found out about the murder, I talked to more neighbors. They admitted it happened. Some said they saw that boy's image in the complex after it happened. One neighbor thought she saw him sitting in a chair in her living room!"

Well, it looked like Juanita had conducted her own psychic investigation and maybe already had some answers. It was time to confirm them with the authorities and find out what we could do to help.

We thanked Juanita and her husband Carlos for their time. We promised that Lorraine and I or Officer David would get back to them.

Police Perspective

We found our coats, walked back out the dank hallway, stepped into the brisk air, and crawled back inside Officer David's car. Officer David agreed to tell us more about the case upon our return to the precinct, before falling silent. He was obviously doing his own thinking on the short ride back.

When we returned to the main house, we settled around a battered, wooden conference table with borrowed mugs of coffee and tea. It felt good to hold something hot in our hands and to sip the warm liquid. Officer David put down his mug, made sure we had sweeteners and cream, and then left us for a few minutes. He returned with a stained, dog-eared folder. "Okay," he said, "what do you want to know?"

"You look upset," Lorraine observed. "Did something happen tonight to upset you?"

"She never told me all that before. How would she know? She wasn't even here and no one else would say anything?"

Lorraine probed gently, "She didn't know what?"

Officer David gave a large resigned sigh and began the story. "About a year ago, a young boy was found dead in the ice-cold brook behind the apartment complex we just came from. The autopsy report showed he died of exposure and from a loss of blood.

"He had been beaten, stripped, and brutally cut with the pointed end of a small bottle or can opener. He was left to die in the swollen creek on a bitter cold night. We found grass in his hands that he must have grabbed in his struggle to crawl out of the creek. Here are the crime photos, if you can stand to look at them," Officer David said as he pushed me the folder. I opened it up.

Lorraine glanced at the glossy prints and looked away. They were as terrible as Officer David had warned us. "Why?" I asked.

"Apparently this poor, simple-minded kid insulted this other kid's mother. You were right, Lorraine, he was mentally handicapped. A few weeks after the insult, the insulted boy tricked the offending boy into coming to the apartment complex, where another friend was waiting. They led the kid to a shallow ravine behind the complex, jumped him, beat him, stripped him, cut him, and left him to die in the creek. We found the weapon, and we recovered plenty of fingerprints. They confessed in exchange for a lighter sentence."

"What did Juanita reveal tonight to disturb you?" Lorraine asked again. "Have you any idea why this soul might be so tormented?"

"I think I may know the answer," offered the officer, still standing and clenching his fists. "According to the autopsy reports, this boy took a long time to die. He tried to get out of the numbing water. He must have kept calling for help. You can hear a private conversation in the parking lot through those walls. Surely, someone must have heard something. Yet, no one claimed hearing anything. They must have closed their windows, doors, and hearts and let this kid bleed to death."

"That's terrible," Lorraine said with tears in her eyes. "The poor boy probably didn't know why they did it. He was so hurt...he couldn't understand why no one helped."

Ghost Tracks

"All I am saying ..." began Officer David with a firm mouth, "if that had been me, I'd be haunting a few people, too."

"But he is not doing it to punish anyone," Lorraine said. "Otherwise, why would he be bothering this woman who was not even there when this terrible thing happened? No, he is still confused and struggling for help and attention. He doesn't know he can move on. His mental handicap in life and confusion as he died are holding him back in death."

"Do you really believe all those other things she said happened?" Officer David asked.

"Yes, yes," Lorraine said. "I felt his presence there just like I did at the diner. He was trying to protect his new territory during her Ouija board session just as he was protecting his territory at the diner."

"He was probably playing with the lamp for attention and with the TV because it was new." I added. "His stomping around, following Juanita and Carlos and playing with the lights and other things would be something an immature child would do. I'm not sure what happened in the bedroom, but he may have been trying to hug Juanita and started to hurt her, which, of course ended up terrorizing her and her husband.

"The few blades of grass Juanita found in the living room seemed significant to her and to me. You just told us that this poor boy grasped at the grass in his struggle to get out of the creek, before giving into the cold and loss of blood."

"You know I have a hard time believing in all this ghost stuff," Officer David admitted. "But how else can we explain it all? Assuming there is something to this, what do we do now?"

"Are you a religious man?" asked Lorraine.

"Well, yes, I guess. In order to do this job, I have to believe in something," Officer David said.

"Good. That's good," Lorraine said. "It's important to believe in something outside this world. I bet you see things all the time in your job that other people wouldn't believe."

The officer nodded.

"Well, so do Ed and I."

The office laughed and finally cracked a smile. "You got me there. So what do we do?"

"We need to try to talk to this poor soul," Lorraine said. "We need to convince him to leave this painful world behind and cross over. Is there a chaplain at your precinct who can say a few words at the murder site?"

"Yes, there is," Officer David said.

"Great," I interjected. "Let's arrange it."

"One more thing, Officer," Lorraine said. "Was I right about where the first altercation took place...by the diner near that strip mall?"

"Yes," the officer admitted. "I don't think that bit of information even made the police file. It is just something I know from interviewing the animals who murdered that boy so ruthlessly."

Our hot drinking mugs had grown cold. After looking at the autopsy reports, we had all lost our appetites—and for me, that's saying a lot. Our heavy wooden chairs scraped on the old checkered linoleum as we all stood up to leave. Officer David had to finish up some paperwork before the end of his shift. Lorraine and I had a long drive ahead of us, and hungry pets to feed.

We said our good-byes, shook hands, and got on our way.

Epilogue

When we checked our schedule, we found ourselves booked back-to-back with lectures at colleges crisscrossing the country. October is always our busiest season, lecture-wise. We arranged to send some of our psychic researchers back to the site to resolve the case as quickly as possible. Their objective was to initiate contact with the haunting entity, confirm its identity, and help put it to rest.

Although we don't recommend it, they used a Ouija board to make contact, since this is apparently how the boy communicated before. As our students, they knew how to ask for protection before using this dangerous tool. Meanwhile, thanks to Officer David's efforts, a police chaplain was also present to help keep our students safe and lead the tormented soul to rest.

Contact was made. The ghost confirmed his human identity as the murdered boy by describing exactly where he had lived. Because of his learning disability, however, he was unable to give a clear street address. The researchers reassured the earthbound spirit and encouraged him to move on. The police chaplain blessed the site and prayed for the boy's restless soul. No one has seen or heard from the boy since ... but we do hear from now Lieutenant David from time to time.

Case Study #3
A Ghostly Interview

All names and places in this true story have been changed or modified to protect the privacy of clients. Ed Warren describes the case.

A Ghost Story

Our book, *The Demonologist*, had just been released and it provoked a call from a family just over the Connecticut border in New York State. The family consisted of a husband, wife, three children, and a dog. Their home was a large three-story structure that was approaching 200 years in age at the time. They loved their house, but it had its share of ghost problems.

Shortly after they moved into their home, the husband kept getting thrown out of bed, things thrown at him, and pushed by an invisible force. Sometimes he'd hear a Celtic voice in his head that seemed to shout, "Tool, tool!" He had no idea what this ghost was trying to tell him, if it was a ghost. Concerned for his own sanity and desperate for a good night's sleep, he and his wife called in a well-known parapsychologist.

This haunting was resolved, but since then the family would occasionally see the ethereal image of a young woman on the stairs. Other times, the family and their guests would hear footsteps, a ball bouncing, or someone falling down the same steep stairs. Upon investigation, there was never anything visible.

Ghost Tracks

Compared with their last ghost, this ghost was easy to live with. However, they had read our book about evil manifestations, and were concerned that their mysterious resident might not be all that harmless. Based on what we heard on the phone, and the fact that the family felt comfortable with their ghost, Lorraine and I believed there was no need for alarm. However, we agreed to go to their home to confirm this and see if we could find what was causing this new haunting.

We drove out one summer evening so the husband could meet us after work. The tall home was an imposing brown structure surrounded by an acre or two of lawn and deep woods along the back. Just inside the front door was a steep staircase that immediately caught our attention. The stairs seemed to go up forever. They led to the bedrooms and continued up to the attic.

It is not surprising to us that a home over hundred years old would be haunted. This is because back a hundred years ago, people would often die at home of old age or other natural causes. And a hundred years provides ample opportunity for someone to die suddenly in the home as the result of an accident, murder, or suicide.

Any of these events could create "ghosts." The events themselves could leave "psychic impressions" that replay the deeply emotional and physical trauma over and over. Those who die suddenly or by surprise might not know they are dead ... or are likely to have some unfinished earthly business. In the case of a suicide, the individual may think he or she is "not allowed" to cross over, or his or her agitated state of mind may continue beyond physical death.

Lorraine and I have found that it is the emotional aspects that keep spirits trapped on our earthly plane.

Cheryl A. Wicks

We find it ironic that the science of parapsychology—the study of the paranormal—began as an offshoot of psychology. It was thought at the time—and many skeptics still agree—that all mysterious manifestations were delusional or mind controlled. However, the great Dr. Freud was fascinated with parapsychology late in his career and took extrasensory perception quite seriously. Lorraine and I have met a lot of ghosts that could have used the good doctor's help.

As it turns out, the entity that first plagued our client's home was one such ghost. We were curious about their first haunting, because sometimes the conditions that accommodate one ghost make other spirits feel comfortable as well. Some researchers feel there may be some sort of vortex that allows spirits easier access into and out of our physical world at particular locations.

We just know that "like seems to attract like." Sometimes a living person may share physical, emotional or habitual traits with the ghost. Circumstances might be similar. Someone living might be mistaken for someone in the ghost's long past. Or some disturbance triggers a ghost's long memory and angst. We also know that evil behavior begets evil, and sometimes ghosts simply attract other ghosts.

At the client's home, Lorraine explored the stairs. Using her light-trance psychic abilities, she reported to us verbally what she was seeing, hearing, and understanding telepathically.

"It is the spirit of a young woman," Lorraine told us. "She committed suicide by throwing herself down these stairs. Her father was a minister, and she had become pregnant while still unmarried. She killed herself to protect her and her father's reputation.

"She feels terribly guilty," Lorraine explained, " ...for killing herself, her baby, and getting pregnant in the first place."

Speaking out loud to the spirit, Lorraine said: "It is all right to cross over now. All is forgiven. Your father is waiting for you on the other side. He is not angry. He only wants you with him." She repeated words like these for a few more minutes. Finally, Lorraine smiled and said, "She's crossed over."

The air in the entrance hall suddenly felt lighter and fresher. We each commented on that, and we all grinned at one another. The husband suddenly laughed and said, "Well, it looks like I have some more research to do."

He explained that after the parapsychologist's visit several years prior, he had researched the history of the house and community to find credible data that supported what was revealed through the deep-trance medium. Deep-trance mediums allow the spirit to speak through them. Some people call this "channeling." Other people call it malarkey.

Lorraine and I had begun our paranormal work by simply listening to other people's ghost stories. We were curious about this one. The homeowners agreed to share it with us, and the wife went to find the audio recording that had been made. After listening to it, we were so fascinated about what it revealed about the nature of ghosts, that we asked for a copy and for permission to share it with our students and readers.

Cheryl A. Wicks

The Ghost

The first time we heard this tape was at our client's home. After our quick resolution of their more recent haunting, we all moved into the client's comfortable living room brimming with antiques. The homeowners offered us lemonade as they set up the recorder. We settled down into soft chairs and prepared to listen.

We were reminded that the investigation was triggered by the invisible harassment of the husband and the mysterious words: "Tool, tool!" Our hosts also explained that on the tape, the parapsychologist was doing the interviewing. Although the responding voice was deep with a heavy Scottish brogue, we were told the medium was a woman with a normally soft, high voice.

Our clients explained that as the medium began to fall into her trance, she started to mumble something about a son being killed in a war and about someone named Maddie.

"Who is Maddie?" we heard the interviewer ask.

In a deep Scottish accent we heard, "My dearly beloved. Now she comes here, too."

Apparently the interviewer assumed the "dearly beloved" is a wife, because next he asked, "What was her maiden name?"

"She says 'Go, go, go!' every time she comes here now," answers the voice.

"What was her maiden name when you married her?" persists the interviewer.

"Benedict, Benedict is my name," answered the ghost.

Realizing he has been misunderstood, the parapsychologist presses, "But before, when you first met her ... What was her father's name?"

The voice goes from almost a dreamy state to one of annoyance. "She has been with me since the year fifteen, she is with me a Benedict. Who are you?"

"I have been sent to help you," answered the interviewer.

"O'Toole?" asked the ghost.

"No," said the interviewer. "Who is O'Toole? What did he do? What work did he do? Did you employ him?"

"No, no, no!" shouted the ghost.

"Did he come here later?"

"I do not know *something* like him," the ghost said with contempt. The words sound as if they were practically spat out.

"But who was he? Can you tell me more about this so I can recognize him?" asked the parapsychologist.

We heard four thumps and then the ghost softly asked: "You are not him?"

"No, I would like to help you find him," the interviewer clarified.

"Him…not here. I know that now. But you come new," answered the ghost with resignation and newfound understanding.

"I am new," the parapsychologist agreed. "I am a friend trying to help you straighten things out."

In a weary tone, the Scottish voice said, "Old bones of one like me are so decayed, it is not so good to find again, but young bones of grandson that has been always with me ... Help me find them."

Agreeing to help, the parapsychologist says, "We'll try to find your grandson's bones. Tell me, were they consecrated by the church? Were you a member of a church?"

"All things consecrated, huh ha!" the ghost said with a sarcastic laugh. "Consecrated!" he barks, followed by a long moment of laughter. Then we hear: "It has never come for me, even though consecrated. Ho, ho consecrated!"

"I know what you mean; but can you tell me the name of your church?" the scientist persisted.

The ghost was just as stubborn. "What consecrate? It's one thing I don't like anymore," he said with disgust.

"Even so… Do you remember what the church was though?"

"No! I will not remember what I don't like anymore," the ghost shouted.

Referring back to what the ghost apparently muttered when first making contact, the interviewer calmly asks, "Is your son with you?"

We heard two slow thuds and then the soft, sad words: "Ah, you bring to me sorrow… You bring to me sorrow…. You bring to me sorrow." This was followed by a long, despondent groan.

"What is your son's full name?" asked the interviewer, still seeking verifiable data.

"Steven," the voice said and then whispered: "Help me, help me." Growing much louder, the ghost said: "Oh remind me not, remind me not. Ohhh…" This trailed off into more groans that seemed to carry the sorrow and anguish of ages.

"Did your son serve in the army?" asked the interviewer, drawing on the war reference made as the medium began her trance.

"Ohhh! He gave his life. He gave his leg. He gave his bones. Ohhh."

"Do you remember what regiment he served in? Who he served under?"

"Oh, I don't remember. I don't remember."

Pushing for material that could be verified, the scientist pushed: "It's important. What regiment did he serve under? What general, what commander did he serve under? Do you remember what commander?"

"Ohhhh," the ghost said, followed by another series of sorrowful groans.

"Did you serve in the army, too?"

The ghost seem to chuckle and said, "No—only my son."

"Do you remember the regiment that your son served in? Was it cavalry or infantry? Was he on foot?"

"Foot," the ghost said abruptly.

"What number regiment, do you remember that?"

"One…six."

"Where was he stationed?"

"North."

"How far north, what town?"

"Oh, I don't know," said the ghost, becoming annoyed again.

Yet, the parapsychologist persisted. "What rank did he hold?"

"I don't remember."

"Was he a soldier or an officer?"

Finally the ghost exploded: "Young blood, young blood! Who are you? Who comes to destroy my peace?"

To keep the ghost from breaking contact, the parapsychologist changed his focus. "You shall have your peace. And you shall have all that you wish," promised the interviewer. "The house now belongs to someone else who takes very good care of it for you."

"I don't care for it. I'm here. I am for always," the ghost explained. After a slight pause, we heard, "O'Toole?"

"No, I don't know who O'Toole is. But I will help you find your grandson's bones, if you will just bear with me," the interviewer responded.

Softly, the voice said, "I will have my revenge."

"You don't need that," advised the interviewer.

"Ohhh, not!" the ghost argued.

In a soothing voice, the scientist said, "A lot of time has gone now."

"Time?"

"Years ... many years have passed," the interviewer said.

"It is quarter to six," said the ghost.

"Why quarter to six? What happened at a quarter to six? In the morning?" asked the parapsychologist.

The voice whispered, "Yes, it was dawn."

"What happened then?"

"O'Toole…the fiend O'Toole came. O'Toole comes here!" After shouting, the ghost suddenly whispers, "Ah, he came here."

"And then what happened? What happened to you?"

Softly the ghost said, "Not to me ... to my grandson." Growing louder, he said, "He dug the bones. He disturbed the grave of my grandson."

"But a lot of time has gone on since then. Do you understand this?" asked the interviewer.

Whispering again, the ghost said, "Ah, what could we do?"

"Nothing," said the parapsychologist.

Still whispering and sounding hopeless and lost, the ghost laments, "Nothing ... right ... always."

"You must accept this," the scientist tried to tell him. "I want you to accept these things."

But this ghost was carrying a grudge against more than a man named O'Toole.

A Ghost's Ghost Story

The parapsychologist had been encouraging the ghost to let go of his anger when the voice seemed to change the subject again. We heard: "No longer, no longer, no longer! I need Steven. See a bloody stump. We see him. We see him. And they have not accepted him."

We paused the tape to discuss what we just heard. These last words seem to indicate that in life, the ghost and his wife may have seen the apparition of their son as he crossed over from death in the battlefield. The father misinterpreted this vision as evidence that the son's soul was denied entrance into heaven.

When we started the recorder again, we heard the interviewer telling the ghost, "You must pray for him. You must ask that he be accepted the same way that you are. And you must ask this whether or not you believe in a church. By asking for it, you will receive it."

The ghost repeated: "We saw him. We saw him."

"I believe you," said the scientist, understanding the phenomenon.

"We saw him, but he was not here in person," the ghost further explained.

"I understand," said the interviewer with sincerity.

"And Maddie cried when we saw his bloody stump. Oh, where is he?"

Cheryl A. Wicks

We stopped the tape again to discuss this bizarre turn of events. This poor soul was a ghost because he didn't believe in ghosts! "Transition spirits" are the second most commonly reported ghostly phenomenon. Obviously, this man never knew that in life. Instead, he assumed this vision meant his son was exiled from the other side. Consequently, the man exiled himself. He wouldn't go where he thought his son was not wanted.

Good-bye, Ghost

The interviewer now had the challenge of trying to convince the ghost that his son had crossed over and was waiting on the other side. This was something the ghost had to want. Human free will is more powerful than most people realize.

Resuming the tape, we heard the parapsychologist say, "I want you to follow my words, and you will be helped. But you must listen very carefully now. I want you to repeat after me ... 'I ask that I be taken over to my beloved ones ...'"

"O'Toole?" said the voice.

"No, I will take care of O'Toole for you," the interviewer said sternly. "Your grandson's bones will be looked for if I can find them. I want you to repeat after me..."

"I'll revenge you!" the ghost shouted, reverting back to believing the interviewer was O'Toole. It is hard to keep a ghost from a century-old habit of hanging onto the past and anger.

The interviewer ignored him and said, "That's not necessary, I have sworn an oath ..."

"You are O'Toole!" insisted the ghost.

Ghost Tracks

Now it was the interviewer's turn to lose patience. "No! Listen, the bones will be looked for. If they are found, they will be interred. But a lot of time has gone on—over 150 years. Do you understand that? It doesn't matter anymore."

Softly now, the ghost asked: "Maddie?" A second later, the voice joyfully exclaimed, "Maddie!"

Perhaps she had come from the other side to help him cross over. The parapsychologist thought so, too, because he said: "She's with you. Ask for her. Call to her."

"Maddie, oh Maddie!" There was uncensored delight in the ghost's voice through the medium. Listening, one could only think how lonely he must have been.

"Good," the interviewer said. "Now will you call for your son? Call for your son, please."

"Maddie?" The voice faded as Maddie may have been fading away, too.

The interviewer pressed: "Call for your son as he was. You want to see him as he was. Ask for him as he was before his injury."

"He'll be bloody! Maddie will cry," admonished the voice.

"No! He will not come bloody any more," the interviewer assured him. "Ask for your son as he was before the war. Ask for him as he was."

Then we heard a voice, full of exasperation and carrying over a century of pain and grief, call out: "Ohhh ...if there *is* a God in heaven, let me have my son without the bloody stump!"

"Good! Now ask for your grandson," the interviewer pressed.

The ghost moaned, "Ohhh!"

"Ask for him. Ask for him. Now, now!"

This is followed by nothing but silence. The interviewer says in a less frantic and more soothing voice, "All right, now hold on to your thoughts about your family. Hold them! Good."

Suddenly the ghost exclaims, "Oh, my son!" There is so much genuine joy in his voice that it brought tears to our eyes and goose bumps to our flesh.

Wearily, the interviewer says, "He's with you, he's with you, now. Go with your family. Take them on over, take them across."

"Oh ..." the ghost said, as if finally at peace.

And that is where the tape ends, but not the story.

Epilogue

The husband was never harassed again. Apparently, their ghost had mistaken all men in the house for "O'Toole," who had disturbed his grandson's grave. The homeowners told us they discovered something quite interesting when they researched the history of the house. According to town records, a John Benedict did own the house—about 150 years earlier. He and his wife Maddie had a son Steven, who married and had a son of his own. During the Revolutionary War, Steven sustained a direct hit in the leg by a cannonball. He bled to death on the battlefield.

It was also discovered that after a full life, Steven's son was buried in a community graveyard that was later relocated to make room for a four-lane highway. The head engineer's name on the project was O'Toole.

This is one of the best true ghost stories we have heard, although Lorraine and I have heard quite a few over the last fifty years. We thanked our hosts for bringing it to our attention, and for giving us a copy of the tape along with permission to share it with others. They thanked us for confirming the harmlessness of their woman ghost on the stairs and for bringing her closure.

We offered our help should there be a recurrence of this activity, or any new one. We never heard from the couple again. Since we know they are still living in the house, we can only conclude that their home is finally ghost free.

Case Study #4
Water Poltergeist

All names and places in this true story have been changed or modified to protect the privacy of clients. Ed Warren describes the case.

Umbrellas Needed

It was a few days after a lecture we gave at a university in Pennsylvania that we received a phone call from a woman who had been in the audience. She sounded both wary and weary. She said she and her extended family had been experiencing the mysterious and sporadic appearance of water in unlikely places. Something other than her tone kept me from directing her to a plumber and roofer. Lorraine and I had investigated other cases that involved the strange manifestation of water. This could be another.

What made this case immediately unusual were the woman's claims that these strange events began in her father-in-law's house, followed him to his daughter's house, and even occurred outside. There had also been some escalating episodes of physical damage such as broken windows, lights, and knocked-over furniture. As a demonologist, this didn't sound good. A thousand questions came to mind, but they would have to wait until the investigation.

I tried not to sound too concerned when I told the caller that thanks to a recent lecture cancellation, we could be at her father-in-law's home the next day. She was too grateful to question the unusual break in our schedule. She gave me driving directions, and we agreed to meet at about 11 a.m. After we hung up, I called two of our researchers, asking them to join us, and I told Lorraine I was ready for lunch. All she said was, "That's nice, dear."

The next morning, our researchers showed up at our house with all their gear, just as Lorraine and I were finishing breakfast. We loaded cameras, video equipment, and other sensors in the back of my station wagon. My tape recorder, tapes, and some extra batteries for the recorder sat in the front seat. Lorraine held the map and directions on her lap. We were off!

It was mid-December and cold enough for snow. Roadside puddles were frozen over and frost whitened the fields and grass outside our windows as we traveled the highways with light early-morning traffic. Once we were off the beaten path, we stopped for a break. Lorraine had a cup of tea while the rest of us had another cup of coffee. I treated myself to a slice of homemade apple pie. Meanwhile, our bright morning had turned cloudy and took on a raw feeling.

We left the tiny rest stop and continued on our way. It became considerably more rural as we followed the directions past farmland through thickening woods. We found the three clustered mailboxes we were looking for a few minutes before eleven. The hilly land was cleared enough to see three small, square, well-kept but worn white houses. Two were practically across the street from one another. The third could be seen off into the distance. We were told to stop at the larger and slightly newer home on the right.

We did this. I barely put the car in park when the two back doors opened, and our researchers jumped out. Lorraine and I moved a little more slowly. My knee was stiff from the drive, and it felt good to stretch it. Looking about, we saw a picnic table in the side yard sheltered by huge oak and maple trees. Across the street, the tiny white house had a large, neatly-stacked woodpile and towering pine trees scattered about. Some distance behind the smaller house were some power lines with a row of tree stumps underneath.

The front door of the larger, but still small house opened. Out poured so many people that I thought of those tiny cars crammed with more clowns than you would think possible. There was a big man and a plump woman in their early thirties with a teenage son. Behind them stood a middle-aged woman and a stooped old man with pure white hair. The younger man, woman, and teenage son approached us while the other two people retreated back into the house.

"Hi, I'm Sarah Bentley. I'm the one who called you," chirped the dark-haired woman while she offered her hand to Lorraine and me. She introduced us to her husband, Ken, and her son, John. I introduced her to everyone who came out of our car.

"Across the street is my father-in-law's house—where it all started," Sarah told us. She explained that her sister-in-law had a record of everything that had happened, and invited us into the house. I grabbed my tape recorder and we all followed her inside.

Sarah's sister-in-law Ann was a tall thin woman with deep blue eyes and short blonde hair. She wore work boots, jeans, and a bulky green sweater. We were welcomed into her home and directed to the few but comfortable seats in her living room. I set up my tape recorder on the coffee table. Our researchers and the teenager John stood at the doorways. Looking out the windows, it appeared we had timed our arrival well. The sky had suddenly become gray, and freezing drizzle now coated the windows.

I began by speaking into the recorder myself. "For the record ... We are in Pennsylvania and today's date is December 16, 1990. We are in the house of Ann Bentley, daughter of Harry Bentley, who lives across the street and is currently eighty-four years old. Harry's son Ken, daughter-in-law Sarah, and grandson John live in another house nearby. Mysterious events involving water have driven Harry to move into this house with his daughter Ann. Is that all correct?" I asked the family.

Everyone agreed and I asked Ann, "How long have you lived in your house?"

"This is my thirteenth winter," she said.

"It is my understanding that all the strange things happened at your Dad's house until he moved in with you. Then they started happening here as well. Is that right?"

"Right," she said and nothing more. She looked nervous, fidgeting with the papers in her lap and anxiously looking outside as if she wanted to run. Some people are afraid we will think they are kooks; others think we are. A few fear Lorraine's clairvoyant abilities make her a mind reader and invader of personal thoughts.

I pressed on, "How long has it been since these strange things have been happening?"

"This is going on the third year."

"When was the last time something actually happened?"

"August of this year was the last time. About three and a half months ago."

"I cannot help but notice that there are a lot of water marks on your ceiling. Are they from a leaky roof?"

"No," Sarah answered for Ann. "We checked that all out. There seems to be water squirting in the air coming out of nowhere. We can't explain where it comes from. It comes from the ceiling. It comes from the air."

"Okay, Ann," I said. "Could you tell me when these things happened and where?"

She bent her head to the papers on her lap and said, "I have three calendars here. Events happened several times before we started taking notes. Ken asked me to start keeping a record."

"Let's hear what you have," I encouraged.

Sequence of Water Events

Ann shuffled through her notes and began. "Okay, over two years ago, in November of 1988, my mother was hospitalized with Parkinson's disease."

Ken interrupted. He was a tall, robust man with sandy hair and callused hands. "When our mother was hospitalized, it seemed like just her body was there. Some days she would know me. Some days she wouldn't."

Ann continued. "The water started on the twentieth of December over at my father's house. His whole house was saturated—beds and everything were soaked. I had to go over, and he moved out the same day."

Ken clarified: "He said when it started it was small, little spritzes. He would feel one drop and look around wondering where the hell it was coming from. My dad would start the wood stove and get the fire blaring. Then there would be a splash of water that would put the whole stove out. That did it for him. And every time he tried to move back, water would reappear within a few hours' time."

Ann agreed and continued. "When we couldn't find anything broken to fix, he stayed here. He'd go back to check on the house and light a fire every other day. But there was always water in his house."

Sarah added, "When we say water, I mean an inch all over the floors. Everything just dripped water. When we mopped, it would produce a wave. It wasn't just a puddle. It ruined the dining room floor. We had to put down a new floor. If it landed on tables or other flat surfaces, it would evaporate very quickly. Otherwise, we tried to get it up off the floors as quickly as possible before it rotted the floorboards away."

"Did it leave a sticky substance?" I asked.

"Yup," Sarah agreed.

"Did the water have an odor?" I asked.

"No," she said.

The old man finally spoke for himself in a deep gravelly voice. "It would happen in the kitchen all the time ... the oddest thing. It looked like grapes hanging, and then got bigger and bigger, then boom! Then another one ... and another one. Everything in the house filled with water. Boy oh boy! Then the lights would go out. The lights went out here at my daughter's a couple of times, too."

"Did you ever have an ozone odor in the house ... the smell you have after a thunderstorm or find in an electrical bus yard?"

"I know what you're saying," Ken said. "No, there was never an odor like that."

"Was anything ever broken by this phenomenon in Harry's house?" I asked.

Cheryl A. Wicks

Sarah answered, "The only things that broke there were the light bulbs from his kitchen light fixture. It filled with water and the light bulbs exploded."

This damage seemed to be more consequential than intentional. It was also a good sign that no one reported any foul odors or an ozone smell—strong indicators of an evil presence. Yet, something preternatural seemed to be involved. The sticky residue was just one clue.

Ann resumed her litany of events. "Dad agreed to stay with me through the winter, hoping we could resolve his problem in the spring. We started getting water in my house just after the New Year, on January 17, 1989. Yet, most of the water was still in Harry's house.

"He would try to move back into his house, but there would be water in his house. He'd move back here, and a couple of days later, I would get water in my house. Like Dad said, water would form at the ceiling—in the kitchen mostly ... and then the living room ... and finally in the bedrooms. It was water bubbles—clustered like grapes. They would wiggle around, and bang! They would fly at you. Finally we told Harry to stay away from his house."

"Were you ever able to find a physical cause for any of these things?" I asked.

Ann shook her head no and said, "Ken is a carpenter. He went up on the roof, into the attic, and under the house into the crawl space. Everything was dry. There was no reason for it to be wet inside either at Dad's or my house."

Sarah volunteered, "We had all kinds of engineers out and all kinds of experts in plumbing, heating, and electricity. No one found anything. Everything was always dry as a bone."

Ann's dad Harry added: "We had the house checked two times for gas. Two times we called them."

Ghost Tracks

Ken explained: "We called the gas company, figuring the disturbance was related to gas. They came in with their meters that could read fifteen different gases, but they said 'no way.'"

Sarah added, "I'm so tired of hearing 'gas'. Everybody had this theory. We also checked for radon. One man said it was methane gas ... sewer gas. We looked into that. We checked the sewer vent pipe. There is no gas."

"I even called the weather station," Sarah said.

Ann explained. "When things happened, it always seemed to be when it was sleeting or raining like today. When we get this kind of weather, we tend to get very uneasy."

Sarah continued. "I called the weather anchor at the local TV news station. I didn't give him my name, because I didn't want him to think I was totally nuts. He was sweet and agreed to talk to me. I told him what was going on and asked him 'Is there any kind of atmospheric thing that could create this?' He laughed and said no, not to his knowledge."

Ann returned to her calendars. "On February 7, 1989, my mother died. We were getting water in both houses—little squirts escalating to bigger ones. Later that month, Sarah and I went over to Dad's house to clean out my mother's clothes. Water started shooting out of her dresser drawers. When I went outside to load the stuff into my car, I got soaked. You could wring out the hair, and it was sticky."

Sarah clarified: "It almost felt like she had put hairspray on her hair and then went out in the rain. It felt like the sticky residue from hairspray."

"Could you tell me what exactly what happened with the dresser?" I asked.

Sarah nodded and said, "Ann and I went over to Harry's house to clean out my mother-in-law's clothes. As Ann began to open the bureau drawers, water shot out of the drawers, hitting her. It sprayed us both. Up until then, there had never been any water in my mother-in-law's room.

"As we were sorting through the clothes, we'd say 'This is nice, I'll keep this ... this is for the Salvation Army ... and this is for the garbage.' Every time we'd say 'garbage,' Ann would get hit in the back of the head with water! I started laughing, then Harry joined us, and we ended up laughing until the tears rolled. I said 'If we don't laugh, we'll cry.' That was the one and only time we ever got wet in that room."

The teenager John had moved closer toward the recorder during this discussion. He had his father's build and mother's coloring. His fine, shiny, straight hair lay below his shoulders. He volunteered, "When Aunt Ann left the house with the clothing, I was sitting in the yard. As she was pushing the stuff for the Salvation Army into the car, she got totally soaked. It was like pails of water got thrown on her. It was lots and lots of water."

"So the water would materialize out of nowhere outside as well?" I asked, concerned.

Sarah agreed and added, "It would follow Harry across the field when he left his house. As he was walking, water would be hitting him. One day it started to get wet in the house, so John and he went out into the woods to finish work on cutting a clearing among the power lines. Dad got hit with water over there in the woods. So wherever he goes ..."

Ann offered: "When we were sitting outside at the picnic table, and we would get water there a couple of times. Once when Sarah and my brother were driving over here, they got some water in their car. The inside of their car was wet. It followed them right up to my front door."

That reminded Ken of another incident. "With all of the water in his house, Dad's woodstove became rusty. He and I went to buy a new one. In the truck on the way back, Dad says he just got splashed. I looked over and his face was wet. It was a snowy day like today, but the window was closed. I thought that maybe something came in from the vent. I made sure the vents were closed, but he just got more and more wet."

"How could you explain the water coming from nowhere outside as well as inside the houses?" I asked.

Ken answered. "We couldn't. That is when we started saying 'There is no logical explanation. It can't be.'"

Ann resumed her sequence of events. "The next month, in March, Ken installed a vent and fan in Harry's house, hoping to improve air circulation. This when we began to try all sorts of solutions—testing for gas, removing the siding—but nothing worked. It was always water, water, water in both houses.

Ken explained, "I put the vent and fan in between his kitchen and living room to get the air circulating better. Dad would have the woodstove hot in the kitchen while the other rooms would be cold. One of our theories was that it was too hot in one room and too cold in the next, which was causing condensation. But the vent and fan didn't work."

Ann said, "We thought the problem in my house was maybe related to the coal stove. After Dad moved in here, my coal stove was always going out. We added to the chimney, making it higher to create more draft. It didn't work. The stove still kept going out. Later, we discovered that the toilet vent on the top of the roof had a pinecone shoved down there. We thought maybe it could have caused the problems. We fished it out but nothing changed. We even went so far as to take some of the siding off Dad's house, because we figured it was too airtight."

Ken explained, "After all these years of living here, nothing like this ever happened before. 'What changed?' we asked ourselves. The only thing we could think of was our putting metal siding on the back of his house. We took it off, figuring the house needed to breathe. You know, condensation, water build-up ..."

"It certainly takes a lot to convince you people that something unnatural is involved, doesn't it?" I asked.

"Did you ever call the university where we lectured?" Lorraine asked.

Sarah answered: "Well, I go to school there. I asked my chemistry teacher about it. He just said, "Yeah, sure, uh huh." He thought it was totally off the wall. He never heard anything like what I described."

Ken added, "I kept figuring it was something basic. I asked the guys I work with 'Hey, you ever deal with this? I got water flying through the air.' They thought I was nuts. They all had a good laugh for a couple of days, but after that, I realized I wasn't dealing with something normal here."

Sarah agreed. "You keep thinking if you talk to the right person, they are going to say 'Oh yeah, I know what that is.' Well, we've talked to lots of people, and all that happened was they thought we were crazy. You have no idea the repairs we made that were probably unnecessary. We threw out a gas stove thinking it must have some sort of leak. We got rid of Dad's refrigerator when somebody said Freon might be causing it. We were trying everything that anybody would suggest. We got to the point where we would consider anybody's idea."

Turning to the boy, I asked, "So why do you keep causing all these problems for your family, John?"

He laughed.

"At first, Harry actually did blame my son," said Sarah. "He thought John was playing a prank on him. John is fifteen, and has long hair and everything, but he is not a prankster or a wise guy. Yet, these things always seem to happen when my son is home from school. Harry would be home all day and everything would be fine. John would walk through the door in the afternoon, and everything would break loose."

"It is logical for parents and other people to say, 'The kid did it,'" I admitted.

Sarah agreed. "Yes, everybody has said that. He was getting to the point where he was thinking he had another life and didn't know about it. Somebody asked him what he told his friends about all this and he said, 'Nothing, I've got enough pressure without that.'"

"Were John and Harry always together when these things would happen?" I asked.

Ann said, "Usually, but not always. Sometimes Harry was alone. It rarely if ever happened when John was alone."

Lorraine turned to Ken and said, "What was John's relationship with his grandmother?"

"Very, very close," Ken answered. "I think she was probably closer to John than she was to anybody. He was very good to her, and she was really good to him. John was always close to both of my parents."

"How old was John when all this strange activity began?" asked Lorraine.

Sarah answered, "When it started, he was thirteen and a half, almost fourteen."

"About this time, did you notice ...if I can be personal enough to ask ... if you felt your son was sexually active?" Only Lorraine could get away with a question like that. I would be labeled a pervert.

"I don't think so," said Sarah. He'll talk to a girl on the phone once in a while, but it was her idea—not his."

Ken added, "Yeah. He is a little bashful yet, you know. He's into lawn mowers and cars, but he's not into the girl thing yet."

I could see that poor John was very uncomfortable with the direction this conversation was going, so I changed the subject. "What happened next?" I asked Ann.

"The following month, April, was dry. The water seemed to stop when the seasons changed. On May 27, 1989, my dad moved back into his house. Everything was fine from April through July. We thought that by removing the siding, opening the blocked roof vent, and a few other things we did, that we had somehow addressed the cause."

Sarah pointed out, "We also thought that these disturbances were winter related. It only seemed to happen on miserable, horrible, disgusting days. During the summer, we felt safe. It had never happened in the summer.

"But we did put our situation in the paper, asking for advice. We got two letters from people who claimed to be knowledgeable about what they thought it was. One was a guy that I had gone to school with. In his letter, he quoted things from Shakespeare relating to fire, earth, wind, water, and all that stuff. Both of the letters came through with exactly the same ideas. It was almost like they talked to each other before they wrote the letters. The other letter was from someone we didn't know."

I asked, "They were saying the spirits were elementals?"

Ann agreed. "Right, they said we were haunted by elemental spirits. We figured it could be worse, it could be fire!"

I concurred. "That's right. There are fire poltergeists. We have actually worked on such a case. Fortunately they are rare. Either that or they burned down the place before it could be investigated!"

No one seemed amused and Sarah continued. "I tried to get in touch with a man who taught a credit-free course entitled, 'Do You Believe in Ghosts.' I called and left my name and number repeatedly, but he never got back to me."

Ann added, "Hannah Croft came here from New York City. She said she was a psychic ... that she can feel things. She's got a home up here someplace."

Lorraine asked Ann, "What did she say she felt about this place?"

"She said she felt very heavy in my living room. It was like she couldn't breathe."

"That was it, heavy? Did she say what this heaviness was due to?" I asked.

"No. She said she would go home to meditate and think about it. That's the last we heard from her."

Lorraine asked, "Has anyone ever used a Ouija board before or after all this started?"

Sarah answered, "No, no one. I don't care for those things. They scare me."

"That's good," I said. "Those things can unintentionally invite dark spirits. Now to summarize, in April there was no unusual water. When did the problem come back?"

Ann resumed, "On January 23, 1990 of this year, the water started again in my father's house. He moved right back with me. Five minutes after it started, he's out of there. He shuts the door and says 'Good-bye.'

"The next two days—January 24th and 25th—both me and my brother had a few water squirts in our homes."

Ken interjected, "In my house, there was just enough to let you know something was there ...very little water."

Ann continued, "On January 28th, my father was hospitalized with severe nosebleeds. He has always been prone to nosebleeds. It was so miserable out. He was confined in the house with the dry heat. Plus he had a really bad head cold ... then you add nerves and everything else ... The water started again when Dad returned the very end of January. After that, just about every day there would be some water in Harry's, Ken's, or my house."

Violence Erupts

Ann shifted in her seat, put some papers on the floor and said, "On February 6th of this year—the day before the first anniversary of my mother's death, we had a priest out to bless the houses."

I let Lorraine ask all the sensitive questions, while I stuck to the chaos and mayhem. She asked, "What are your religious beliefs?"

Sarah answered, "Well, we're Protestants, but Harry is Lutheran. We're not religious people, but we thought a priest might help. He came with five or six prayer followers that morning. They walked around and blessed both houses, while they were saying prayers and blessing rooms with holy water. Harry said 'Just what we need, more water!'"

"Did the priest think that something preternatural was involved?" I asked.

"He really didn't say," Sarah said.

"Was he sympathetic to your problem?"

When everyone said the man seemed genuinely concerned and sympathetic, she asked, "What happened after he left? Did things stop, or did they increase?"

Ken admitted, "We had been warned by people that if the priest didn't know what he was doing, things could get worse. But after trying everything else, we figured, how much worse could it get?"

Ann inserted, "Well, a week and a half later, we found out. That is when all hell broke loose. My kitchen window blew out... knick-knacks got busted ..."

"Okay, this is important ..." Lorraine interrupted as she moved to the edge of the couch seat. "Prior to the priest's visit, you never had this kind of damage. Exactly how many days after the priest was here did this happen?"

Ann rustled through the papers on her lap, paused, counted, and answered: "Nine."

"That's three, three, and three," observed Lorraine.

It is our experience that malevolent spirits like to do things in multiples of three—as an insult to the Holy Trinity. According to Ann, the time between the priest's visit and a violent outburst consisted of three periods of three days. Was this coincidence or something else?

I signaled for Ann to continue, and she explained, "Nine days after the priest's visit—on February 15, 1990—my kitchen window blew out and a lot of other damage was done. I wrote down here that it was raining and sleeting. It was terrible out. The roads were a mess."

Sarah elaborated, "My son had gone with his grandfather over to Harry's house. While they were there, they went to make coffee and hot chocolate. Water came from nowhere and put out the stove and knocked the cup out of my son's hand. The mug flew right over his head. His grandfather also got hit a few times in the back of the head. Sometimes there would be water behind it, and sometimes it was just a dry force.

"Did John ever get hit?"

"Yes, he had a lump in the back of his head ... an actual lump."

The old man looked like he was sleeping, so I turned to the teenager and asked, "John, could you sit next to your grandfather, closer to the tape recorder, and tell us your version of what happened that day?"

John approached the coffee table, settled down next to his grandfather, and began to tell his story. "There was no school that day. The cup was knocked out of my hand at Grandpop's house, just like they said. When Grandpop started getting hit in the head, I made him put on my football helmet. We started to walk back to my aunt's house."

Harry, now wide awake, interrupted: "Then the helmet flew off my head while I was outside! Something hit the helmet, and it flew off my head about sixty feet. I bent down, picked it up, and put it on again. Boom! Down it went again. This happened three times."

John agreed. "Yup, the helmet rolled all the way to the house here. It kept rolling and rolling. He got hit in the head about three times."

Sarah added, "Harry later told me that if he hadn't had the helmet on, the force would have knocked him out. That dumb helmet probably saved him."

"Then what happened?" I asked John.

"We were sitting in my aunt's house, when all of a sudden the dog—normally very friendly—began snarling at us. We had never seen him growl at anyone before—bark maybe, but never growl. All of a sudden, the dog stared at the back door and snarled again. This time showing teeth. We opened the door to see what was outside, and the dog took off."

Sarah interrupted, "That morning, Ann's dog and cat both left and didn't come back until my husband and I got here later in the day."

John continued. "Then other things began to happen. There was such a splash of water around my aunt's sliding glass doors that the curtains were knocked off the wall. Pictures were knocked down, frames were broken, knack-knacks broke, and everything was knocked off her countertops."

"What time of day was this when this happened?" I asked.

It was Ann who answered after looking at her notes. "This had gone on from about 10:30 in the morning until 4:30 in the late afternoon. I didn't know anything about this until I came home from work. John and my father were hiding in the shower all day and were too afraid to come out even to call."

John agreed. "This will sound stupid, but we hid in the shower so we wouldn't get wet. Water was flying all over the place. We still got wet from the open top of the stall. Then we heard a big crash. I got out of the stall

Cheryl A. Wicks

and peeked through the keyhole. That's when I saw the kitchen window was broken."

Sarah interjected, "I asked him why he didn't call me to come home. He said he was afraid to leave his grandfather alone. It was so rainy and miserable outside—cold and snowy. He didn't want to take Harry out on the ice."

Turning back to John, I asked, "What did you find when you finally came out of the shower stall and bathroom?"

"It was like a tornado came through here," John said. "Even the detergent box on the washing machine was spilled over. There was soap powder all over the place."

Ken offered, "I came home from work that night, and as I pulled into Ann's place with the paper like I normally do, John came running out and said: 'You're not going to believe it. You've got to see it.' I walked in here, and he was right. I couldn't believe it. This place was a mess. I telephoned my wife Sarah and told her to come over."

Sarah agreed and added, "Yeah, it was like a bomb hit."

Ann went into more detail. "Fluorescent lights were broken. There was glass all over the place. Sparks were coming out of my outlet over there by the wall. Everything that had been on the tables was just wiped off. My bed and Dad's bed were both soaked—right through to the box springs."

Sarah explained, "When we first went in, we felt the beds and found the blankets on top were dry. So we said 'Oh good, at least the beds are dry.' But when we pulled the blankets back, the bottom sheet, mattress, and box spring were soaked. The same was true with the plaid rug runner. The runner wasn't wet, but there was a puddle underneath it. It does no good to cover things up to protect them. It doesn't help."

Ken added, "I also felt a mysterious, invisible force when I was sitting on my sister's couch right after all this happened. It was like a small golf ball rolling up my neck. I knew something was there, but nothing was. It only lasted five to seven seconds, but there definitely was something."

"I can understand why you would find all of this very disturbing," I commiserated, but then tried to refocus the report. "Can we go back to the broken kitchen window? Where was the broken glass, on the inside or the outside?"

Ken answered, "Outside. That window blew outside almost a foot. And it broke into thousands of pieces ... kind of like a busted windshield."

Ann added, "And it blew out round ... in a round shape about the size of a basketball. I have a picture of that. I still have the new sticker on the replacement window. I haven't scraped it off yet."

I had noticed the window stickers, but just thought it was a home improvement. Ann passed around the picture of a window with a large, gaping, perfectly round hole. Lorraine and I have seen this sort of thing before, and it wasn't from kids playing baseball.

"What happened next?" I asked.

Ann continued. "The next day, February 16th, we made plans to send my father down to Florida to stay with my other brother. We figured we'd get Harry out of here for the winter months. He was a nervous wreck and eager to go.

"The day before he left, February 23, 1990, there were only some small water squirts in my house. Nothing happened after he left. While he was away, I would go over to his house almost every day to check. Both his house and mine stayed dry.

Ken laughed and said, "My brother and I each agreed to drive Dad down to Florida halfway. He drove up halfway, and I drove down. When Dad got there, he said, 'If I'd known how long a drive it was, I would have flown.' We were ready to kill him. The only reason we drove is because he said he was afraid to fly."

The mood in the crowded living room lightened up a little and Ann continued. "On June 2, 1990, Dad came home from Florida. He flew this time. Nothing happened in June or July. We didn't expect anything to happen in the summer months. Nothing ever did before. However, on August 15, water started showing up again at Dad's house. Five minutes after it happened, he moved back in here with me.

"I noted that it was hot and muggy that day. The day before, we had a big thunderstorm. The day after Dad moved back in with me, it was humid, horrible weather. That same day, my front windows blew out. Six windowpanes out of the nine, by the front door there, blew out with perfectly round holes, but it never pushed the molding out. I've got pictures of that, too."

She passed around pictures that showed baseball-size holes, so clean and round it was like a glasscutter made them. The windows broken were not all together but scattered.

"Did anybody see this happen?" I asked.

"John and my father were here," Ann said. "My father saw water squirting from the sink to that big window there," Ann added while pointing to the sliding doors. "That's almost twelve feet away. Both Dad and John saw the windows around the front door blow out."

"What did you see, John?" I asked the teenager.

"My grandfather and I were sitting at the table out on the porch. We heard this sizzling sound, and all of a sudden, it was like a baseball came through the window! The sound was like a hiss. The window was coming out at us. Glass was falling out of the house. They didn't all break at once. One, then down one, then back up one, down again, and then the middle two."

After a moment of silence, while we all tried to absorb what we just heard, Ann continued reading her log. "A few weeks later was the last time anything happened. It was August 29th of this year—a little over three months ago. My house had water all over the place and everything was wiped off the table. A cake box and lamp were on the floor. The sheets I have covering my couch against the pets were pushed back and soaked. The beds and rugs were soaked. Everything on my dresser was overturned. A brand new coffee can was tipped over, the grounds were knocked out, and the inside of the coffee can was wet."

Ken offered, "It looked like someone came in here with a garden hose for about fifteen minutes. It also looked like someone took an arm and just went down the counter, wiping everything off in one direction."

"That time, we even called the troopers," Ann said. "I felt we should get something on record. When the policeman left here, however, he had no idea what he was going to write for the record. His job covered burglaries, vandalism, and those types of things. At least we got it on record that someone came out. The trouble is, if there was major damage, my sister couldn't file an insurance claim."

I asked Ann, "So, you haven't been able to collect insurance money for any of this damage?"

"No, no. The first thing they are going to ask is, 'How did it happen?'" she said.

These people were not making up this wild story just to collect insurance money for home improvements. In fact, they had spent an awful lot of money they probably didn't have trying to identify and remedy the problem.

Sarah added. "The other thing we worried about was my father-in-law's getting hit on the head and our being blamed for it. He had been knocked down a few times. He's eighty-four years old. We were afraid that one day he was going to get hurt. If no one knew that this stuff was going on, they were just going to say, 'He was hit on the head with a blunt instrument.'"

Ann agreed and continued. "September 4th is when I got the dehumidifier."

"Did you think that was going to suck up all the extra water appearing everywhere?" I asked. "That would be like trying to empty the ocean with a bucket, right?"

"There was a lot of water here when I first plugged it in," Ann responded with a straight face.

Sarah jumped in. "She swears it is a cure-all, but she is still trying to think logically, and there is nothing logical about this. This is just the calm before the storm. At any moment, I expect something—especially when the weather is bad. I tend to get very edgy in weather like this."

Ann wrapped it up. "In December, Sarah heard about you at college, called you people, and today, December 16th, you are here."

I asked the family, "Of everything you tried and all the people you asked for help, was anyone able to find out what was happening? Did they actually resolve anything?"

Sarah answered. "No, nobody. There have been many ideas and suspicions. Two or three years ago, if you told me about this, I would have said 'Ah, it's a bunch of hooey.' Now I suddenly believe a lot more than I used to believe. It has changed our lives a whole lot. It has also made a mess of a lot of things."

Lorraine asked, "Like what? Tell us. It's important." She was looking to see if the phenomenon was putting people at odds with one another or bringing them closer. Sarah's comment sounded ominous.

Sarah explained. "Well, it just creates a lot of turmoil between myself and my husband. His father looks to Ken to fix it. If the roof flew off, he could fix that. But he can't fix this. He doesn't know where to start. Ken gets aggravated and upset, so he takes it out on my son and me."

Ken said, "When I'm at work, I don't know what's happening here. So when I come home, I never know what to expect. When you can't fix it, you feel helpless. It spills over to your whole life. You think it has to be something basic like gas turning into water vapor or something. When it's not, it's very frustrating."

Lorraine asked Ken, "Do you feel it has caused a great deal of animosity between family members, or would you consider yourself a close-knit family?"

"Actually, despite our frustration, we're very close," Ken said. "The turmoil has brought us closer. It's a problem we all face together."

Sarah concurred. "Yes, my husband, myself, son, along with his sister and father are the ones experiencing it. Because we have all experienced something, we know we are not Looney Toons. Believe me, for a long time, I thought I was crazy."

"So, even though you began to associate these events with Harry, you never thought of dumping him?" I asked, smiling.

Lorraine was not amused. "Oh, you are very subtle, Ed," she said.

"Well, we did send him to my brother in Florida," Ken admitted. "But that was more for Harry's sake than ours. And nothing happened to him while he was in Florida."

I continued exploring. "Has anyone ever seen anything like a ghost here or a strange dark, black shadow?"

Sarah said, "No, not to my knowledge. I don't think anyone has ever seen anything." Ann, Harry, Ken, and John all nodded their heads in agreement.

"Okay," I said, paused, looked around the room at everyone and said: "I think I'm ready to tell you what I believe is going on here. I cannot tell you why it is happening until we conduct a psychic investigation with Lorraine. But I can tell you what seems to be happening. Anybody interested?"

The room vibrated with a loud chorus of "Yes!"

"Okay, I'll tell you, without asking you to bake me a cake first."

Lorraine groaned and everyone else just laughed.

Ed's Summary Impressions

"Well, folks," I said, "it seems you have a genuine water poltergeist here. Lorraine and I have seen this type of phenomenon before. Years ago, people in Missouri would be in their house, and it would be as if someone threw a bucket of water right at them, and let it splash all over the place. Another house we were in looked as though it was raining in the kitchen. In that case, it was very similar to yours where they would get globules of water and so forth on the ceilings.

"In both of these cases, water would appear apparently out of nowhere and leave a slightly sticky residue. You are more apt to have this happen when it's humid, raining, sleeting, or snowing because the water is being teleported. Water is being transported from the outside inside, or from some place else to wherever you are outside. The events themselves and the sticky residue are clear signs of teleportation.

"But let me explain a few other things first. 'Poltergeist' is German for noisy or mischievous ghost. In your case, the entity is not noisy but is mischievous. And, as I just explained, it probably is not a ghost. The term 'ghost' usually refers to the spirit of someone who lived and died here on earth, but has not yet crossed over to the spirit world. Those souls that have crossed over and those spirits that have never been human can also interfere with the living. Some of the 'never human' entities are good, and some of them are bad.

"In most poltergeist activity cases, 'ghosts' are seldom seen. This is because 'ghosts' are seldom involved. It takes more knowledge and power than any earthbound ghost we've seen to move gallons of water, disturb heavy furniture, and do other significant damage, particularly in more than one place. 'Ghosts' are always linked to one place and area. Your entity followed Harry outside, to Ann's house, and to vehicles. Yet, it didn't follow him to Florida. Although this force is not tied to the area, its interests seem to be.

"Sometimes, poltergeist activity can be attributed to a person who is disturbed, hurt, or angry, particularly a teenager. Yet, even science has to admit that this is not always the case. And I don't think it applies in this case. John seems like a good kid who is well-adjusted. While I think he is bright, I don't think he has engineered a secret, elaborate sprinkler system in all these places in his spare time. I cannot reasonably believe he is orchestrating all these events—consciously or unconsciously.

"I also don't think you folks are creating a hoax. There are water stains on Ann's ceiling. You have pictures of window damage that is unusual to you, but familiar to Lorraine and me. The hissing sound you described is also familiar. As you might have guessed by now, these are all hallmarks of paranormal activity. You folks are not becoming rich from this experience, nor do you seem to be seeking attention. This is not a scam for some free home improvements. 'Acts of ghosts' tends to come under the 'acts of God' clause in insurance policies and Lorraine's and my endorsement won't change that."

I heard a few weak chuckles and continued. Now it was time to get serious.

"Actually, most poltergeist activity can be harmful, and some can be downright deadly. Your boy John got hit so hard, he had a lump on his head. Harry was forced to wear a helmet. They both had to hide in the shower to avoid being hit by flying objects. You admit to being afraid Harry might be knocked unconscious one day—or worse. People have been hurt. Harry and John are lucky they weren't hurt more seriously, or killed. This is nothing to fool with. I know. I have been slashed on the arm. I've been thrown across the room—all 106 pounds of me."

Lorraine couldn't let that stand. "Sure, honey. Slight understatement, very slight."

"Did I say 'pounds'?" I said innocently. "I meant to say 106 kilos." No one was buying it. "Joking aside, you have a serious problem here. Sometimes events like this end as fast as they start. But from what you people told me, this has already stopped for months only to resume again when conditions are right.

"We are dealing with something here that is unseen, intangible, and has skills and powers beyond human experience. It has the intelligence to target Harry and this area for some reason. Psychic energy can build up quickly in a small area. Your dad's house is extremely small. Ann's house is not much bigger.

"John is an ideal age to be a trigger or agent for poltergeist activity. Trained scientists and we field researchers have found that this type of activity requires an enormous amount of energy and often occurs where there is an adolescent present. We just tend to disagree with science regarding the reason. Science feels agents are always the direct cause while we feel they are sometimes the indirect cause. I believe that is the case here.

"As an experienced demonologist, I'll tell you what has me concerned, and then I'll tell you some of the conflicting, but more positive signs I see here. First, my concerns: It is very disconcerting to learn that the activity has turned violent and that it made this change following the house blessings by the priest. This entity has the ability to follow Harry outside, to Ann's house, and to Ken's truck. It is powerful enough to blow out windows and consistently teleport large volumes of water. These are not good things.

"On the conflicting and optimistic side, however, you all have experienced some of the same phenomena. The entity and problem didn't follow Harry to Florida. No one has complained of foul odors, felt they saw an unusual black shadow, or complained about something trying to gain control of their body. You tell us no one here used a Ouija board, held a séance, tells fortunes for a living, or practices black magic. Looking at you, I'm assuming Harry's deceased wife was not a Satanist either."

There was no dissent, so I continued. "Despite everything that has happened, you are not at each other's throats. Now there were probably quarrels. Everybody has those. There is no way to get out of it. While you don't have any strong religious convictions, I can see you are positive people. You don't go around kicking animals, or throwing Harry and John out into the street in order to keep your homes dry."

Sarah added, "We try to support one another and remain hopeful. We even went so far as to get John a puppy in September, and we named him Spirit!"

I laughed. "And you have a sense of humor, too. That's also good. Inhuman malevolent spirits or 'devils' like to frighten. They want to create animosity among you and usually do this by isolating and harassing one person. The rest of you start to blame that person. When completely different things begin to happen to different people, and you start blaming one another. These activities tend to escalate over time. Eventually, the entity will try to take control over one person. Through that individual, more deadly damage can be done. These maleficent spirits also react violently to any type of religious intervention.

"You can begin to see why I am still not exactly sure of what you have here. Malevolent spirits are also very deceptive. That is their biggest strength. The other question is, why did this activity start and why is it directed at Harry? Since we are dealing with something not from this world, the only way to find out what is here and why is through a psychic investigation.

"The priest and so-called psychic that were here were well-meaning, but not knowledgeable. They were unable to discern what was causing these problems. This is what is important. You can't operate on a person unless you know what you are operating for. You just don't take a scalpel and open somebody up because he has a pain in the stomach. You have to know what you are doing and why. That's what we have to find out now.

"In order to do this, we need a psychic. Fortunately, I just happen to have one with me today. Lorraine's psychic abilities have been verified, validated, and categorized at UCLA. Science is now doing that these days. It helps discern those with credible psychic skills from the crazy or opportunistic. Lorraine might be crazy for marrying me, but her psychic abilities are real. I think we need to look into your situation further because unfortunately, I don't think you have seen or felt the last of your unwelcome visitor."

Ann volunteered: "Oh, I agree. I've been getting this creepy feeling lately."

Lorraine added: "See, the problem has never been rectified, really. It has never been identified or corrected. It has only been tabled temporarily or circumvented."

I turned to the older man and asked, "It might be uncomfortable, but do you think you could go back into that house with us now?"

"No, no, I don't want to go near the place!" he exclaimed.

I explained that it would be easier for Lorraine to reach the spirit with Harry and John around, because the entity was already attracted to them for some reason. Sarah coaxed Harry: "We'll all be going with you. Not just you, everybody ... all of us."

Harry held firm: "No, I don't want to. I might get soaked. I don't want to go in the house."

Ken persisted. "Five minutes, that's all. We'll all be there. Then you can show them the ceiling and everything."

Harry was stubborn. "You people show them the ceiling. No, I don't want to go. No, I'm not going."

I spoke up: "Okay, your father doesn't want to go. He is really afraid. He's eighty-four years old, and he could have a heart attack. John, would you be willing to go with us?"

"I guess so," he said with little enthusiasm. "What are you going to do?"

"Lorraine is going to try to contact the spirit and find out why it is upset, and what it wants. Depending on what it is and what it wants, Lorraine may be able to convince it to leave. If not, we can recommend or arrange other actions to try to resolve this problem for your family. Are you willing to help us?"

"Okay," John said, with eyes as large as saucers in his suddenly pale face.

"Good!" I reached into my pocket and pulled out a handful of religious medals. "Now I know you people aren't Catholic, but I am what is known as a religious demonologist. That does not make me a religious leader of any sort. What it means is that if an extremely bad entity in involved, it is my observation that science has never been able to relieve the situation. Only religious rituals seem to have any chance for success. It doesn't matter what religion, but how much faith the investigating person has does matter. These medals have been blessed with a ritual exorcism and are ascribed with prayers against evil.

"Please take one of these medals to hold in your hand. It is not so much what you believe as what Lorraine and I believe. This is what works for us, and this is the best way we know to protect you. We still don't know what we have here, but it is better to be on the safe side."

As we all stood up, everyone took a medal. Except for Harry, all of us shrugged into our coats and found umbrellas. We became drenched just dashing across the street in the sleeting rain. If someone was watching us run as a clump from house to the other, they would have thought they were watching some sort of bizarre Chinese fire drill.

Lorraine's Psychic Impressions

Ken opened the door of Harry's tiny house and let us inside. It was dry, but not much warmer than the raw weather outside. Once again, I set up my tape recorder. Then I explained what would be happening.

"With your permission, Lorraine is going to wander through the house to see what psychic impressions—if any—she receives. If she senses something, she may be willing to go into a light trance to try to communicate and find out what it is and why it is causing these disturbances."

Ken interrupted: "Before we start, can I ask you something?"

"Of course," I said.

"I always feel unusually cold in this house. I mean this coat I'm wearing is good to minus ten degrees, but I'm practically freezing. I think it's warmer outside than it is in here. Is this to be expected?" Ken asked.

I explained: "If there is some sort of ghost or spirit involved here, it may be drawing energy from our body heat. This is why someone can feel cold spots in haunted houses and yet see no difference in temperature reflected by thermostats. The house may actually be warmer than it feels to us."

Lorraine took off with our researchers to explore the other rooms. The rest of us walked into the kitchen to study the water spots on the ceiling, and we remained huddled in that small room talking about the upcoming holidays.

A few moments later, Lorraine walked to the kitchen door with the researchers following in her wake. "It's following me to this point," she announced.

"What's following you?" I asked.

"Well, I'm not sure, honey," she said. "In the bedroom area, it doesn't feel that bad. But the living room area and little vestibule where you come in... it's just powerful."

"There is something here in this house?" I asked.

"Oh yes, something is still in this house. It feels tremendous aggression, violence. Here in the kitchen, I feel like I'm in the midst of an argument. People are just bickering, fighting, and screaming back and forth at each other."

"Would this have any meaning for this house?" I asked the family.

Sarah answered. "Ken's father and mother fought mostly nonstop. Not actual fights, but they chewed, bickered, and picked at each other for everything. Their relationship was like that since I first met them."

Ghost Tracks

Lorraine continued, "If the grandfather, Harry, were to come back in here again, it would give energy to what is here. The same thing would happen again. It seems to follow him from this house to the other house. But it is here. It is here, now ... especially in the other room. The living room and the vestibule are really the focal points. I don't feel anything in the bedroom areas ... not at all."

"Okay," I said. "Let's go back to where you were."

We all traipsed into the small living room. As we crossed from one room to another, one of our researchers said, "I think I just got a drop on my head."

The other researcher pointed to water that wasn't there just moments before on the coffee table. Suddenly that same researcher said, "I'm feeling ... my body is so cold right now. I don't know what I'm feeling. The cold is coming up through my legs. Unbelievable!"

Suddenly he flinched again and I asked, "Did you get it again?"

"Yes," he confirmed.

We were all crowded into the living room with our winter coats, which were still damp from the weather outside. Lorraine had the teenager John stand next to her. She stood still, looked down and inward, and clasped her hands together. It looked like she was praying. She was. Silently, Lorraine and I said the St. Michael prayer together to protect everyone present from evil.

After a brief moment, Lorraine spoke, "Harry's wife is here," she announced, "but only out of concern for her husband's state of mind. She is not the one causing these disturbances. She has crossed over and came back to help.

"There is someone else. He has also crossed over, but has many powers. He is very upset. He was an Indian brave in this life. He fell in the water as a child and came up laughing. His name is Waterfall. He likes to play in the water, splashing others. The tribe he belongs to is very attached to the land. They do not wander like other tribes. Instead they stay and work the land, and hunt from here. They have been protecting this land for generations, and still do.

"There was a big stand of trees—pine trees. These have been cut down. This brave is angry about that. He is angry with Harry for having the trees cut down and for burning the wood in his stove." Lorraine asked the spirit: "What can we do to correct this?" She waited, then said: "He says new trees must be planted. He is going now, but he is forever watching. Unless this is done, he will be back and only more angry."

The heaviness and coldness in the air seemed to lift a little as Lorraine shook herself out of her light trance. "Does any of this mean anything to any of you?" she asked the family. They were all looking at one another with both surprise and wonder on their faces.

"Wow, it's incredible, and we never even thought ... Yes, it does," Ken said. "The electric company had been after Dad to cut down the row of pine trees under their power lines. My mother was a nature lover and wouldn't hear of it. That was one of the things she and my father kept fighting over. When she was hospitalized, Dad went ahead and with John's help, cut down the trees. Even though I tried to tell him pine is not the best fuel for woodstoves, he figured he wouldn't have to buy firewood for a few years. We figured he just needed something to do to keep his mind off Mom."

"Is that the row of stumps I saw way behind this house?" I asked.

"That's it."

Ann laughed and commented, "This certainly would explain the timing for all the water activity ...and why Dad and I had a hard time keeping our stoves lit. I guess it also explains the water. Good thing the Indian was not named Fire-starter or Rock-thrower!"

We all laughed in agreement and John said, "The time it followed us out in the woods, we were chopping those downed trees for firewood."

Sarah said, "And I guess that spirit was very protective of my mother-in-law when we were cleaning out her things, because she was protective of the trees."

"So," I said, "you see, there is a logical explanation! We humans just need to look outside this dimension to find it. The good news here is that this spirit is not looking to possess or destroy you. It is looking for restitution of those trees. Will you be able to plant new trees there in the spring? If they are seedlings, it will be a generation or two before they will interfere with the power lines again."

"Maybe we should leave a note for subsequent generations," suggested Sarah half-seriously.

"That might be a good idea," I said, smiling. "We'll follow up with you in the spring to see what happens. Until then, do you think these people will be harassed again, Lorraine?"

"The spirit was angry about the trees and about not being heard or understood. That is why the activity kept escalating. You were not the only ones frustrated! Now that he knows the message has been received, I think he might wait to see what happens. Maybe not. I recommend you plant those trees as early as possible."

Sarah observed, "I guess it will take another year or so before we are sure we have found strange cause and solution."

"I'm afraid so," I said. "Remember, spirits literally have all the time in both our and their worlds. Call us if things continue or get worse. There still may be another spirit here trying to take advantage of all the anger and fear. We don't think so, but you never know."

We stood around for a little more chitchat while I sent the researchers out to warm up the car and scrape the windows. Age does have its privileges. When they signaled that the car was ready, I interrupted a conversation Lorraine was finishing to ask: "Where is there a good place to eat around here?" We got directions and were on our way.

Epilogue

We didn't hear from the Bentleys all winter long. In May, we called them. Harry had stayed at his daughter's house for the snow season. Except for a few spritzes, there was no more water or violence in either of the houses. When we spoke to them, the Bentleys had just planted a row of pine seedlings near where the mighty pines had stood. Harry was moving back into his own house, but was more confident in the warm weather than in the new trees protecting him.

It turns out Lorraine and I have a mutual friend with the Bentleys. It is through this acquaintance that we learned years later that the Bentleys never had another unexplained disturbance. The spirit Waterfall apparently had been appeased by our contact and by the planted trees. Once again, both the natural and supernatural worlds were at peace at the Bentley compound.

This case also reminds us how interconnected we are with nature, as well as, the living and the dead, along with the past and the present.

SECTION III

Evil: Beast or Behavior?

Once again, Ed and Lorraine Warren stood before the eclectic group of students of the paranormal. Lorraine got everyone's attention and began the evening by saying the St. Michael's Prayer—a Catholic prayer for protection against evil. She then introduced the night's topic.

"Tonight we're going to talk about a controversial subject in the field of paranormal research. Even today's religious leaders are sweeping it under the carpet, and science likes to think the whole topic is nonsense. But it is not. We wish it were. Ed is the demonologist, not me. He is going to give you the religious history and then tell you how you can discern evil phenomena and what to do about it."

Ed jumped in, "What to do about it is easy. Run as fast as you can as far as you can in the opposite direction! Actually, that is never enough, because evil can follow you. You can never run fast or far enough. As with all destructive forces, the best defense is avoidance and prevention. We'll get to all of that later. Meanwhile, I'd like to start with what religion tells us about the dark forces.

"According to the biblical story, the archangel Lucifer was cast out of heaven due to wanton insolence and arrogance. A third of the angelic host left the heavenly choirs to become part of Satan's diabolical legions—with demons being more powerful than devils. The Greek term 'Daimon' referred to all spirits with divine power. In the

Bible, however, the term 'demon' refers to evil spirits, while 'angel'—or messenger—refers to good spirits.

"'Satanism' has its roots in early Christianity. As this religion grew in power, it imposed more and more rules on its followers. The 'anti-Christ' movement started as a revolt against the Church. Christian rituals were parodied. The Lord's Prayer was said backward, the crucifix was hung upside down, black candles were used, and a Black Mass was held.[11] Those that worship Satan today follow many of the same rituals. Regardless of what they do, how they do it, and even why, they are inviting evil into their lives. And if invited, he will come. He just won't leave as easily."

Lorraine spoke up, "So, are devils and demons real? According to a Gallup Poll taken in May 2001, 57% of Americans eighteen or older either believe in evil possession or at least have some doubts about the possibility.

"Reprinted in *L'Osservatore Romano* in November 23, 1972, is the following quote from Pope Paul VI when addressing a general audience on a few day earlier on November 15, 1972. 'What are the greatest needs for the Church today? Do not let our answer surprise you as being over-simple or even superstitious and unreal. One of the greatest needs is the defense from that evil which is called the devil…Evil is not merely a lack of something, but a positive agent, a living spiritual being, perverted and perverting…'"

Ed added, "In January 1975, a closed-door, invitation-only conference was held at the University of Notre Dame in the U.S. The topic was 'A Theological, Psychological, and Medical Symposium of the Phenomenon Labeled as Demonic.' The twenty-four scholarly papers presented confirmed the austere reality of diabolical oppression and possession.[12]

"Sociologists argue that many individuals are driven to vile behavior by their environment and circumstances. Demonologists warn that these same situations attract and invite evil spirits. Psychiatrists and psychologists argue that rather than 'evil possession,' many individuals have a chemical imbalance or other mental disorder. However, even these professionals admit there are some cases that defy clinical diagnosis or solution.

"Doctors can identify multiple personality disorders, schizophrenia, and bipolar personalities. Yet, they know of no mental or physical disorder that triggers drastic and abrupt physical changes or the spontaneous development of unusual skills. While exploring poltergeist activity, science has been able to link telekinetic activity to emotional issues in many of the cases. The exceptions are infrequent, but scientific professionals admit relief in these rare cases only comes from religious intervention ... regardless of the victim's religious beliefs—or lack thereof.

"In his 1980 book, *Minds in Many Pieces,* psychiatrist Dr. Ralph Allison revealed that patients—particularly multiple personality disorders—can benefit from exorcism as well as conventional treatment."[13] Ed stopped and reached for the tall glass of diet soda Lorraine had placed in front of him.

Lorraine took this opportunity to address the group. "The conundrum with evil is it is a master of deception and misinformation. It counts on others not wanting to become involved. It thrives on fear and confusion. Whether it is human or inhuman, evil preys on the ignorance and trust of others. It seeks complete control, and takes pleasure in using its power to do harm.

"We may chuckle at people who are quick to blame 'the devil' for their self-serving acts—like the character created by comedian Flip Wilson, who whined: 'The devil made me do it.' However, it is not funny when people we thought we knew suddenly become lurid and homicidal ... with no physical or psychological reason. It is not funny if you are the one who feels oppressed, beaten, or violated by something malicious, powerful ... and unseen.

"Since recorded history, priests, rabbis, lamas, shamans, witch doctors, medicine men, psychics, and psychiatrists have been consulted regarding the removal of negative thought and energy that seems to be independent of the individual. As early as the first century, rabbinical literature mentions exorcism rituals."

Ed offered Lorraine a seat and regained the floor. "The Greek term 'exousia' means oath. An exorcism invokes a higher power to compel the malicious power to accept an oath contrary to its wishes. The formal exorcism rite for Catholicism is known as 'Rituale Romanum.' Its text was authorized by Pope V at the beginning of the seventeenth century, and only can be applied to people—not places.

"However, Anglican priest Reverend J.C Neil-Smith of Hampstead, England claims to have performed 800 successful exorcisms of both places and people.[14] Rev. Neil-Smith feels—and the Warrens strongly concur—that exorcism success depends on the faith, motive, and conviction of the exorcist."

Lorraine spoke up, "Of the more than the 3,000 paranormal cases Ed and I have investigated over fifty years, almost 600 have benefited from an exorcism. While we are willing to help people of all religious faiths, we ourselves are Catholic and seek the same evidence the Catholic Church does before recommending an exorcism. This is what makes Ed a religious lay demonologist. Although he is not a priest or minister, he believes in the power of God and seeks to validate phenomena based on rules of evidence for our particular religion. This includes levitation, superhuman strength, speech in a language not previously known, and a physical discomfort with religious words, rituals, and articles."

Ed explained, "The exorcism itself is a dangerous and unpleasant business. Waves of heat and cold fill the room. Objects are thrown about. Without the individual being touched by anyone or anything, the possessed often suffer pain along with unbelievable physical contortions and spasms. They experience disgusting body noises, diarrhea, spitting, vomiting, and spontaneous cuts. The victim utters strings of foul swear words. The exorcism reveals what had been happening to the person under the evil force's cunning and usually more discrete control.

"The Catholic Church considers exorcism as private as confession, and abhors any publicity. Authorities are often forced to label evil phenomena a hoax. The alternative is to cause panic or attract relentless attention to a specific home or community. Even those who actually perform exorcisms, or are firsthand witnesses to the violent and bizarre events, will resort to the 'hoax solution' to avoid ridicule or attention. These actions, of course, only make it harder to sort reality from fiction."

Lorraine added, "Evil entities are resourceful, intelligent, and devious. They will often represent themselves to be something they are not. That could be someone with whom you are likely to sympathize ... or maybe even someone you knew.

"For example, two nurses had in their possession a Raggedy Ann doll that developed the ability to move and talk on its own. (This was the first clue that something was not right, even for paranormal activity.) They were told the doll was possessed by the spirit of a little girl who died in a car accident on their street. They verified that a little girl had in fact died there, and proceeded to call the doll by the girl's name—Annabelle. (Evil used its supernatural knowledge of this information for its own purposes.)

"The nurses began to treat the doll like a child, 'inviting' it to become part of their lives. When physical slashings occurred as a result of a boyfriend's challenging the doll, the Warrens were called in on the case. They confiscated the doll, but before it could be placed out of reach, behind glass in the Warrens' occult museum, it was responsible for a policeman's early retirement, a priest's near-fatal car crash, and a young man's death."[15]

Ed continued, "We have captured many horrific hauntings on film, as well as, on audio- and videotape. This material documents rappings, bodiless voices, large and small objects moving by themselves, and even the trauma of an actual exorcism. We are willing to write and talk about these experiences because we feel people should be aware and forewarned. Lorraine and I have nothing to prove, only to report. Our objective is not to frighten, but to inform. After over five decades of observation, interviews, and research, we are completely convinced evil entities exist. As powerful as these demonic spirits are, however, they have vulnerabilities and follow predictable patterns."

Lorraine began, "The first step in the demonic process is **attraction** ... also known as encroachment or invitation. Understandably, the Warrens are asked to investigate only after violent events begin to happen. What preceded the disturbing events may indicate if the phenomenon is dangerous. A violent or malevolent act that occurred some time ago at the scene may have either caused the event or been attracted to it. If witchcraft or black magic were practiced, evil was encouraged. If a Ouija board, séance, or tarot cards were used, evil might have felt invited ... even if it was unintentional. And, in extremely rare cases, the good and pious may be 'chosen' for a diabolical attack as a challenge to the religious community and to God. Unintentionally giving recognition to an evil-infested inanimate object also invites trouble, such as with the Raggedy Ann case."

Ed introduced the next stage. "The second step is what is called **infestation**. Sounds such as knockings and footsteps, along with objects that move on their own and mysterious odors start to occur. Inanimate objects or even animals have been known to speak. (They aren't really. The devil just makes it look that way.) Usually just one member of the family or a pet witnesses these things initially. These strange events won't happen when an outsider is present, but may become worse after the outsider leaves—particularly if that someone was a priest or minister. People sense 'something' is trying to scare them or drive them crazy. (People with earthbound ghosts in their home may feel startled and uncomfortable, but not the same sense of dread or panic.) There are certain patterns to these manifestations that allow the Warrens to better determine legitimacy. The time of day, number of knocks, type of odors, and other indicators are all clues to the trained investigator."

Lorraine continued, "The third step is what is called the **oppression** phase. Air temperature might change and the disturbing sounds and activities increase, making sleep and peace of mind difficult. More people in the household may be affected in varying degrees. Also, family members are less motivated to leave the home, despite the discomfort. Bigger objects are apt to move by themselves. Teleportations can occur. This is when objects disappear only to reappear somewhere else—apparently in and out of thin air. Levitations and physical assaults may start. The weaker and more frightened the victims become, the stronger and more frequent the phenomena ... occurring even in the presence of outsiders. Such phenomena are often labeled 'poltergeist' activity by investigators who witness them. After ruling out fraud, telekinesis, a restless earthbound ghost, or an angry spirit, that leaves the presence of evil."

Ed wrapped up the sequence. "The fourth step is **possession**. This occurs sooner if sought out through black magic or if specifically conjured by black magicians to control others. Nonetheless, one's physical body is temporarily taken over by another entity. Invisible physical assaults, levitation, and speaking in a much different voice or unknown language can occur. The victim's physical appearance may change, including physical bone structure and eye color. The possessed suddenly start doing things they never did before such as demonstrate superhuman strength and athletic abilities. Meanwhile, they just as suddenly are unable to do the things they always did such as find their way home, drive, or even sit. Their behavior changes drastically, including cursing and lewd activities way beyond the casual joke or spontaneous moment. They start talking about harming themselves and those they once loved, and actually begin to take steps to do so.

"The final step is **death**. The victim either commits suicide, murders, or both. There is also a risk that the victim—and those helping—might die in the process of attempting an exorcism. After gaining control, evil's intention is to destroy as many people as possible, as well as its host. Why? Evil rejoices in death. Its objective is to destroy God's creations. However, it needs us to do it. It needs us to invite it into our lives."

Ed reached behind him and held up a newspaper. "In April 2000, the *New York Times* profiled 102 killers in rampage attacks over a fifty-year period and found: 'They give lots of warning and even tell people explicitly what they plan to do. After their violence, they do not try to get away. Half turn their guns on themselves or are shot dead by others. They not only want to kill, they also want to die.'[16] The *Times* study admitted that virtually all the killers demonstrated serious 'mental health problems.' It was also noted that rampage killings are increasing while other murders are decreasing.

"If bullying and higher expectations in today's more impersonal world are triggers for this alarming trend, evil might also be a factor. The demonic is attracted to anger and frustration and self-destructive behavior involving drugs and alcohol. It feeds on fear. Those who feel trapped or abuse themselves may inadvertently invite more than other abusers into their lives."

Lorraine nodded in agreement and spoke. "As a clairvoyant who can see auras, the aura of a possessed person is much the same as that of someone with a strong addiction. In both cases, the individual has relinquished free will. Ironically, a belief—and better understanding of—evil might bring about more good. With a better appreciation of the power of human 'free will,' mankind might be less likely to blame God, fate, or others for its own behavior and tolerance for mistreatment."

Ed added, "It has been demonstrated that bullying only survives when the majority who aren't bullied look the other way. In schools where children are encouraged to frown on bullying, regardless of the victim, the problem has all but disappeared.[17] Remember that evil likes to isolate its victims. If everyone ignores it, bullying can thrive and evil has an opportunity to gain control.

"An amazing truth of the human mind is that if we expect pleasure, we'll find it. And if we feed our minds with trivia and violence, then trivia and violence will appear in our window of life. Schroeder, in his book *Hidden Face of God*, tells us quantum physics reveals that there 'seems' to be an underlying force and intelligent power behind all matter and energy ... leading to growth, complexity, and diversity. Anything that works against this in nature—as well as in societies—tends to be relatively short-lived.

"In his book, *The Cancer Ward*, Solzhenitsyn proposed: '...that the question of any frontier would be not how much the action enriches us or strengthens us or raises our prestige, but only: How moral would it be?' Later he added, 'The wild animal gnawing at his prey is happy, but only humans can love, and this is the highest thing man can achieve.'[18] This is what religion has been trying to tell us for centuries—with the caveat that one follows all the separate rules, regulations, and rituals of a specific religion and shuns or attacks those who differ. Historically, religious wars have been the cruelest and bloodiest."

Lorraine interjected, "Evil, of course, would delight in this irony and may be instrumental in perverting the message of love ... distorting it to one of abuse and control. According to observations throughout the ages and based on our own experience, evil is extremely opportunistic, but requires an invitation and recognition from its victims. It is a master of deception and makes its first steps when no one is looking, undermining the victim's credibility. It grows in confidence and control until it accumulates enough power to destroy.

"Evil needs for its victims to be weak and for others to look the other way in order to gain control. And, it needs control of our bodies to do its dirty work, which destroys the host in the process. Evil's only real vulnerability is pious religious intervention from those motivated by love, a firm faith in a higher power, and the dedicated desire to help. Those motivated by greed, the need for attention, or other carnal obsessions are not going to fool or scare the devil."

Ed reiterated, "Blind and stubborn denial regarding the existence of evil as a separate power can be dangerous unless proven otherwise. The Warrens point out, if those who don't believe in angels or God, and experiments with prayer, the risk is only that they'll be pleasantly surprised. However, if those who don't believe in evil and devils, and experiments with witchcraft and black magic, they risk a ruined life."

Lorraine confirmed this. "The most physically and emotionally damaging cases we've investigated have been the result of someone playing with Ouija boards, tarot cards, séances, or consulting an inexperienced, uninformed psychic. Such tools 'open doors' to both benign and bad spiritual entities. If a bad entity responds to an 'invitation,' it won't leave until it gets what it wants or is successfully exorcised.

"Ed and I and other researchers advise trusting one's 'gut instincts' and common sense. If it makes you feel uncomfortable, avoid it. It doesn't matter if it is an activity, place, or inanimate object. Also beware of any inanimate object that seems to take on a life of its own or have its own intelligence. Credible researchers agree that a human spirit will never take up residence in an inanimate object. Even J.K. Rowling in her *Harry Potter* series warned: 'Never trust anything that can think for itself, if you can't see where it keeps its brains.'" [19]

Ed also warned the students, "Exercise caution when seeking spiritual or psychic help. Ignorance and inexperience can make things worse—much worse. It is important to know what 'spirits' are involved if paranormal activity is present. Just because someone has a religious calling or psychic ability doesn't mean they understand all the possibilities and ramifications. Religious intervention is likely to provoke any negative forces that may be present ... once you are left alone. An inexperienced clairvoyant might be able to describe the lamb's clothing, but not the wolf lurking underneath.

"Always protect yourself with prayer. Don't allow possible doubts about religious dogma let evil make a fool out of you. As Lydia M. Child wrote in her *Letters from New York* (1852): 'It is right noble to fight with wickedness and wrong. The mistake is in supposing that spiritual evil can be overcome by physical means.'

"And, as I like to say, 'You might not believe in God, but the devil does.' Do evil entities exist? Let's explore the following cases, and I'll let you decide for yourself."

♦ **Case Study #5:** Amityville: Hoax or Horror?
Ed and Lorraine were the only psychic investigators invited into the Lutz house shortly after they fled in terror. Since then, this has become the Warrens' most famous

case, even if it is not the most horrific. An interview with George Lutz clarifies discrepancies and reveals new information and insights.

- **Case Study #6:** Haunted by Evil
A woman recounts what it is like to struggle with an unseen enemy. The Warrens point out what they look for to determine credibility and what patterns are cause for concern.

- **Case Study #7:** Like Someone Possessed
After a routine business trip, a man experiences drastic physical and personality alterations. His wife chronicles these changes as she seeks medical, psychological, psychic, and spiritual help.

Case Study #5
Amityville: Hoax or Horror

*The Amityville case in now a matter of public record.
The following is based on the transcript
from an actual phone interview between
Ed Warren (with Lorraine) and George Lutz.*

Ed Provides Background

On November 13, 1974 at approximately 3:30 a.m., my mother passed away. After overcoming alcoholism and cancer decades before, her death at that time was sudden and unexpected. Lorraine and I were away at a lecture at the time.

Also on November 13, 1974 at approximately 3:30 a.m., Ronald DeFeo Sr., his wife Louise and their children Dawn, Allison, Mark, and John-Matthew were shot to death with a high-powered rifle in their home in Amityville, Long Island. The only survivor was Ronald DeFeo Jr., who was in his early twenties at the time. He was charged with and convicted of the murders.

My mother's death, coupled with these tragic murders, are just two of the many "coincidences" linking this Amityville case and us together. Since Lorraine and I were out of town and distracted with the news of my mother's death, we didn't immediately hear about the horrible DeFeo murders. We first learned of them early in 1976, when a New York television news station called, asking us to investigate a house on Long Island. Allegedly, it was so haunted that the family fled in terror.

We agreed, but only with the permission of the current homeowners. George Lutz met us at a restaurant about half a mile from the house he and his family abandoned just twenty days before. He refused to go to the house or to tell me what happened. He wanted us to see for ourselves. He seemed genuinely frightened, but also confident that whatever it was, it was not his imagination. He wanted only experienced and credible investigators of the paranormal, who were less likely to get hurt and more likely to understand the phenomena. Regardless, he and his family had no intention of returning to the house or taking anything from it. This man had seen more than a ghost.

George and Kathy Lutz moved into the Amityville house December 1975 excited with the prospect of providing a nice home (despite its tragic history) for their family and business. They were aware of the home's tragic history, but that only made the price too attractive to pass up. It was a large home, in a desirable neighborhood, on the water with a boathouse and a swimming pool. This was more than they hoped for, but still well within their budget. This was the home where they planed to raise their children and retire. Yet less than a month after moving in, they left the house, relinquishing all their belongings along with their business. A few months later, they left family and friends to move to California and put as much distance between them and that house as possible.

The book and movie entitled *The Amityville Horror* created their own set of problems. They attracted thrill-seekers and all kinds of pseudo-experts, after the fact. Some tried to capitalize on the notoriety while the town struggled to play it down. Details in the book and movie were scrutinized and debated. Finally, it seemed in everyone's best interest to a claim "hoax." Despite losing court cases based on details, the George and Kathy Lutz maintain that it was not a hoax, and we believed them.

We were constantly being asked about this case by the media and our lecture audiences. We could only answer based on our own experience investigating the house in 1994. We could not answer regarding the details of what Kathy and George experienced. Also, the notoriety of the case had brought all sorts of people out of the woodwork, claiming they had investigated the house. It was hard to determine who had been truly involved and who just wished they were. Again, only the homeowners could verify this information.

At a scheduled day and time, I got George on the phone to help clarify details related to the case. Both Lorraine and I picked up extensions in our home. With George's permission, I taped our entire conversation.

"George," I began, "this is one of the most controversial cases Lorraine and I have ever investigated. It sure is keeping us on our toes."

Lorraine interjected, "We have some questions we would like to ask you concerning what took place in your Amityville home on 112 Ocean Avenue, questions that have been asked of us whenever we lecture."

Clarification Regarding the Priest

According to the book *The Amityville Horror*, researched and written by Jay Anson, Catholic priest Father Ralph experienced unpleasant and strange events as a result of his effort to help George and Kathy Lutz by blessing their new home in Amityville. Later, he denied this. In my experience, this might be due to pressure from the Church, which abhors publicity of any sort, never mind the attention this case drew.

Lorraine said, "According to the book, while the priest was blessing your home on the day that you moved in, a voice told him to get out. Did anyone else hear this voice? Were you with him? Could the priest have heard this voice psychically ... in a telepathic way?"

"I think he probably heard it audibly," George said, "but we really wouldn't know. We weren't with him at the time. He never told us about it. He never told us any of the problems that he experienced after blessing the house."

"Do you feel this was because he felt he didn't want to burden you with anything that he was experiencing as a result of blessing your home?" Lorraine asked.

"All he said to us," George answered, "was 'I would appreciate it if you would not use one room as a bedroom.' We told him we were planning on using that particular room only as a sewing room."

"Did he tell you why he felt that you shouldn't use that room as a bedroom?" asked Lorraine.

George said, "He said he felt something there that he didn't like. He also asked us to keep the door shut as much as possible. We thought it was a bit strange, but we agreed and thought, 'Okay, no big thing, we're just going to use it for sewing.'"

When Lorraine and I investigated the Amityville house earlier, Lorraine accurately discerned where the DeFeos' bodies were laid out prior to being picked up by the morgue. Remember, we were not around when these murders took place, and had no prior knowledge of the case details. As Lorraine climbed the stairs during our investigation to research the upper floors, she felt an invisible force. She said it felt like she was pushing her way through water. Upon entering this room that the Lutzes once used for sewing, she exclaimed, "This is as close to hell as I want to get!"

Clarification Regarding Levitation

Lorraine asked George, "How long a period of time were you in your home before levitations took place to any member of the family?" It was important to clarify this critical clue to demonic involvement.

"That didn't happen until the last few nights we were there and after we left the house," George answered.

"Did every member of the family have problems with levitation, George?"

"No, mostly Kathy, and me once. However, one night the children's beds were slammed around. The beds moved up and down, and were dragged across the floor. While this was happening, I felt like I couldn't move in bed. Kathy was in what appeared to be in a sleep trance, but rigid, and sliding away from me. And the same time there was a lot of noise going on downstairs."

The immobility George described, and Kathy's rigid, deep sleeplike state are what is known as "psychic paralysis." It is frightening to the person who experiences it, and frustrating. The one who is conscious cannot believe that the loud noises and other disturbances aren't waking up the other person so they can help or witness the experience. Psychic paralysis is not uncommon in evil-infested environments—night or day. I myself have experienced this powerlessness. One such occasion was while investigating the basement in the Amityville house.

I said to George, "In the book, you came into the room and saw Kathy levitating and you grabbed her. Could you tell us about that?"

"This happened when we were meditating at Kathy's mother's house," George explained. "I looked up, and Kathy was rigid and sliding right up the wall like she was being hung with her hands as if they were tied together. I had just come out of meditation and couldn't believe it. It didn't even register. I grabbed her and pulled her down, and woke her up. She had huge welts on her tummy. I called her mother in to see them.

"Another time, Kathy and I had been asleep, and we were flying around in the room."

"Were you conscious of this?" I asked.

"Yes, he said. "When we looked down, the bed below us was empty. It was immediately after we had moved out of the house that this happened. When Kathy levitated in our Amityville house, there was so much going on, I just grabbed her down, and pulled her back."

"Was it hard to pull her down, George?"

"No, she came right back down."

"Was she conscious at that time?"

"She woke up right after that."

"Was she frightened?"

"She was surprised, not terrified like I was. But she could see the terror in my face."

"How many times did you and Kathy actually levitate?"

"I levitated a couple of times with Kathy at my mother-in-law's house. I didn't levitate at all in our house. Kathy levitated twice in our house in her sleep."

"How long did you actually levitate?"

"It felt like a long time, but it was probably no more than five minutes."

"And one time when you and Kathy were levitating—I remember you told me you looked over to Kathy and said, 'Do you believe this?' Am I quoting you right?"

"Yes, we were talking to each other. We just couldn't believe it was actually happening. We were flying, floating around, looking down at the bed, and seeing it empty where we had been. We have never experienced anything like that before or after."

This is consistent with what Lorraine and I have heard and witnessed elsewhere. The Lutzes could have been well-read or tutored in the occult and made up the story, but based on what we felt and experienced in the house, we felt these experiences were not only possible, but probable.

An Evil Pig

According to the *Amityville Horror* book, the youngest daughter, Melissa, is the only one who "sees" and befriends a large pig she names Jodie.

Lorraine introduced the subject by asking, "George, you mentioned the furniture once moved around the children's room, and terrified them. What else did the children witness in the Amityville home?"

"When Missy (Melissa) told us about her pet pig, we dismissed it as a child's imagination. But then one day she came down the stairs and asked, 'Do angels talk?' We said, 'What are you talking about?' We got a little alarmed because Missy was fairly levelheaded as far as six-year-olds go. We figured it was still her imagination, though.

"However, I saw the eyes of this thing looking up from the boat house. Kathy and I were sitting in the living room one night, when we saw the eyes peering at us from outside."

"What did the eyes look like, George?"

"They were just two red, beady eyes."

"You could actually make them out as eyes?"

"Yes, they were definitely eyes, but there was no form behind them."

Lorraine asked, "And the windows you were looking out were very high?"

"Yes," George answered, "so it had to be something *very* big ...very tall."

I asked George, "I think Kathy said something about ...footsteps?"

"We saw footprints in the snow that we couldn't attribute to anything other than a cloven-hoofed animal. The prints went right off into the river ... right off the boat dock, and right into the river."

Mysterious Substances ... and "Monsters"

"What other frightening things happened to you in that home, George?" I asked. "What about the substance that came out of the keyholes that looked like blood?"

"That stuff grew," George said. "It actually grew ... right out of the keyholes. The drips got bigger and bigger. We never saw them grow at night, but they would be hard in the morning. The playroom, where the most flies were, didn't have the substance, but the rest of the rooms did."

"Did you ever have that substance analyzed?" I asked.

"We couldn't get it off," George explained. "I couldn't get it off with a knife. It was like epoxy—like a black epoxy—but shaped like a tear. We would describe it to each other as a tear coming out, because it would look like a big, long, sad, tear.

"Was this the same substance that was in the boat house?" I asked.

"No. There wasn't a substance in the boat house. But we dumped some stuff that we scraped off the carpet out in the boat house. We had another substance that looked like drops of green oil or bits of Jell-O on the red carpets ... just going from room to room. It looked like some sort of tracks ... going from room to room. The trail would go up and down the stairs, but most of it would be between the sewing room and our bedroom.

"Did you ever touch the green oily substance, and if so, what did it feel like?"

"It felt sticky. It would go away during the day and be back the next morning when we woke up. All of a sudden, they were there. The night before, they weren't. Well, at first we blamed it on the children.

"We tried—easily for three weeks—to explain all the strange things that were happening. We didn't believe in psychic reasons for it. When it got to the point that there was so many things happening that we could not attribute to physical causes, what could we do? We just had to leave."

The book *The Amityville Horror*, recounts how the two boys were startled by a "hooded monster" that was seen moments later at the top of the stairs by George as he gathered his family to flee the house. I asked, "In the book, George, the children see a creature. What was that?"

"Only Missy talked about a pig. What the other children saw was something else—the same thing Kathy and I saw in the fireplace."

"Could you describe that?" I asked.

"It looked something like a Ku Klux Klansman with half of the hood blown away, with no face. The first time I saw it, it was just an outline of what the fire made into the fireplace brick, but it stayed there for days. The next time I saw anything like it was the very last day—the morning we were trying to get out of the house itself. I believe you and Lorraine also saw something in the fireplace when you investigated the house."

"Yes, I do remember, Ed," Lorraine interjected. "I remember it was when we went into the home at night with Dr. Oasis and Dr. Tanis. When I looked in the fireplace, I remarked about how what was there so closely resembled what we saw in a West Hartford home." That West Hartford case was another horrific haunting.

Disturbing Sensations, Noises, Odors, and Damage

"What did you find particularly disturbing while you lived in the house, George?" I asked.

"It would play tricks on your imagination. You'd close a door, and it would be open. You'd open a door, and it would be closed. The very last night we were there, something got in bed with us. You could actually see the impressions right in the bed. You could see the footprints, you could feel the weight, and you could almost hear the breath, but there was so much noise going on elsewhere in the house."

I asked, "What kind of noise, George?"

"It sounded like a demented marching band ... like a whole bunch of musicians, each one going in their own direction, playing their own song. The first time it happened, I thought it was a clock radio or something that went off downstairs. It wasn't a clock radio. As soon as I got downstairs, everything went quiet. I expected to see the carpets rolled back downstairs based on the clomping of the feet sounds I heard. At the same time, it sounded like every door and window downstairs was being opened and closed as hard as it could be."

I asked, "The book said that the front door was almost ripped off the hinges. Could you tell us about that, George?"

"The front door was a very heavy door. I imagine it weighed 150 pounds, at least. You knew when that thing was closed, no matter where you were in the house you could hear that thing slamming. I just came down one morning, and that was the way it was.

"Where the garbage cans were, there was a whole enclosure. Each one of the enclosures had bi-fold doors. One morning we came down and found all of them were open. The next morning when we came down, they were all closed. Eventually half of them were all ripped off their hinges."

"And what about the sounds that sounded like gunshots?" I asked.

"It only sounded like gunshots when all the doors began slamming ... just about every door in the house," George explained.

"Your aunt Mary had been on a radio show, and she said she had seen the front door boarded up with plywood where the door had broken off. Now, is she talking about the storm door or the other door?" I asked.

"She might be talking about the back door. There is a very large back door almost the size of the front door that we had trouble with while we were there. I didn't hear what my aunt Mary said, so I really don't know what she was referencing. I know she was at the house there on Christmas Day with the rest of our family."

"What about bad smells?" I asked. "The priest in the book refers to very sickening smells that developed in his own home. Did you have anything like this?"

"We had what we called a 'cheap perfume' odor," George said. "It was nauseating, but it wasn't a putrid, horrid smell. We did have an odor in the basement for a couple of days that wasn't very pleasant, that's for sure. It smelled like somebody had been sick."

Oppression

Lorraine asked, "George, there seems to be some confusion about the time that you bought and moved into your Amityville home. Was it December the 18th or the 23rd?"

"As I look back on it, we moved in on the 18th and I think the 23rd is when things started happening ... when we became alarmed. You have to remember, while we were living there, we tried to explain away everything—fluctuations in the heat, the cheap perfume odors, and our changed behavior.

"I stopped taking showers and going to the office. Kathy lost all interest in Christmas shopping and would not leave the house. It was like we were too depressed to do anything, and for no apparent reason. We had a new home, I enjoyed my own business, and the holidays were coming.

"But it was wearing us down ... doors slamming ... always waking up 3:30 in the morning ... flies in the middle of the winter ... just all these strange things."

"What happened with the flies?" I asked.

"We killed hundreds of them, and they just kept coming back," George said. "They were mostly in the playroom; but we found them in the sewing room as well."

"Did you ever inquire of your neighbors if they had flies like that in their home?"

"I spoke to the neighbors once across the backyard fence, just to introduce myself. We really never had any rapport with the neighbors or really met them formally. They never really came over to the house, or anything like that."

There was nothing unusual about this. The Lutzes moved into Amityville just before Christmas and were busy unpacking. They and their neighbors were busy preparing for the holidays. People are also apt to stay indoors in December in the Northeast.

Lorraine and I had prior experience with sickening-sweet perfume smells, sick room odors, interrupted sleep, fly infestations, and dramatic behavior changes, unexplained loud sudden noises, and even the "demented marching band." They could be brought about by psychic telepathy or actual physical manifestations created by some invisible force. Either way, the intent was to frighten, oppress, and gain control. The Lutzes would have had to be well-tutored and gifted liars to make all of this up. Yet, that possibility always needs exploration.

Clarification of Motive

"Weren't you concerned about moving into a home where six members of a family were murdered?" I asked.

"No, we had felt they had died there, and that was that. The house itself had nothing to do with it. Based on what happened afterwards, however, we wanted to warn others and try getting our own heads straight. We wanted to explain why we moved out and why we didn't move back."

Lorraine asked, "Did the church support you as far as believing your story and trying to help you understand what took place in that home?"

"I believe if it wasn't for the church's concern, my family and I would probably be dead right now. I have no doubt about that," George answered. "I think as a family, we were not ready to give in to it; and we were not able to talk to anyone about it. We considered ourselves rational people. When we couldn't find one physical cause or another, we realized it had to be something else. The church was there when we needed them.

"Fortunately, at the time, Kathy and I could talk about anything and not be afraid of what the other would think. Kathy would say to me: 'I felt like my hand was grabbed while I was meditating.' And I'd say, 'Oh, okay tell me about.' And she would. And we'd both say it was probably our imagination.

"But when you have all the noises, and you have the odors, and the flies, and everything else going on as well ... And then you can't even get up out of bed, like that one night when I was making different sounds ..."

"You were making different sounds?" I interrupted. This, along with being able to speak a language not previously known ... or talk backwards is one of the hallmarks of possession.

"I was making a noise that seemed like a physical impossibility. I made two distinct unnatural sounds from my mouth. I was awake and sitting up in bed when this happened. It was like more than one wild creature was inside of me."

"That doesn't sound good," I admitted. "Would it be too personal a question, George, to ask you how much you lost by leaving that home and never returning? Your family's clothing, personal items, valuables collected and handed down from generations were all left behind. You never went back to get those. Is that correct?"

"Yes, but to answer that question I would have to look at two parts," George said. "One part would be the down payment on the house itself, and our being unable to wait for the best time to market the motorcycles and our two boats. We had just bought a speedboat, which we had never even used. I had three custom choppers—each bike was very valuable ... fully chromed and custom painted. I also had recently converted my motorcycle trailer so it could carry motorcycles as well as tools.

"The second part of the loss was my business. We sold the business just to get away from everything and to get out. Anyone who knew what the business was worth couldn't refuse it. Its market value was entirely different from what it was sold at.

"Regarding the house, the bank put $40,000 in escrow. Kathy and I put a down payment of $20,000. The closing fees and everything came to an additional $8,000. So, we put down $28,000 altogether, which we lost when we walked away from the house."

I pushed for a total number. "When I asked you earlier how much you thought you lost when you fled the house, you agreed it was around $100,000, is that correct?"

"Easily, that amount," George confirmed. "What does that have to do with anything, though?"

"Well as you know, some people claim you created a hoax. People don't lose 100k trying to create a hoax," I offered.

"When Kathy and I moved in, we got a mortgage. At the time, it was hard to get a mortgage for any kind of house on Long Island. Nonetheless, we qualified for a mortgage on an $80,000 house with almost $3,000 a year in taxes. We were very happy with it and the house. We didn't have any problem figuring out how to afford it and still be able to save. I was planning to move my business there. Previously, Kathy and I had been keeping up two houses—one in East Cypress and one in Deer Park, whose values came very close to the Amityville house."

"Tell me this, George: if you wanted to get out of this deal, couldn't you have thought of a better way to get out of it than making up stories about monsters and losing $28,000 to $100,000?"

For the first time that evening, George laughed. "Sure. I could have burned the house down for one. It was insured for much more than it was worth. It was insured for its replacement value, which would have served us quite well. Instead, we lost well over $40k in the furniture, boats and everything else. Those things were not our concern when we fled."

When Lorraine and I investigated the house just a few weeks after the Lutz family had left it, we found the kitchen refrigerator and freezer completely stocked. The closets and dressers were full of clothes. Silver servers that they inherited from family and other valuable gifts they had accumulated throughout the years remained where they left them. We took and kept pictures of these things to show us that the family's departure did in fact seem sudden and unplanned.

One must remember that the values George estimated were based on 1976 prices. Kathy and George eventually moved into a smaller house and never again enjoyed the nice things and financial success of the short time they lived in Amityville. The book and movie generated more income for the writer than for the Lutzes, and the money they did get hasn't even covered legal fees.

Clarification of House History

There have been many stories attached to the Amityville house the Lutz family fled. The benefit of time—and more complete research possible over that time—has uncovered discrepancies that have also been used to dismiss all the claims Kathy and George made. One such historic story involves someone called John Ketcham (or spelled Catchum). It was said he fled Salem, Massachusetts during the witch trials and came to live at a house on that lot where the Lutzes lived. Rumor had it that his house was haunted; but when the house was moved off the lot, the hauntings in that particular house stopped. Other stories about the property were linked to Indian legends.

"According to the *Amityville Horror* book, George, it says that the Shinnecock Indians once inhabited that area, and had an enclosure on your land ... and that John Ketcham was buried there. What can you tell me about this?" I asked.

"Kathy and I tried to research some basic things regarding the property through the Amityville Historical Society. Some things were given to us by an investigator for William Weber (the attorney for Ronald DeFeo) and also by a criminologist by the name of Paul Hoffman. We could never verify this information as being true or not. We did, however, find some things referenced in books my brother-in-law had, but evidently there are very few copies of these books.

"As far as the Shinnecocks are concerned, I don't know. I honestly don't know whether they settled there or not. However, I do know Alex Tanis apparently made some statements about Indians when he went to investigate the house. I'll read you the section from the *Book Gallery Magazine*, December 1977, written by Donald Newlove quoting Mr. Tanis' psychic feelings at the time he explored the house:

> "When Tanis, Oasis, (meaning Dr. Carlos Oasis and Alex Tanis) and I went into the house, we had been told nothing about the murders, only that the house was haunted. We were all kept in ignorance, even Oasis, so that Tanis' psychic powers—we were testing—would not read our minds about the mass murder, or anything about the house. Without help, Tanis located the rooms where the murders had taken

place. (He had not even known that there were murders there.) He found columns of cold air and had flashes about the land the house was built on as being an unhallowed Indian burial ground. He went into a trance, and saw some white settlers—Dutch—attacking and killing some Indians on the site while they were having a wedding. A dying Indian doctor or Indian chief cursed this ground of slaughter. 'This house,' Tanis explained, 'was not so much haunted as cursed or on cursed ground. The Indians did not want the whites to enjoy their stolen land.'"

"We also had been told that Indians dying from yellow fever were taken, tied to trees, and left to die in that area."

I asked, "Is this information according to Amityville Historical Society's records which you saw yourself, George?"

"No, as far as I know, it is all hearsay."

"Yet, according to Anson (the author of *The Amityville Horror*), these were in the records of the Amityville Historical Society," I said.

"I really wouldn't know about that. That might be true based on his research," George offered.

Clarification Regarding Other Investigators

Steven Kaplan was one of the persistent people who claimed the Lutzes' story was a hoax. He apparently made this pronouncement after George Lutz refused him permission to go into the house with a TV crew to perform an exorcism. From that time on, Kaplan has been against

Lutz all the way. Any time we or the Lutzes would appear on television or radio, Kaplan would demand equal time ... claiming he knew more than us, without having ever stepped foot in the house near or at the time of the disturbances.

Our research found that Kaplan ran about six different organizations in Long Island. He described himself as founder and director of the Parapsychology Institute of America, the Werewolf Institute of America, the Vampire Institute of America, and the Ghostology Institute of America ... all of which he ran from his apartment in Long Island. Yet, the recognized organizations and college that we work with regarding parapsychology did not know of Kaplan at that time.

We also found that Kaplan's doctorate came from the Pacific Correspondence School in California, whose founder and director served time in prison for fraudulent activities. Up until then, apparently anyone could get any kind of document they wanted from that school for a nominal fee.

I wanted to hear how Kaplan and the Lutzes became entangled. "What was your initial contact with Dr. Kaplan regarding investigating your Amityville home? How did you meet him? What transpired?" I asked.

"On February 20, 1976, I talked to Mr. Kaplan on the phone," George answered.

"Did you call him or did he call you?"

"I'd have to pull out my tapes to remember that, but I believe that I called him."

"And why was this? Had you read about him or something?"

"I had either read about him or seen him on the news commenting about some houses on the south shore of

Long Island—having paranormal problems. He claimed that what I was experiencing was nothing new. He also made a statement saying, to some extent, that people should stay away from the house, because they could be dealing with something dangerous. He wasn't confirming or denying the existence of something unnatural in my house, but only being cautionary."

I asked, "Did you give him permission to investigate your house at any time?"

"No, we did not. However, we did make an appointment to meet with him around March 5th or 6th of 1976. He met with Kathy and me at a restaurant and brought someone he referred to as a 'white witch.' They both wanted to investigate the house."

"And then what happened, George?"

"After the meeting, I called Duke University, two research associations in Manhattan, and the State University in Stonybrook to find out about Mr. Kaplan. Kathy and I wanted to make sure that any investigator we allowed in the house was known and respected by other people in the field of psychic and paranormal investigation. For our own sanity and the safety of others, we didn't want any quacks in the house.

"Well, the American Society for Psychical Research on West 73rd Street in New York and the Parapsychological Foundation, I guess it is, on 29 West 57th Street New York, both denied knowing—or ever hearing about—Mr. Kaplan."

"So you couldn't check out his credentials?" I asked.

"No, I could not. Duke University and Stonybrook didn't know about him either. No one had ever heard of him."

"So, what transpired then?"

"I called Mr. Kaplan back to tell him we decided against letting him investigate the house," George said. "He got a little upset on the phone, and wanted me to explain why we didn't want him in the house. I told him that we were trying to organize a professional investigation of the house. I explained how were not able to verify his experience in this area. I tried to make it clear that I wasn't making any kind of insinuation against his character or credentials, but that we just wanted to be very sure of the people who we worked with on this case."

"Did Kaplan mention anything about an exorcism of the house?"

"I believe he said one possible outcome of any investigation that he would make with his 'white witch' would be an exorcism, which she could do very well. However, the idea of any kind of 'witch' to Kathy and I really turned us off. We preferred to have a scientific investigator.

"First of all, I couldn't ascertain that he was a professional parapsychologist ... not from anyone in the industry that we could reach. And second of all, he was adamant about bringing in a 'witch.' At the same time, we didn't want anything to do with witches. So, we just said no, thank you; and we haven't had any further direct contact with him after that."

"George, Kaplan has often referred to your mental state at the time you moved into the Amityville home. He claims that you were under psychiatric treatment just before. Could you tell us about this?" I asked.

"I don't know what he's talking about, unless he is referring to what's known as group therapy or marriage counseling. After my divorce in 1974, I went to group counseling with a guy with a master's degree in social work.

There was whole bunch of people there, who were trying to learn from the disappointment of a failed relationship. No one told me I had to go. It was something I wanted to do. I have never had any psychological problems that I know of.

"Ed, that reminds me that I found this article in the Book World section of the *Washington Post*, dated December 9th, 1977:

> "Dr. Steven Kaplan of Parapsychology Institute of America in Queens was also called repeatedly by Lutz; and he undertook an investigation of the case over several months. Kaplan is now convinced that the story is an obvious hoax. He became suspicious when Lutz couldn't keep his facts straight from one story to the next. He suspects there is a very 'strong possibility' that the Lutzes invented much of their story because of financial worries. 'This is a couple that had great financial dilemmas,' Kaplan says, 'who had been looking at $30,000 to $50,000 houses and suddenly found themselves up to their eyeballs in debt for an $80,000 house.'"

"It's unfortunate that things like that are allowed to get in the newspapers."

"According to that article, George," I commented, "you couldn't even make the next mortgage payment."

"We paid the mortgage through July and August of 1976," explained George. After that time, our negotiated agreement with the bank was for them to keep our equity, take over the house, and sell it."

"So, you left the house on January 14, 1976 and the mortgage was paid up right up through July and August?" I asked.

"That's right," George confirmed. "We were living in California and still making payments on the house. We were concerned about our credit. We were also quite concerned about the house itself. It had been broken into and vandalized. Part of the reason for this were newspaper articles like I read you quoting people like Kaplan. They caused us tremendous problems. And, evidently there are a few others ... people that say they have investigated the house, and they haven't."

"It doesn't matter what they investigate now, George," I offered. The thing is, they did not investigate during the twenty-eight days that you were there or go into the house immediately after you left, and this is what we're talking about. Lorraine and I and other experienced investigators went into your home while the furniture was still there and the house was as it was when you lived there. Kaplan, Moran and no one else can say that."

"Well, I don't know Mr. Moran," George admitted. "I really don't know who he is. Yet, I understand from an interview he did with the *College Point Tribune* awhile ago and he says—at least this is what I understand—that he investigated the house over a four-month period and discounted quite a few things in the book.

"The problems that Kathy and I have with this kind of thing is the same one we had with Mr. Kaplan. Who is Mr. Moran? Is he a knowledgeable person in this field, or someone who is trying to make a name for himself? So, I don't know."

Cheryl A. Wicks

Clarification Regarding Police Involvement

The *Amityville Horror* book indicates that Sergeant Pat Cammarato of the Amityville Police Department witnessed the wrecked garage door and cloven hoofprints in the snow. Invited into the home, he was shown a secret red room in the basement and was told of some of the strange occurrences George and Kathy were experiencing in the house.

I asked George, "Was there ever a detective in your home, or were the police ever called into your home?"

"No, Sergeant Cammarato evidently was incorporated in the book from newspaper accounts.

"I want you to realize, we created problems for Jay Anson (the author) in writing the book. First of all, we wouldn't let him go to the house. We felt he would be much safer—and it would be much better all around—if he didn't have direct contact with the house. Therefore, he was dependent on the tapes we had done and on newspaper accounts. And as we know, the newspaper accounts are not always accurate. Sergeant Cammarato was quoted in the papers as being there, and that's how that got in the book."

"We created problems for Anson regarding accuracy even with the tapes. They weren't the best quality by any means. They were just on a little recorder. The information was just so Kathy and I could remember it ...for our own purposes. We never expected these tapes to be heard by anyone else, or anything like that. When the idea came up for the book, we hoped the tapes would keep us from having to relive all that. We didn't want to go through it all again."

Clarification Regarding the Book Idea

"George, could you tell me when was it that you got the idea that your case history would make a book, and when you contacted somebody about it?"

"William Weber (DeFeo's attorney) asked us to come into a deal that he was putting together. He had gotten Ronald DeFeo to sign over all his rights to the story of what had happened to him and what had gone on in that house with the DeFeo family.

"They approached us with a contract that had to do with three movies and three books. We said no. We didn't want any part of that kind of thing. We weren't interested in that kind of commercialization. They sent us a contract. I admit we said we would look at a contract, but we really weren't interested in something that incorporated three movies and three books. It was not something Kathy and I wanted to see happen at all.

"We were quite concerned, however, that there was no reference of this kind of phenomena ever published ... other than *The Exorcist*. There was not anything about a house. We agreed that a book might help Ronald DeFeo ... perhaps help him get the psychological help he needed. We also felt that if a book was put together, it could help other people going through the same thing. They would know they weren't crazy, or whatever ... that these things do happen. This would be very good ... even if just helped one person.

"Eventually, a friend of ours said, 'Look, let me call Prentice Hall and see if they will want to talk to you about a book.' We agreed and went into New York City and met Tom Mossman, who had Jay Anson sit down with us to talk about a book and our reasons for it. That is how the book came about."

"So you didn't buy the house with the intention of pretending you had a haunted house, get a book written and make a million dollars?" I asked.

"We would have to be the best liars in the world to do that ... and pretty stupid not to put some things in storage first or wait until later to buy the new boat." George said.

"Based on our experience, you'd have to be the best clairvoyants, too," I commented.

"Right. We would have had to pay off each of the individual investigators before they ever went into the house. For example, we didn't go to you. Channel 5 brought you people to us. When it came to the investigators themselves, we didn't tell them anything when they went into the house. You know that yourself. They went in all on their own. Whatever they discovered or didn't discover, that was up to them. It wasn't our place to tell them."

This much Lorraine and I knew to be true. Initially, I was frustrated when George would not tell me anything. He also refused to return to the house with us. As soon as Lorraine and other sensitives stepped into the house, they understood why. Whatever was still there at the time was not at all friendly and extremely dangerous.

Escalation of the Paranormal Attacks

"George, for the entire twenty-eight days that you lived in that house, did you feel you were under some type of paranormal, supernatural attack?"

"No, not until we got the idea from a friend of ours to kick it out. One of his sons had a problem with something in his room that frightened him and wouldn't go away. My friend had gone around his house and said a prayer in every room. He opened the window in each room, told it to leave, and that was it. We tried to do that. Things were quiet for about an hour ... but then things became much worse."

This is what Lorraine and I call religious provocation. For the trained investigator, it provokes the evil entity to show itself. For the unsuspecting, it can be dangerous.

George continued: "The thing is, the *(Amityville Horror)* book presents it differently because the first few weeks would have been boring to recount; and in the last week, so much happened, no one would believe it. But it wasn't twenty-eight days of terror we lived in, by any means. It was the last week that we lived there that was very bad for us. It was totally impossible to stay there any longer. We didn't have any problems of a serious kind until we tried to kick out what was there."

I clarified, "So okay, George, it was the blessing that you and Kathy tried to bring about in the different rooms of the house that really brought on the phenomena that frightened your whole family ... forcing you to leave that home?"

"Yes," George confirmed. "That and the fact we could no longer explain away all the different things that were happening. It was nothing we could fix or fight. We just had to leave. Kathy's hands were touched a few times, she would pass out and levitate, the toilets were turning black, flies kept reappearing, weird substances or whatever ... those were things that we could no longer rationalize."

"George, when we first met, you wouldn't go any closer than four blocks to your Amityville house. You left it and very valuable possessions behind. You are also an ex-marine. You are not the type of a guy that frightens very easily. What was most frightening to you in that home?"

George's voice became soft as he answered, "It takes a very long time for me to lose my temper. It takes a very long time for me to get to the point where I don't care what the outcome is. I was willing to break down walls or do whatever I had to do, to be done with this problem. I just yelled and screamed at this thing to come out and fight me and let's have it over with, because I wanted my house ... I wanted my family left alone. It wouldn't. I felt the thing was smarter than I was."

Signing Off

"Okay, George, I think we've got enough ammunition here to answer the questions we've been asked and try to counter the misinformation."

Ronald DeFeo Sr. meet a Father Rain while at a shrine in Canada, seeking relief from what he told neighbors was "a devil on my back." He came home with religious statues he placed all around the house and had masses said in the house. Shortly thereafter, he and most of his family were killed. The Lutzes spoke with the Father after their own ordeal and George indicated he had a message from this priest for us when we first began our phone call.

Lorraine remembered and asked, "Did you say you had a message for us?"

"Yes," George said. "They—the things in that house ... the words from Father Rain were, 'They never let anyone get away that has been there.'"

"In other words," Lorraine said, "They get to you one way or the other?"

Ghost Tracks

"One way or another or eventually," George sadly agreed. "They aren't going to let anyone escape if they have anything to do with it. And you have an idea how strong and powerful that 'they' is ... okay?"

"Yes, dear, I understand that," Lorraine said.

George continued: "So I guess it's their word of warning, or whatever. But those are the words. And they don't surprise me. This is why I never want you to go to Suffolk County again."

I understood, too. The evening following our investigation of the Amityville house, Lorraine and I witnessed two dark psychic cyclones in our home ... in two places at once. This was a first for us, despite our decades of research.

Much later, we were driving a new rental car along a scenic road aptly named Promised Land in "The Lord's Valley." It was a beautiful, bright, clear day. I couldn't resist commenting: 'Even the Amityville Horror couldn't reach us here.'"

Immediately, our car started fishtailing on the dry pavement in broad daylight. The car flipped and went into a ditch. While this was happening, we called on Jesus and his Mother Mary. Somehow, we walked away from this terrible crash.

A truck was behind us when all this happened. A state officer overheard the trucker's radio account of the bizarre event. The policeman arrived, observed the accident scene, and couldn't believe anyone survived. No physical cause was ever found.

In the afterword of his book, *The Amityville Horror*, Jay Anson says: "During the preparation of this book, one of those primarily responsible for it reported feeling weak and nauseous upon sitting down to work on the manuscript—whenever he did so in his office on Long Island. But doing the same task in Manhattan, across the East River, he experienced no ill effects at all."

Research done in the year 2000 for a History Channel update of the Amityville Horror event uncovered a disturbing bit of news connected to the Amityville case. It seems virtually every male (including camera crew) who was involved with our investigation of the house, later suffered a heart attack. I survived mine, but many did not. Anson, who wrote the book *The Amityville Horror*, died at age 58 following heart surgery.[20] Also, the young man who lived in the house after the Lutz family fled and the bank sold it, died of a heart attack. He reportedly was only twenty-eight years old at the time.

Epilogue

This case has remained the most controversial one we have ever investigated. As far as evil manifestation is concerned, it is one of the worst ... but there have been others. Yet, because of the visibility of the book and movie, the quiet town of Amityville attracted a lot of unwanted attention. This triggered lawsuits, which only attracted more media attention. The pressure to disperse thrill seekers by saying it was a hoax was great. Suddenly, "experts" appeared to support that claim and capture a moment of fame for themselves.

Meanwhile, many questions regarding the DeFeo murders themselves have also kept the controversy alive. Why didn't the DeFeo family wake up when the first gunshot was fired? Why didn't the close neighbors hear anything? Some researchers claim actual forensics and testimony tell a different story—one that eliminates these questions altogether. Meanwhile, Ron DeFeo, who was charged and convicted of the murders, has claimed everything from his sister did it and he shot her in self-defense ... to the devil made him do it.

Despite numerous lawsuits and their relocation to the opposite of side of the country, George and Kathy Lutz still maintain that they were driven out of their home in Amityville by unseen forces. Kathy's story was analyzed on a psychological stress evaluator shortly after they fled their home, and the conclusion was that she was apparently telling the truth.[21] The Lutzes have never enjoyed the financial success—or peace of mind—they had before moving into Amityville. In a History Channel interview aired in October 2001, the Lutzes were divorced. Kathy was on oxygen and looked frail. Yet, they both stuck by their stories.

So do we. I know I was talking to a very frightened man when I first met George. I also know what I saw and felt in that house shortly after they left. This family left with virtually the shirts on their backs. Down in the basement, upon religious provocation, an unseen force knocked me to the ground and kept me there. Lorraine felt and saw things she had no way of knowing beforehand. Yet, these feelings and images coincided with what is now controversial about the murders ... and some of what is still controversial about the Lutz family experience.

Like the Lutzes, Lorraine and I have been hurt and disappointed by many of the people involved in the case. Some who investigated with us have claimed they were never there—although we have pictures. And of course, there are those who were not there, who claim they were.

Cheryl A. Wicks

Controversy frightens off a lot of good people ... and can attract a lot of the wrong people.

Who did what the night the DeFeos died is less important than the horrific fact that six people—ranging in age from nine to forty-three—died violently. Whether evil influenced the events or came as a result of them, something extremely unpleasant felt comfortable and welcome in that home. The courts have even recognized this likelihood.

Connecticut law requires home sellers and their agents to disclose if there has been any tragedies or alleged hauntings on the premises. This law came about as a result of another case we had. A single mother and her son were also driven out of their rented house by unseen forces. We investigated and testified on her behalf in court when the landlord refused to let her break her lease. She won her case and a precedent was established that is now reflected in real estate law around the country.

The historical accuracy regarding witches, Indians, and the former home or property inhabitants is more entertaining than enlightening in determining what actually happened in the house while the Lutzes lived there. Lorraine, a validated and proven clairvoyant, accurately picked up on the murders, but did not sense any disturbing history beyond that. However, she did discern an evil presence in that home at the time we explored it.

Was a hoax planned? Were agreements broken with Ron DeFeo's lawyers? There is nothing in the Lutzes' background that we could find that would lead them to know how to contrive and describe such a hoax. Which came first, the book deal or the story? Did DeFeo's lawyers approach the Lutzes with a collaboration idea for this story? Did the story become all too true? A lot of nasty cases we've investigated started out as a game—séances, Ouija boards, tarot cards, or experiments with witchcraft. While we personally don't believe this was the case with the Lutzes, what matters most is that for some reason, evil felt invited to play.

Evil doesn't stick to plans or any rules. Evil doesn't go home when everyone else wants to stop. Nor does it pose for pictures or perform for the evening news. It likes to torture the few so the majority will continue to have doubts. Its strength is in ignorance and fear.

Were there factual problems and discrepancies in the book? Yes, in one case, the book's story was spread over the full twenty-eight days. The real horrific events escalated in just the week following religious provocation. This does not make for a believable or entertaining movie or book. Naturally, this rearrangement of events would not coincide with actual weather reports, etc. Also, the book's author was handicapped by not being physically familiar with the house and grounds. He depended on the research and quotes of others.

Finally, if someone is frightened, confused, and oppressed, he or she is not thinking straight, never mind remembering straight. The tapes were allegedly first created for the Lutzes' sanity ... not as a matter of public record. In trying to protect the sanity of others who might possibly be terrorized by similar events, the Lutz story became public record. This development created problems for the little town of Amityville. It also attracted thrill-seekers, nitpickers, fame-seekers, and an opportunity to cry hoax.

We are constantly asked, "If evil was in the Amityville house, is it still there?" Evil spirits—like all spirits—have a different perception of time. They can wait out a century or two. Renovations or other changes, ignorant interaction with the spirit world, or physical and circumstantial similarities with the past can trigger manifestations. It is interesting to note that some people have seen a striking resemblance between the faces of Ron DeFeo and George Lutz. Maybe something else did as well.

We don't know ... but we know enough about this type of phenomenon to believe something wicked did indeed come to Amityville in the mid 70s. This case did not conflict with others we've seen ... with similar disturbances we witnessed directly. This case also followed an all-too-familiar pattern. Invitation: the murders themselves, or what led up to them. Infestation: unexplained sounds, smells, substances, and disturbances. Oppression: interrupted sleep, depressed behavior, and escalation after religious provocation. Possession: levitation, multiple voice sounds.

Someone could have researched and created this tale, but he or she seldom get all the details and sequence right. They also could not have planted the clairvoyant images in Lorraine's head ... or the images that appeared from pictures taken at the time we explored the house. In one photograph, the face of Padre Pio—a renowned, pious, but deceased exorcist—appeared along with Lorraine and others in the room where the DeFeos' bodies had been laid out before being moved to the morgue. And we have a picture taken with infrared film during our investigation when there were no children present, where we see by the stairs the dark image of a child with glowing red eyes.

(See the pictures on pages that immediately follow.)

"The devil is no damn fool.
He is a damned angel.
And he'll make a damn fool out of you."
—Catholic Priest, Jamesburg, NJ
Easter 2000

Cheryl A. Wicks

Psychic Researchers Ed and Lorraine Warren Investigate the Amityville Case

Except for the portrait photo of Padre Pio, Gene Campbell took all the photographs as part of the Warrens' research team, during the 1976 investigation.

The house in Amityville, Long Island, New York, as the house appeared at the time DeFeo and Lutz families lived in it and when the Warrens investigated it. Subsequent owners have remodeled the home.

Ed and Lorraine Warren in the Lutz dining room at the Amityville house in 1976.

Infrared photograph taken of the staircase leading from the foyer to the upstairs of the Amityville house. Note the boy with the glowing eyes in the doorway, at the stairs. This image was not visible to the eye of the photographer or other investigators when the picture was taken.

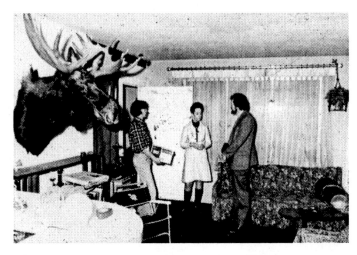

In this sunroom, Lorraine had a vision (later confirmed) of the murdered members of the DeFeo family laid out prior to being transported to the morgue. Lorraine is clutching a holy relic of Padre Pio. The gentleman on the right is an unidentified reporter. The man on the left is Paul Bartz, a researcher with the Warrens. Note the two images that seem to be in the moose antlers.

Ghost Tracks

This close-up of the moose head was taken at the same time as the previous picture. There appears to be an image of a man's face cloaked in black looking at Lorraine from the center of the antlers and the head of another man at the tip of the antler. The latter has been identified as the image of Ron DeFeo.

Cheryl A. Wicks

This picture of Padre Pio was taken from the book of an Italian priest who served with Padre Pio in Italy. This priest validated the image in the photograph taken in the sunroom at Amityville as the image of the pious Italian priest Padre Pio—renowned for his stigmata, miracles, and exorcisms. Padre Pio died in 1968 and was beatified by the Catholic Church in 1999, which is the first step to being recognized as a saint.

Case Study #6
Haunted by Evil

This case is based on correspondence between the Warrens and their clients. All client names and places referenced have been changed or modified to protect their privacy. Ed Warren introduces and discusses the letter's contents.

Not believing in the paranormal is a luxury many of our clients don't have. This is particularly true if the invisible entity is evil. Weeding out the frauds or those in need of psychiatric or medical care still leaves more than a few cases that Lorraine and I (and religious leaders) consider diabolical.

This particular case involved the wife of a policeman. I'll let her tell you her story in her own words. I had been counseling her in preparation for an exorcism and had arranged to visit her again during one of our lecture tours. Below are excerpts from a letter she wrote me just before our trip.

Dear Mr. Warren,

How wonderful of you and your wife Lorraine to offer to see me during your visit to our city. It's a lifeline for me and I wouldn't miss it for anything. However, the reaction from these foul creatures has been most violent.

These entities are intelligent, with a knowledge spanning thousands of years and miles. I was once working on a demonic case in England, when an evil entity told me what Lorraine was doing in Connecticut. She had just moved an evil-infested object in our museum. When I called to make sure she was all right, she was shocked to learn I knew exactly what she was touching. After all, Lorraine is the clairvoyant one.

Mr. Warren, I no longer fear this. It took a year of terror; but through our Lord, I've learned to fear no evil. I fear this presence less than I ever feared anything. That is why I shall take a deep breath and be strong as the last step approaches. I will do anything to free myself of this foul thing—with yours and the Lord's help.

She is saying she is ready for an exorcism. Evil thrives on fear. The less fear, the weaker the stronghold and the more likely an exorcism will be successful. Evil will not relinquish control without a fight, however. Therefore, the client has to be emotionally (and spiritually) prepared. Unfortunately, an exorcism is often the only way for someone possessed to reclaim peace of mind. These are the cases where the best psychiatry and medication have no effect.

It's true; I would eventually go mad. God has kept me sane through this indescribable nightmare. The feeling of gagging in my throat ... rape and sodomy are still present. This must end, or I will certainly develop another hideous pelvic infection.

The voice no longer goes through my own throat. I have become strong enough that it may not use my throat to speak, but I can hear it speaking occasionally in my head (it is always rebuked in the name of Jesus of Nazareth when

I hear anything)—threats, boasts, foulness, etc. I won't give it credence by elaboration. Nor will I allow it to speak through me ever. (If it chooses to take the risk of speaking to anyone other than me, independent of me, that is another matter.)

She is referencing the assaults she has endured and is still experiencing, and the advice I have given her to fight this thing and build strength. Notice how she describes what it is like to have something use her voice or speak to her in her head. Speaking in inhuman voices or previously unknown foreign languages are key signs of possession and possession attempts that are hard to fake. She also alludes to the cleverness of this entity. At the beginning, it usually targets, isolates, and torments one person without speaking out for others to hear. This, of course, makes it hard to rule out mental illness.

It covers my features and attempts to change my expressions. I will not allow it.

I pray constantly, read all appropriate passages in the Bible. I invoke the names of St. Margaret, Padre Peale[22], Archangel Michael and our Lady of the Immaculate Conception, as well as constantly proclaiming that Jesus is Lord. I make the sign of the cross and anoint all areas of affliction with holy water.

I, through the divine intervention of the Lord and the infusion of the Holy Spirit have grown very strong—strong enough to handle anything that may happen. I fear the upcoming possible situation, but do not fear the cause for the exorcism ever again. Mr. Warren, I truly believe this case to be either unique or something that generally isn't known.

At first, she describes what it feels like to have her physical features changed. Some of these changes are structural as well as cosmetic. This is another sign of possession that is virtually impossible to fake.

She recounts all the things we suggest she do to protect herself as much as possible. She also doesn't want to give "recognition" to the "cause for the exorcism," because to do so can be interpreted as acknowledgement and acceptance by these foul entities. Unfortunately, her case is not unique, but she is correct that these cases are either dismissed or covered up in secrecy or by claims of a hoax.

> *Let me try to explain the circumstances involving what happened to me (as clear as crystal in my now unclouded mind).*
>
> *I have been psychic since a child. One year before my mother became ill I knew she would be dead within the time span of one year. She was... 11 months later. After she died, I went to a card reader—a good honest woman who saw my "ability" and taught me to read cards.*
>
> *I was an excellent card reader, and I never gave a reading I was ashamed of. I always gave my best and prayed for the client. I also looked carefully for signs of health trouble or substance abuse. If the client was very troubled etc., I would always suggest the Problems For Daily Living Clinic at the hospital. I never over-charged or abused the trust these people had in me.*
>
> *I had a very high accuracy rate—between 70 and 90% with some people. Often I would tell them things about their relatives who had crossed over—things I couldn't know even by being a*

"good detective" (which a discerning reader must be). I was never troubled by real disturbances. If I felt an "oppressing" force, I would send it away. (However, my religious education did not teach me to proclaim this in Jesus' name. I knew zero about demons and evil spirits, save for reading The Exorcist 10 years ago! I did not know about the possibility of rape, sodomy, and torture. I was vulnerable to a sickening degree.)

Ignorance and out-of-hand dismissal of anything "demonic" is what keeps demonologists and exorcists busy. Whatever your religious belief, we all sometimes have to call upon a "higher power" for help. Neither we nor even the most pious religious leaders are as strong as evil, but God (or whatever your name for this power) is stronger.

After my mother died, I visited another woman, who spoke to spirits, had spirit guides, etc. She was very "religious" in that she read her Bible, advised a course of Bible study, claimed Jesus as Lord, etc.—a little grandmother type. She believed Ouija boards to be so dangerous, etc. However, it is my gut and heart-felt belief that it was there where I picked up these creatures. It became so important to speak to my mother. My husband was the one in which the voices and answers initially went through—never me. He didn't hear actual voices, but got messages in his mind.

During one visit, Mrs. E (who knew I was "psychic" and a reader) advised me to try automatic writing—mistake #2. The compelling urge to write became so strong—unbelievably so—from all sorts of people. I was never hurt during these times, however.

Then one day when I thought my mother and I were "speaking" about what happens to murderers, I mentioned a famous murder case I knew my mother had heard of before dying. My "mother" (who said she spent much of her deceased time working among the sick and trying to help reform the criminal element) said she had seen the victim. My mother said: "She's very sad and confused. She doesn't understand that she can move on (fly, as it were). Will you talk to her?"

I said yes, and about 5-10 minutes later, I was in the presence of the very frightened and suspicious victim. She wanted to know why I was talking to her, etc. She kept writing "nonono" like that. I said I cared about her and wanted to help her. I asked her if she wanted to talk ...to tell me anything that might make her feel better. "She" felt the need to confess. (How I wish I had all the over 50 notebooks written during that time. But alas I destroyed them as proof these creatures had no power over me.) "Her confession" was so sad and shocking. As best, I remember it went ...

"She" drew arches for some reason and wrote: "He picked me up at the station. He said his mother was gone and I could sleep on the couch. He didn't drive me there. He drove me to the beach under the pier. He raped me and said he was sorry. Would I forgive him? I said no, and he took me to a building. He hung me upside down naked and hurt me so bad. I screamed and screamed. He put cloth in my mouth; and he laughed and laughed.

I saw blood and then I felt such a bad pain in my stomach. And I cried and cried, but nobody came. And then I heard something fall, but it wasn't me, it was something else. And then I watched him and he did other things. Do you know what I mean ...in my mouth and hair? And then he wrapped me in a blanket, I think. And I tried to follow him, but could not."

Earthbound spirits are "bound" emotionally where they died ... were buried ... or where they lived and frequented. For the same reason, it should have been suspect that this deceased victim would be available to "speak" through this automatic writer. Also, we have never met an earthbound spirit that recounts its human death in such detail. This is yet, another example of how evil takes advantage of ignorance and good intentions.

Then the writing stopped, and my "mother" began to write frantically. She had no idea the victim would write that. Nobody knew that about her. Was I upset? My mother was sorry, etc. I said to let the victim finish her story.

The victim resumed saying she was now so ugly, so sad, and how she hated "him." And then the pen dropped down and drew first a pair of glasses like this ...

And then filled in the rest of the picture. (I can draw very well, much better than this. This is close, but slightly different from the original.)[23] *"He's young and ugly, wore glasses—I hate him", she said through me.*

And that was the beginning of my talking to "people who needed help." I talked to a wide variety of people. Each was unique—some crabby and

> *suspicious. I was always asked if I could see their families and friends who were still on the earth plane. Without exception, the suicides—including my own Uncle Charles, asked if they'd been sent to hell for killing themselves.*

The **Attraction**—At this point, she has "opened doors." There are a few more clues that the "spirits" writing through her are not what they say they are. Those who "cross over" have the ability to see and be with former families and friends at will. It is also our experience that the only suicides tormented after death were linked to demonic worship, oppression, or possession during life ... otherwise the same emotional issues apply to cause a spirit to remain earthbound, regardless of cause of death. The only difference is, suicides won't be in denial about their death ... a common cause of earthbound hauntings.

By referencing "Uncle Charlie," the entity got this woman's attention and sympathy, which invited recognition and involvement. Evil spirits can read information telepathically and use it against you. This is why exorcists have to be pious people.

> *I was hurt twice ... slapped and pinched by a man and woman first who, after doing that, had no idea why they had and were very ashamed. Mr. Warren my theory is many of those "people" (spirits) were indeed real, but became possessed by the horde of demons that were waiting, and watching. They planned to use those spirits I knew and trusted, so they could get close enough to me to take me over and do things I would not question. Eventually, even in my raped and dazed condition, I wouldn't question—only beg for help from these*

"other" spirits. The plot thickens and gets so sick and sad.

Infestation and oppression—Notice how those who "pinched and slapped" her quickly apologized and expressed shame? This same thing happens with spousal and child abuse. Both spiritual and physical abusers use fear, confusion, and doubt to control someone else. The other spirits she references are probably demonic, too, but pretending to be human. This is why séances, Ouija board games, and witchcraft done for fun can be so dangerous.

Then one day when I spoke to my "mother," she sounded different and was "angry" with me. I was dumbfounded. I began to feel the most awful pain. The writing got abusive and called me a bitch. Then I was attacked. I was so scared and hurt. I had a funny ache between my legs in my thighs and pelvic bones.

The spirit was never her mother, but played the woman along. Next it pretends to be the murderer to justify its behavior and to cover up its real identity and intention.

Shaking and terrified I called Mrs. E who said: "That's not your mother. It's someone who must want your help, who needs release. He may be trapped. Let him talk, and then send him on his way!"

Later, with my husband present, I asked: "Who are you and what do you want?" The writing changed and this is approximately what it said:

"My name is R. P. Are the police after me now? I didn't mean to hurt her so bad. I had hurt others like her, whores like her but never so bad. I'm truly sorry I hurt her." Meanwhile, my husband (who does

> *not like to talk about it) heard a very unpleasant man's voice in his head that said, "I want her dead because she's helping people." As God is my master, he heard that. I did not.*

Possession—Sexual attacks, levitation, temporary but drastic voice, language, behavior, and physical changes are all signs of possession. It might not be complete or constant, but the diabolical is exercising its ability to take control at will. The words in the husband's head were designed to demonstrate power and scare him off. It is easier to gain full control of an isolated victim.

> *And now the most difficult part of this oh, so unbelievable story (nightmare). During my talks with all these people, I met someone truly special. His name was M. He'd been famous here, and was very suspicious when I spoke with him. I learned all about him, his past, his career, his family, things too intricate and intimate to have been murky mimicry from a demon. He is brilliant and soft and funny and sad and fascinating and we spent much time talking.*

She is underestimating the knowledge, power, intelligence, and cleverness of the diabolical.

> *Mr. Warren, it's my horrifying belief (hang onto your hat) that while I was possessed by one (or more) devil, Monty was also possessed by one or more demons. It was like hideous layers of possession—too horrific to even contemplate. It's my belief that these demons often use these oh, so innocent bodies to give them the outward appearance they desire at the time.*

This sort of attack is incomprehensible to most people. The evil entity can manifest it in your mind and create both pain and physical evidence. It can also manifest itself as either a pleasant or horrible creature ... or even someone you know. Apparently, this demon was successful in convincing her an "innocent" spirit was misused in this attack. Her "friend" M. was not possessed, but a wolf in sheep's clothing.

More than one evil entity is usually involved in infestation, oppression, and possession cases. They can control and torment earthbound spirits who had invited evil into their human lives. However, devils and demons are quite capable of deceit and deception all on their own. It is like terrorists posing to be merely flight passengers.

Mr. Warren, after hundreds of hours of deep, painful thought, I feel a demon will inhabit a woman's body only to torture her and to have the experience of being present while another demon(s) rapes her. They feed on fear and crave pain—the hideous suffering and pain they can create.

Absolutely! This is why demonic possession usually leads to rape, murder, rampage killings, and suicide. It uses—and needs—the human body to bring about the most fear, pain and suffering to the most people. (This is not to say, however, that the devil can be blamed for all such violent acts.)

A demon will use the body of an attractive spirit as a go-between—to torture and rape and feel pleasure through—and if the mortal and spirit involved are emotionally attached—oh, then the ensuing emotional and mental torture experienced by both victims is just what they want. They worked so hard setting up the whole thing.

And so, the year passed—a year of the most unbelievable physical and mental pain imaginable. There were months when M was totally surprised; and then when the demon(s) lost interest temporarily until they decided on their next (oh dear God) game ...as they called it. His terrible suffering would come through —his torture and misery and total bewilderment.

The torture would always get hideous after any communication passed between us. M will not speak to me. The creature attempts to imitate him, but cannot do this successfully. It's like a Chinese box—endless springs and catches and hidden things.

The evil entity has less reason to hide his true character at this point, so the M personality only seems to be pulling back. Meanwhile, this woman was so confused and oppressed; she continued her automatic writing and let at least a year go by without seeking outside relief. The diabolical spirits were toying with her and breaking down her will. As any torturer knows, sometimes the best way to break someone is to let them see (or think they see) someone innocent being hurt.

Mr. Warren, my theory cannot be any crazier than the reality of possession itself! I have never been under the care of a psychiatrist, have always been mentally strong and healthy—never suffered severe depressions until this creature. Never hurt myself ever. I always loved living, being alive, and looked forward to each new season, each New Year.

November 1st was the first real attack, but I know now I was "watched" for years. Natural predators will wait as long as necessary, if their plans and numbers are sufficiently large and complex. I opened the door, and have begged God's forgiveness. I've been forgiven and get nothing but strength and guidance—witness you and Mrs. Warren.

I know this letter is hopelessly long, but it's as condensed a version of four years as I could manage. I cannot wait to see you and Mrs. Warren. I shall be free, with yours and God's help.

She is correct in that evil has eternity on its side. It can be very patient and calculating. Sometimes these creatures become dormant ... and reappear years, decades—or in the case of infested places or objects—even centuries later.

Lorraine and I referred this woman to Father LeBar in New York for a Catholic exorcism. The evil entities within her were forced to reveal themselves during the execution of this rite, and were successfully cast out. It helped that beforehand this victim came to better understand what was happening, and how it happened. As you can see from her letter, she had already begun to take steps to regain control.

However, like a deadly cancer in remission, these creatures can always come back. It is not easy to find or convince a qualified exorcist to relieve this torment. The ordeal of an exorcism is traumatic itself, and may require multiple efforts. This is why awareness, avoidance, and prevention are the best advice Lorraine and I can give people.

Unfortunately, there are not many people like us who would take such an ordeal seriously ... or are able to offer any real help.

Cheryl A. Wicks

> **"The devil can cite Scripture for his purpose."**
> Shakespeare, *The Merchant of Venice,* Act I, Sc. 3

Case Study #7
Like Someone Possessed

This case is based on correspondence between the Warrens and their clients. All client names and places referenced have been changed or modified to protect their privacy. Ed Warren introduces and discusses the letter's contents.

It was in the late twentieth century when a woman first contacted Lorraine and me out of concern for her husband. Based on what I heard, I warned her at that time that her husband was becoming dangerous to her, their children, and himself. I advised her to put some distance between him and the rest of the family until the problem was resolved. Here are excerpts from the letter we received a few years later documenting her ordeal. She took our advice and was writing while living apart from her husband. She enclosed pictures along with other documentation.

Dear Ed & Lorraine,

Do you know any real exorcists? When I last spoke to your wife and you, you told me that my case could be serious and that our lives may be in danger.

I couldn't find anyone else to take my situation seriously except for a lay person who prays to Jesus and has special healing hands. The evil creatures in my husband actually pushed this person away, but she said Jesus is stronger than all Hell. He has recovered somewhat, but something is still wrong. At the very least, I wanted to document all that happened, for both your and my benefit.

Background Information

Paul and I met in college and married two years later. When we became engaged, Paul quit the Catholic Church and called religion the "panacea of the masses."

When I went to meet his brothers and sisters in Switzerland, I felt uncomfortable with the coziness and petting among his adult brothers and sisters. While we were in Switzerland, I was walking down the sidewalk with him when a car jumped the curb and pushed me to a brick wall of a funeral home.

I found out later that one of his sisters practices witchcraft. Looking back now I think that this sister doesn't seem to want her brothers to marry. Bad things seem to happen. Just before my husband Paul's youngest brother was to be married, he visited the same sister. Shortly afterwards, he blew his brains out with a rifle right before his wedding.

Included in the material this woman sent us was an aerial photo of the town where her husband had grown up in Switzerland. His childhood home was formerly a church rectory directly across from a cemetery. It is here where Paul's brother shot himself immediately following a visit with the same sister Paul visits later. The family home has since been condemned and the church destroyed.

Up until his last trip to Switzerland, Paul was the top engineer for one of the largest oil fields in Indonesia. He redesigned it to improve production—a redesign worth billions for his employer. Having been so successful in this redesign, he was considering becoming an independent consultant in Petroleum Engineering.

When he left for Switzerland, we just had our fourth child and were very much in love.

He went to Switzerland to explore a business opportunity and visit his sister and childhood home. He came back a completely different man from the one who left.

Sequence of Events

In September, Paul left for Switzerland. While there, he visited his sister and her boyfriend, who practice occult and witchcraft. Before this visit, his sister told Paul to eat a lot of cheese before going to her house. At his sister's place, he was given some "herbal" potions to help him relax.

When he first called me that night, he said: "I must have fallen asleep there. When I woke up, my sister and boyfriend were gone. I think I am losing my mind."

For an educated, accomplished man to say he thinks he is losing his mind, something besides his falling asleep at his sister's house must have happened.

He called me again a little later, and it was strange. He was making a "porn" call to me. He had

> *never talked to me like this before. He was telling me to masturbate, etc.*

When someone is being oppressed by one or more evil entities, the victim often assumes specific evil characteristics. Gluttony and apathy are common. In this case, lust was the primary manifestation, with apathy and gluttony to follow.

> *While still in Switzerland, Paul went to a psychologist—one recommended by his sister—who made him remove any (religious) medals he wore and the scapular[24] of our Lady. He told me this woman doctor blew air—or drug—up his nose; making him feel very powerful. He felt as if he could make a rocket blast off with his voice.*

How professional is any "psychologist" who insists on the removal of religious medals and blows something like cocaine up her patient's nose? Paul was wearing religious medals because he had returned to the church after his marriage, for the sake of the children. One of their daughters was preparing for her first communion at the time all this began.

> *When Paul missed his flight home, he saw his sister again. Since she is a nurse, she could get him a doctor's excuse. He was seen in a Zurich Hospital, and got an extension on his ticket.*
>
> *He finally got on a flight that stopped over in Paris, where he was deplaned and sent to a hospital for observation.*

Obviously, Paul was not acting appropriately if he was deplaned and hospitalized en route. The fact that he was hospitalized twice before he could get home indicates how bizarre his behavior was and how quickly it changed.

The suddenness of these events is not unusual in cases where witchcraft is involved.

> *Later he returned on a flight home to the U.S., but he was acting weird. I had gone to meet Paul at the airport. He was the last one off the plane and moved very slowly.*
>
> *When he got in the car and took the wheel, his driving was different. Usually he was a calm and cautious driver, but he was reckless and jerky. And he didn't know the way home. He thought he could fly over a ravine from one freeway to the other.*
>
> *On the way home, he said, "We must get divorced. It will be hard at first; but we have to." I was completely floored. He then told me he picked up a girl in a bar in Switzerland, and went to her apartment.*
>
> *Later, Paul told me that when he visited his dead brother's grave in Switzerland, he stayed up all night. Afterwards, he felt an evil presence with him in the car he was driving. He told me he knew it was the devil; and when he looked, his speedometer had changed to 666!*

This was very likely one of the events that made Paul think he was losing his mind when he first called his wife from Switzerland. This could also be a drug-induced experience.

> *Back then he would confront things and share his concerns. It was like he was himself, only scared. Sometimes he said: "How will I get rid of all these ghosts?"*

The visions one sees while under a demonic attack are not ghosts. They are more like monsters. They are not human and have never been human. Yet, most victims don't know what else to call them, because these creatures often remain invisible to others.

> Paul lost his great job and got fired from a consulting job when he hung up on the guy. He went to another consulting job and ended up lashing out at the owner for being a spoiled brat, causing him (the owner) to have a bad asthma attack.
>
> When he came home, he told me he stared at all the girls around town, and they looked like models. (He never commented on other women to me before.) Then if I would get mad because of his escapades—cheating on me, etc.—he would get a blank look in his eyes, look up like he was looking at something in the air, and get very strange and bizarre ...not understand English, etc. He spoke Swiss German or something.
>
> He couldn't sit on a chair. He would slither off to the floor, or walk on the furniture.
>
> I took him to a local Emergency Room. They decided to keep him, and transferred him to a psychiatric hospital as a "danger to himself or others." He ran out of the hospital after asking for his handcuffs to come off so he could use the urinal. He was caught by the police and taken back to the psychiatric hospital.
>
> He stayed there about 3-4 days and was diagnosed as bi-polar. He told me that when he was in there, he was in Purgatory or Hell with his brother who shot himself. He saw demons, etc. in his room.

The demonic "trickster" was using the image of Paul's brother to control and torment him.

After his release, I went with him to pick up his medication. While I was at the pharmacy counter, he disappeared a while. I saw him reading Cosmopolitan *magazine—something he never did. When we went to the parking lot, the store manager came out, a young couple, and then the police. I didn't know what was going on. The young lady said he put his hand up her shorts while waiting in line. The police let him go since I said he was just released from the hospital and needed his medicine.*

At home it was scary. He would act like he was tumbling weightless along the walls of the house. He said he would see us out of this house and on the street with no money—or dead. He had to be watched every second. He would bang into people in the grocery store on purpose. I would have to hold his arm.

In a rare moment of slight normalcy after he came home from the hospital, he told me he felt a very dark evil cloud—or feeling—coming over him.

After consulting my parish priest, Paul and I took our two youngest children and flew out of state to see a priest who had seen these things before. The Father had to be secretive about it, since his superior didn't support his involvement with these things.

My husband said the holy water burned him. After three sessions and while we sat in the Father's office, my husband was touching his private parts in front of the priest. The priest asked: "Who did this to you?" My husband said his sister and her boyfriend. The priest asked: "What are you to do?" Paul answered: "Kill my family." The priest asked: "What would this do for you?" Paul said: "The devil promises me sex in Hell forever." He said all this in front of our youngest children (ages one and three at the time).

After we flew home and we got back to the airport parking lot, the car wouldn't start. He thought he could lift the car. When we got home, every mechanical thing Paul touched broke—sweepers, garage opener, etc.

A few days later, I thought he was doing better. He said he was going upstairs to watch football. I went up an hour or so later, and he wasn't there. He had climbed out the bathroom window, scaled a stucco wall, and took off to a topless bar, returning with porno movies to show our thirteen and seven year-old girls. Also, he had his pants on inside out. I tried to take the movies from him; and he stuffed them in the front of his underwear.

Paul said it would be good if he could be with other people for sex. He wanted no protection from pregnancy and a lot of wild sex. (He could have sex forever—permanent erection.) He wouldn't climax, and could go on and on—tore my clothes. Meanwhile, I just had my fourth C-section and it was too unhealthy for me to have another child.

If I went to the playground with the children, I would take him along by the hand to keep him away from other people. He never played with our children in the playground. He would usually just sit. One time he easily climbed a straight pole (like a fireman pole).

All his eating tastes changed. He also thought he lost his sense of smell—and still does. He still doesn't hear well. His eyesight changed, as well as his handwriting.

Paul as described is certainly showing some classic signs of oppression and possession. The changes he is experiencing and others are witnessing are well beyond cosmetic. Beyond the physical and behavior changes, what is significant is his newfound physical abilities and his speaking in another, unknown language.

The pictures this woman enclosed with her letter also confirm the changes. A photo taken just before his trip to Switzerland shows a lean, well-groomed, tanned man with warmth, laughter, and love in his eyes for the family he embraces. Only a month later, another picture shows the same man standing apart from everyone. He looks slovenly and overweight, and has cold, lifeless eyes set in a gray complexion.

I took him to another psychologist, who admitted he felt something unnatural was involved. Paul walked on the doctor's couches and hid in the bathroom with the lights off. He still does this. One day while he was in the dark bathroom, I heard him say: "What now master?"

By mid October, he was always going to our bedroom and locking the door. Later I found wires connected from the electric plug and TV to the metal parts of the bed. Twice I woke up to find he had slipped a belt around my neck. My screaming: "Paul! What are you doing?" snapped him out of it. Later, the gas line on our water heater had been manually cracked and was leaking bad.

You wouldn't think I would have to tell this woman that her and her children's lives were in danger. But as strange as this seems, her behavior was not unusual, either. She was trying to hold her family together, loved her husband and the father of their four children, and could not believe he was not the same man. She was too busy trying to return him—and all their lives—to normal to recognize she and her family may be in real danger.

Also, demonic oppression affects more than the individual targeted for possession. For example, in the Amityville case, both George and Kathy Lutz lost interest in things that were important to them prior to moving into the house. George ignored his business and wouldn't shower, while Kathy didn't want to leave the house or finish Christmas shopping.

> *Whenever I confronted him with the truth, he would become enraged. He knocked my daughter's head two or three times for saying something. On a few occasions, I would ask where our one-year old was, and he would say: "I think I drowned him in the backyard pool."*
>
> *He kept telling me that "the big event"—Halloween—was coming. He was afraid of what might happen.*
>
> *And things got worse. I found him in his underwear on the floor of my daughter's room growling like a wolf. Pastor Dr. D called at this moment. I put the phone to Paul's ear while the priest invoked the Precious Blood of Jesus. I held a statue of the Blessed Mother over Paul, prayed, and invoked Jesus, Mary, and St. Michael. Paul started pulling at the carpet, ripping down the drapes, pulling clothes out, tearing up the beds, and then*

some horrifying evil sounds and moans came from very, very deep inside of him.

This is not good. The behavior and terrible sounds described are probably not human.

While playing with the children downstairs, our dog suddenly went crazy and bit my three-year old. As I got ready to take my son to the hospital, my husband danced around naked in front of our four kids, and then sat on the couch in a weird, cross-legged position.

The dog was probably reacting in fright based on what its instincts told him was present. It is unlikely the dog itself was possessed. Evil entities want human souls ... to control our free will. They have been known to manifest into animal form, but these creatures would never be confused with the family pet.

I took care of my son and had my husband committed. I spent many hours at the hospital trying to get Paul back to reality. He was heavily drugged and slept a lot. I asked priests to visit him.

Paul may have slept, but the devil doesn't. It never sleeps. It doesn't need sleep.

Upon discharge, Paul resented me, the kids, and any work or obligations. During any prayers, rosary, or mass, he would instantly fall asleep.

His reaction to anything religious is predictable with someone "under the influence" of an evil entity. Reactions will either be violent and blasphemous, or completely blank and inert. This range of reactions also occurs during an exorcism.

I had to teach Paul how to do things. He was like a severely retarded person, or from outer

> *space. He did not recognize utensils. He thought to cook an egg, you just put it in the fire on the stove (no pan needed). To rake leaves, he thought you use your hands. During this time, he told me he was going to Hell and would take me there, too. I told him: "No, don't you know the Brown Scapular Promise?"[25]*
>
> *However, something strange happened a week ago when he left the scapular, crucifix, and St. Benedict medal on when he went in for hernia surgery. The nurse said he became very violent after the operation ...scratching his neck bad until he could rip off the scapular and medals. The nurse said he had a very ugly look on him while he did this. This made me feel that his subconscious had showed through, revealing his hatred for the holy "sacramentals" of the church.*

Lorraine and I suspect something other than his "subconscious" was showing through.

> *While he was not acting as "berserk" as before, he became very lazy, resents work, wants to go bankrupt, and does nothing to provide for his family. When one of our sons slipped on the tile floor, banged his head, and screamed, Paul just got up and walked away.*
>
> *The children can't stand to be near him. Either he uses a fake, sweet, singsong voice or a rotten one. They can't stand to be touched by him. They scream if he wakes them up in the morning. His eyes scare me, and his face has turned ugly. He only cares to feed and gorge himself.*

As I stated earlier, common "side effects" of diabolical oppression are apathy and gluttony ... which are often hard to differentiate from depression. Paul's sudden, uncontrolled and chronic lurid behavior, however, is a little easier to diagnose as abnormal. The pictures enclosed with this woman's letter confirmed the physical changes she described.

> *Paul will not say he loves me. Now I feel a lot of pain, resentment, and don't want to "hate"—for that is of the devil. Yet, I find it hard to say, "I love you" to him. I wonder if Paul ever returns to some degree to this body, or if an evil one always waits behind a dark curtain in his mind.*

Summary

> *We have consulted four psychiatrists ... two who, after examination, felt we were dealing with an occult situation. Paul was hospitalized twice in Europe and twice in the U.S. Prescribed medication doesn't seem to have any long-term physical or emotional impact on his strange behavior.*
>
> *I have also sought the help of the church. One Father, now deceased, read a "short exorcism," which had little impact on the problem. Another heard Paul's inhuman growls over the phone. This is the Pastor who gave me your name to contact. A third Father referred me to yet a fourth who feels this is not his expertise.*
>
> *Since Paul's last trip to Switzerland, he suddenly needed glasses. He lost his sense of smell. His hearing has deteriorated. His handwriting is different. His eating habits have changed. (Before he would never eat fast food, and now he loves it.)*

Effortlessly, he can climb straight poles, buildings, and the side of our stucco house. He forgets how to drive, where we live, and how to do the simplest of tasks such as how to use furniture and even how to speak and understand English. He speaks a foreign language I never heard him speak before.

He threatens and puts his family at risk by hooking up electric cords to our bed, disconnecting our fire alarms and breaking them, and other dangerous or negligent behavior.

He has either a violent or blank reaction to confrontation and falls asleep when faced with prayer, a mass, or the rosary. He also has a negative and sometimes painful reaction to religious metals and symbols.

His craving for wild sex and porno is constant and shows a complete lack of respect for our children, other people, and me. He cannot hold a job despite his education and past success as a Petroleum Engineer.

Current Situation

All of this is difficult to talk or write about, but I'm afraid my husband is not free from the evil. I wake up every day with my heart shaking recalling the experience, wishing it were a bad dream. I now need medication for the irregular heartbeat that has come from all this shock. I am worried about my children, a recurrence, and my getting over the trauma myself.

Paul has not been living with us for almost a year. Yet, I saw him over the weekend. We visited a shrine and lit a candle. I think it is a good time to get through to Paul. I trust Jesus will help me for the sake of the children.

I have spoken to the Father who will be saying the Padre Pio[26] Birthday Mass, but he says he is not an expert in these matters. This is why I need someone who is. May Jesus, Mary, St. Joseph, and St. Michael, and all the angels and saints assist you in your courageous work, and may the Holy Ghost enlighten you always.

This woman has described the horror of having someone she loves—and her life—completely change before her eyes while she is powerless to do anything about it. The best scientific minds, institutions, and drugs offered little or no relief. If this is what I think it is, long-term relief can only come from a religious exorcism, calling on the power of God.

I advised this client to keep herself and the children away from this man. He was no longer the same person they once knew. Unfortunately, there was little Lorraine and I could do for him as he had not asked for our help. Even when Jesus was casting out demons, the victim was always asked if he wanted the demon cast out before the demon could be actually exorcised.

Free will is that powerful. You can no more exorcise someone's demon than cure him or her of an addiction without his or her acknowledgement of the problem and desire to correct it.

I'm afraid the evil controlling Paul has not simply gone away, but is lying dormant, waiting for an opportunity to strike. Unfortunately, if there is no religious intervention, the result will likely be death. Paul's health is apt to continue to break down or he may be driven to suicide. Hopefully, no one else will be hurt. If we take a closer look at rampage murders, would we see more cases of a "mental illness" that defies diagnosis and treatment?

Unfortunately, the very people who can help are often reluctant to do so. There are very few trained exorcists because it is dangerous and unpleasant work ... and there is already a shortage of pious Catholic priests to serve the public's more routine spiritual needs. And the church abhors publicity. In some respects, I understand. This is serious business, not a circus. Yet their "secrecy" and "confidentiality" can cover up more than the evil of child molestation.

As this woman says in her letter to us, "May the Holy Ghost enlighten you always" ... and please stay away from *anyone*—including family and friends—who you even *think* worships Satan and dabbles in witchcraft.

"I've been to numerous homicide scenes, including multiple murders that ended in suicide. These have been scenes where things just didn't feel right. The atmosphere in some felt so mockingly evil, heavy and dreadful, that I felt I had to pray for the victims."
Forensic detective, in a letter to the Warrens,
August 2000

SECTION IV

The Unexplained: Real or Ridiculous?

Once again, the Warrens were together with a group of eager students of all ages and walks of life, eager to learn more about the paranormal. Lorraine was dressed in one of her trademark tartans and matching scarf. Ed was looking tough but comfortable in a dark sweatshirt. Lorraine pulled up a tall stool and began to address the group.

"Since the beginning of human history, there have been accounts of 'outside of this world' encounters," she began. "It is easy to assume that our ancestral anecdotes or stories from the Third World have superstitious origins. However, the same tales are told today by educated, credible people in scientifically advanced countries, all around the globe. What is hard to ignore is that the contents of these unexplained experiences are consistent, no matter to whom and in what cultural environment they occur.

"It is one thing to believe our mind is playing tricks on us, but another to believe it plays tricks on us the same way with the same images throughout the centuries and regardless of culture. It is these consistencies that continue to fascinate the open-minded and stump skeptics. For example, people of apparent sincerity and sanity continue to report sightings of hairy humanoid beings in our world's most secluded environments. While description details vary, people are consistently *not* describing woolly mammoths or something that looks like a giant bug. It is the consistencies in what they do describe that warrant further research."

Ed added, "It wasn't so long ago when seasoned fishermen were said to be mistaking floating trees with large root systems for huge animals attacking their boats. Then science uncovered the giant squid. It wasn't until 1847 when the fierce-looking and eerily humanlike 'pongo' was officially recognized ... a creature known to us as the gorilla. Other creatures first dismissed as illusions based on the power of suggestion or as an outright hoax include the giant panda and duck-billed platypus."

Lorraine continued, "It wasn't until 1982 that the science of cryptozoology was founded. This is the 'science of hidden animals.' It recognizes that local populations often are accurately aware of the creatures found in their environment, regardless of how strange and unlikely they are to the rest of the world. Local knowledge reveals key aspects of the appearance and behavior of these elusive and unusual animals. Are they hairy, have scales, large or small, nocturnal, walk on four legs or two?"

Ed explained, "What makes a creature of interest to cryptozoology is that it is unexpected. For example, a penguin in the Caribbean bears further study as much as a long-necked monster spotted in a quiet lake in Scotland."

Lorraine nodded her head in agreement, shifted on her stool, and resumed speaking. "Parapsychology looks at the other 'weird stuff that happens.' Once again, there is too much consistency in diverse testimony to be ignored. This includes ghost sightings, telepathy, telekinesis, psychometry, poltergeist activity, and even miracles. Mysteries surround us. We don't have to go to ancient castles or desolate graveyards to find an unexplained sound, physical event, or image on a photograph. Hardly a day passes without someone substantiated as being sane, sober, and even skeptical, shaking their head after being confronted with the inexplicable.

"Yet, science and scholars have historically failed to acknowledge this significant part of the human experience. It is one thing to demand persuasive evidence and another to be afraid to admit the limits of current knowledge. Weird stuff happens ... whether it is encountering a strange creature while walking in the woods, or having your grandmother announce her passing *after* her death, from hundreds of miles away."

Ed offered, "Human nature is uncomfortable with an explanation vacuum. It is hard to admit that we 'don't know.' Skeptics dismiss paranormal accounts as either ridiculous or unbelievable. Those who are gullible come up with and accept 'far-out' explanations without considering the source, effort, or thought behind the theories. Real understanding comes from exploration with patience, modesty, and a tolerance for ambiguity.

"Comprehending the incomprehensible starts by acknowledging we don't know what is behind all the weird experiences that so many people seem to have. Yet, with an ever-accelerating accumulation of knowledge in so many areas, a rational perspective is apt to be found. Sooner or later, we are sure to learn something new."

Ed stopped to look into the faces of everyone in the audience before he continued. "However, this new information is apt to lead to the discovery of unsuspected perceptual anomalies ... or glimpses of an otherwise undetected larger reality. This, of course, could rattle the scientific community ... and shake the foundations of consensus reality. In short, the implications of discovery in these areas are enormous."

"Yes," Lorraine confirmed. "Remember, it wasn't so long ago that community leaders and educated people found the idea of the earth being round and spinning around the sun as outrageous as space travel. Yet, today's greatest minds admit that there is far more unseen than seen in our so-called physical world."

Ed added, "It is getting harder and harder to ignore the fact that people of all ages, cultures, and educational levels insist they were not dreaming and were fully conscious when they hear and see strange things. At some point, we are going to have to listen to the witnesses.

"Lorraine and I dedicated most of our lives to doing just that. For more than fifty years, we interviewed thousands of others who have had paranormal encounters of one kind or another. At first, it was something people were hesitant to talk about. They were embarrassed about being frightened and frustrated with their inability to find logical explanations for their experience. Over the years, however, people became more curious and open about the weird events in their lives. Through improved communication and sometimes our efforts, they learned they were not alone.

"Unfortunately, there are also those who are so eager for their brief moment of fame that they tell tall tales or fake occurrences. Yet, there are many things that are still hard to fake or create with even an informed, overactive imagination."

Lorraine offered, "What happens in a legitimate poltergeist, haunting, or demonic attack is hard to believe, even for those going through it. There are so many consistencies, however, that they are hard to deny.

Also, these experiences are often witnessed by more than one person, and match thousands of other reports from around the world."

"Nonetheless," Ed said, "Sorting out the real from the enhanced, imagined, or faked is sometimes as much a challenge as understanding the paranormal activity itself. It doesn't help that often multiple 'realities' blend. True paranormal activity might be exaggerated. Someone perpetuating fraud may also be attracting evil. Here is where a 'tolerance for ambiguity' is helpful. The following two cases illustrate the difficulty in trying to both validate and make sense out of the unexplained."

- ♦ **Case Study #8:** <u>Bigfoot in Tennessee</u>

  Motivated by fear and the desire to warn others, humble rural families report multiple sightings of a large hairy, human-like creature standing and walking on two legs. Lorraine's unexpected psychic encounter may shed more light on the recurring mystery regarding this and other strange "hidden animals."

- ♦ **Case Study #9:** <u>Haunted Hotel in the Highlands</u>

  The Warrens were invited to investigate strange occurrences in an isolated hotel in Scotland. A reluctant clairvoyant could be both part of the solution and part of the problem. Readers join researchers in the struggle to sort out the startling from the staged.

Cheryl A. Wicks

Case Study #8
Bigfoot in Tennessee

All names and places in this true story have been changed or modified to protect the privacy of clients. Ed Warren describes the case.

Background

While Lorraine and I were lecturing at a school near the Andrew Jackson Hermitage in Tennessee in April 1976, a professor I'll call Ralph brought a recent article from the local newspaper to our attention. According to the story, people were reporting a nearby sighting of a Bigfoot-like creature. Ralph asked if we would like to investigate. We agreed to an outing in the wild woods of Tennessee early the next day. Years of lecturing have taught us to leave some extra time in our schedule for just such opportunities.

After a restful night, we met Ralph in the lobby of our hotel early in the morning and set off for rural Tennessee. En route, Lorraine chatted nonstop while I wondered when I would ever have my next meal. Every mile took us further from civilization as I knew it—diners, restaurants, and fast food places. We found ourselves in a part of the state and country so remote that migrating birds would need maps.

A long dirt road led us to a tiny community of shacks linked by electric lines to a "street lamp" in the center like a Maypole. Outside of this ramshackle area were thick woods that seemed to go on until the edge of the world. The man who owned all the cleared property was also the sheriff for this isolated bit of community. Living next door to the sheriff were another couple and their two young sons.

The sheriff was a tall, gaunt man with sunken cheeks. He wore overalls and a dark shirt that looked well used. He extended one of his huge, stained but clean hands, and we exchanged introductions. He was an "ah shucks" kind of guy who was extremely polite and respectful, but nobody's fool. He had a soft voice despite his size and spoke in a thoughtful, measured way.

I agreed to conduct the interviews, while Lorraine went with our tour guide Ralph to wander the grounds and nearby woods. She wanted to see what she could discern through her clairvoyant skills without being influenced by what others claimed or thought they saw. I started the interview by inserting a fresh tape in my recorder and directing my questions to the sheriff.

First Interview with the Sheriff

I began by trying to get a feel for the man and the location. "I understand that you are a security guard at a department store nearby, and that you live here with your wife. Do you have any children?" I asked him.

"No, sir, we don't have any children, unfortunately, sir," the sheriff replied.

I continued: "You have a neighbor who lives just a few yards from your own home, but otherwise, there are not too many homes around here, are there?"

"No, sir, not real close there's not. There are no houses, sir, for several miles. There's only a creek that follows a hollow and comes out approximately four and a half miles onto a blacktop road," the sheriff outlined.

"From what I understand, there are some caves nearby that go in as far as a mile, and that the temperature rarely goes under sixty degrees. Is this correct?"

"Yes, sir, I have been told so," the sheriff said, nodding his large head. I have not been in the cave, but I have talked to a neighbor of mine, which lives about ... oh, two miles from my house, sir. He says that there is a cave where this trail leads, according to his description of the area. This path that leaves the house—that we're looking at out here —leads down to the area in which the cave is located."

"So, this would be an ideal location for an unfamiliar creature to survive. Also when I look out at these woods behind your home, I can see that something large could stand hidden there less than thirty yards away. You'd never know it was there."

"That is right, sir. Something huge could hide there, and unless you just walked up on it, you would never see it. That's right."

"Lorraine and I saw a newspaper story of something that happened recently with your neighbor. Could you tell us about what happened to this family who lives next door to you?"

"About two weeks ago, last Monday night to be exact on that, sir ... at approximately 9:30 p.m., this gentleman (my neighbor) came to my house and woke me up. He was real upset and raising his voice and hollering for me to open the door and help him. And he went on to explain that something had almost got one of his little boys down here.

"He said his boy needed to go out of the house, and his wife led him to the door. When he stepped out, some sort of a thing reached out and grabbed at this little boy. His wife jerked the boy back into the house just in time."

(For those wondering why a little boy would need to go outside in the middle of the night, these families still used outhouses.) I ventured: "I understand the boy is four years old?"

"Yes sir, right," the sheriff confirmed. "They have another child. It's a boy, sir. He is five years old, sir."

"Has this family ever seen this creature around here before?" I queried.

"Yes, sir. While they were cutting wood …"

"Out back of where we are standing?" I asked while pointing to the edge of the woods.

"Yes, in the back of the house, which you can see from this point here. There is a whole lot of undergrowth and stuff in there. And one of them said they saw this thing come out. That was approximately two weeks before this incident happened, sir."

"So, in other words, there were two sightings within a month here?"

"Yes, sir, yes sir, definitely."

"Have you yourself seen this mysterious creature I read about in the newspaper?"

"Yes sir, I sure have," the sheriff said without hesitation. He obviously had been waiting for me to ask that question.

"Could you describe what you saw and when you saw it?" I asked.

"Well, I would describe this thing as being approximately seven feet tall. It walks upright like a man, and I would say that at the shoulder part, it ... slightly stoops forward when it walks.

"The first time I seen this thing, sir, happened approximately three and a half or four years ago. I'm sorry I cannot give you a sufficient date on this, but I didn't mark the date on it. The dogs had been raving for several nights, and I hadn't been paying a whole lot of attention to it. And one morning, about 2:30 in the morning—the best I remember, sir, I came out and turned the light on to investigate, and this thing was out in the yard ... just a short ways from the house.

"And it seemed to be afraid of the light. It turned and ran away ... going out of the yard and back into the undergrowth—the forest down here."

I asked: "How much would you say it weighed?"

"I would estimate the thing to weigh from three and a half to four hundred pounds at least."

"Did this creature make any noise?" I asked.

"I couldn't swear that this thing made the noise; but I have heard noises several different times—after this thing and before I first seen it. It sounded like something I have never heard—no human being could imitate it—or animal that I know of in this area."

"How would you describe the sound?"

"Well, I would describe it something like a woman screaming—when she was real upset. Except I have never heard a woman scream just exactly like this. But I would say it'd be the closest thing to it, only a whole lot louder and coarser."

"Is there any smell connected with this animal?"

"I have smelt some unusual scents around with it, sir. Yes, sir, I sure have." The sheriff paused and then added, "Well, I would say a fox-type odor; but not quite the same thing."

"Did you do anything when you saw it?"

"I picked up a board and a stick and chased it into the woods, but I didn't pursue it."

I asked, "Do you think that this creature would harm anybody?"

"Sir, it looks mighty mean. But, as far as I know, there hasn't been anyone hurt by it," the sheriff admitted.

I thanked him for the information and asked if we could use it to inform and teach others.

"Sir, I give you permission to use it in any way. And I would like to thank you very much for your cooperation in this thing and your interest in it. And I appreciate that I finally found somebody to listen to me. I have talked to several people around that don't believe this is happening, and I again thank you for your concern, sir."

"You're welcome," I said. "Now I'd like to interview your neighbors."

He introduced me to two women and another man who stood at a respectable distance, listening to every word. A small assortment of children and dogs also milled about. Both the sheriff and his neighbor lived in dilapidated houses, only a few feet apart, and about the size of a one-car garage. Each home had a front and back door with an outhouse in the back. Behind the neighbor's house was a sprawling pile of cans and other metals. A thin wiry woman, in her mid thirties, wearing a faded flowered dress, was the lady of the neighbor's household. She wore her thin brown hair pulled back and seemed unable to stand still. Her voice was scratchy, as if she spent too much time hollering after kids and animals. I directed my next set of questions to her.

Interview with Neighbors

I turned to the woman, pointed my tape recorder at her, and said: "Please tell me in your own words what happened with your little boy and this strange creature the other night."

She glanced down at her worn shoes and tugged at her frayed dress as she answered: "Well, ah, my son and me went to the back door.

"We were standing there in the door. I was looking down through yonder. I heard something walking on those cans," she said with a sweeping arm motion toward the scattered can pile behind her house. "I kept staring, looking down through yonder, because I thought it might be a dog or something. Then I heard something. It was breathing. It sounded as though something or somebody was standing there that had asthma."

She shifted her weight, glanced side to side, and continued. "I turned to look at the side of the house where the sound was coming from, and when I did, I saw a tall, black shadow standing there. It reached out just like it was going to grab my son. And when it did, I jerked my son back inside and closed the door."

That certainly would have frightened me, I thought. "Could you make out what it was?" I asked.

"No, I couldn't," she admitted.

"Have you ever seen this thing before?" I asked, realizing these people didn't volunteer anything.

"Yeah, when we was down there sawing wood," she said, indicating the tree line. "I didn't see it that day, but I heard it. My husband saw it," she added.

"What did it sound like?" I asked.

"I just heard something walking," she said. "It seemed to be real heavy, 'cause you could hear it. I recognized when its feet hit the ground."

"How did your husband react when he saw it?" I asked.

"He was just scared, you know, the same way I was. He told me: 'Get the gas and saw and run!' I did because I was on the verge of running anyway."

No doubt, I thought. "Have you or your husband seen this creature any other time?" I asked, trying to cover all bases.

"One day we was bringing wood from down there ..." Again she pointed to the tree line. "We drug it up and put it here in this field. We were going to go back down to get some more, but we stopped after laying the wood down in the field and stood talking. I happened to look back down there and saw something."

"What did you see?" I asked.

"Whatever that thing was, I couldn't see it close enough to tell you what it was or what it looked like. The only thing I saw was some kind of hair sticking from behind the tree. As far as seeing it real good to tell you what it is or anything, I don't know, and I don't want to know," she emphasized.

"Are you frightened of this animal or creature, or whatever it is?" I asked.

"I'm not just frightened, I'm pretty well terrified! I mean I'm really scared," she said emphatically.

"Do you think it will harm you?" I asked.

Cheryl A. Wicks

"Yes," she agreed.

I thanked her and turned to her husband. He was a large, husky, strong man, also in his thirties. His deep tan and already leathering skin revealed a life of outside work. He boldly stepped up to the recorder when his wife stepped back. He had a booming voice —the kind that carried, even at a whisper.

"Could you describe the creature you saw, please?" I asked.

He jumped right in, "Well ... it's about seven feet tall, weighs about 300 pounds, and has long hair all over it. I have never seen its face or anything like that, but I have seen its paws and arms or whatever you call them. As to what it is, I don't know.

"I do think it is dangerous," he volunteered, "because it was smacking at my kid. On account of that, I reported it. I know a lot more people around here got kids."

"So you are the one that wrote the warning," I asked before I read:

> "Warning! People in county to be on the lookout for some animal-like thing, 6 feet tall weighs about 300 pounds, half brown, half black, has long hair, walks upright like a human. Considered dangerous?"

"Yes, I felt about it this way ... if one of them was to get their kids taken off and I come up and say: 'Same thing almost happened to one of mine out there,' then they'd say: 'Well why didn't you report it so it wouldn't happen again?' So I decided to go to the paper and report it, and I did."

Ghost Tracks

"In other words, you brought this flyer to the newspaper; they became interested in your story, and they published it. Is this true?"

"That is true," he confirmed. "There is a lot of people who don't believe it and make fun of us for saying it, but it's true. The sheriff here and my wife, and the sheriff wife know what we've seen. We know it's up here. And, people make fun of us account of it. But we know, and we know it's for real.

"I know there is a lot of people that say it's a little old monkey or something. But if they was to see it, it would be different than what they think it is. And a lot of people say it is a bear," he added. "But no bear is going to run up on its back legs all the time. A bear is going to run on all its paws. It's some kind of a different kind of creature than a bear. I just don't know what it is. Like I said, I'd call it a half man and half ape. And, that's about all that I can do. It's hard to believe."

"What kind of sound did it make?" I asked.

"Well, my wife said its breathing is like somebody with a bad case of asthma. Also, I have heard like a woman's scream. I don't know whether it was coming from that thing, or what it's coming from. But, anyhow it is coming from somewhere."

"Tell me your account of what happened with your wife and son the other night," I said.

"It was about nearly 9:30 at night. My youngest boy and my wife were standing there at the back door. She heard some kind of noise in some cans around here. She seen a great big shadow, and she seen it smack out. She jerked the boy back inside and slammed the door.

"She was awful upset and nervous about it and about scared to death. So I told her to lock the front door, and

I run out. And as I run along up there, I hollered to my neighbor. He comes running down, and we went around there to the back to see if we could see it. We didn't see it, because it was done gone.

"And she said she felt something like the breath from it, or something or other. I don't know. I mean, I've never been that close to it. We never said nothing to the boy, but when the news guy asked my boy, 'What did he look like?', the little boy described it as tall, with long hair, and it had 'long toenails'—he called it, but he was talking about its claws.

"So what it is, I mean, I figured I'd say it is between half human and half ape ... is the way I'd describe it.

"As to what it is ... now we've been looking around here. It has a path down yonder. We think it lives down in here behind the house, behind the brush down there, or something like that. And as far as being real close to it, I haven't been real close to it. It would hide behind a tree. There are two caves located down there, according to neighbors."

"You don't want to catch it and put it in a cage?" I asked.

"I don't want to get close to it, because I figure that it is dangerous. That is why I went to town and reported it ... to warn people not to capture it. I don't want nobody going down there and harming it in any way ... leaving it wounded or something."

"You don't want someone to hurt it and infuriate it, is that correct?" I tried to clarify.

"Yeah. It would come up here and destroy us. That's what I don't want it to do. I'd say people who go down to look for it must be ultra careful about it. In my opinion, people should stay away from down there and leave the game warden or somebody that really knows something about it to handle it.

"We are afraid people will get to shooting around, get brave, kill one another, then we would feel like it would be our fault about it. And so I go against anybody going down there, unless they knew what they were looking for and knew how it acted and everything. I'd say for them not to be fooling with it and wounding it in anyway to disturb it."

I asked both the neighbor and his wife, "You don't mind if we use this interview that I just made of you on television or anything?" I verified.

"No, I don't mind one bit at all about it," he said. "I saw the television show last night, and I know that those people down there believed it. They didn't, you know, make fun of anything. And it's like I told the TV man ... I said a lot of people don't believe it, that it is true, but you get it on the TV, maybe they'll believe it then. I'm glad he did, because maybe people will understand now and accept this warning for it."

"What do you want to do about this thing, now?" I asked.

"It has got me worried. I don't really know if it means to hurt us or not; but I believe it does by smacking at my boy. And the little boy that was smacked at, he had come running in the house several times before and told me that he has seen that thing."

"Really?" Here was yet another piece of valuable information they just happened to mention. The little boy was another eyewitness to more than one sighting! These humble people certainly didn't seem to have their stories rehearsed or have any idea how important some of this information was. They just wanted to warn others and be left alone by this creature.

The man admitted, "Well, you know, I didn't pay too much attention to it, but I don't believe the little kid was lying about it. I believe that thing was watching the little kid all the time. And I really believe that the thing is dangerous. It's like I said, I wanted to warn people around here because they have kids like everybody else."

Second Interview with the Sheriff

I turned back to the sheriff and asked, "Have any of your other neighbors seen this strange creature?"

"Well, I would say they have, yes," he answered.

Trying to coax him to tell me more, I asked: "Who are these people and what did they say they saw?"

The sheriff shifted from foot to foot and slowly began his story. "Mr. J. S. lives approximately a mile from this area. From the area we're standing, it would be due west, about a mile. About three years ago, they reported this same creature in their yard. I heard the gunshots. They fired at it with a shotgun and ran the thing off. They told me about it and asked me if I believed it."

"That was about the first time I ever told anybody about my experience with this thing," the sheriff admitted. "I thought I ought to tell them that they were right ... that I had already seen the thing. And that I was also scared to tell anyone about it, because I didn't want people to make fun of me. I feared they wouldn't believe me. So I told these people, after they described what it had looked like, that I had seen the same thing.

They reported that this thing was screaming—making an unusual noise in their back yard at night. They came out and fired on it, and the thing ran off into the woods."

"Wow, that is interesting!" I exclaimed. "Has your wife ever seen this creature?"

"Yes, sir."

"Then I would like to talk with her as well."

"Okay," he said, while he waved her over to where we were standing.

Interview with the Sheriff's Wife

This was a short, plump woman wearing tight pants and an overlarge T-shirt advertising a sporting goods store. She had been keeping in the background behind the others who gathered about me. She reluctantly came forward and agreed to tell me what her experience with this creature had been. Her voice was strong with a "no-nonsense" quality about it.

"Could you tell me what it was that you saw?" I asked.

"I don't know what it was," she said in a surprisingly strong voice. "I was standing up there on my porch; and that thing was standing down here at the corner of this house." She pointed to her neighbor's house directly in front of us.

"What time of the day or night was this?" I asked.

"It was about 9 o'clock at night," she answered.

"And, what did you see?"

"Oh, I don't know. I hadn't seen it before."

I persisted: "What did it look like?"

"It stood ... on two legs and had all shaggy-looking hair. It looked like an old mop!"

"How tall would you say it was?"

"Well, it was taller than you, sir."

"So in other words, it was well over six feet?" I clarified.

"Yeah," she confirmed.

"Could you tell me a little bit more about what you experienced that night?" I asked. "How did you feel about it? What did you do when you saw it?"

"I was only standing on the porch and looked at it," she said.

"Did you feel frightened?"

"Nah, it didn't bother me," she shrugged, looking into my eyes. She was apparently braver than most people were.

"Did this creature look back at you?" I asked.

"I didn't get to see his head. I didn't see that part," she explained. "Just from his neck down was all I seen."

"Was he hiding behind a tree or something?"

"Nah, he was standing near that corner of that house," she said, pointing to her neighbor's home again.

Considering how close the creature had been, I asked, "Have you ever found strange footprints around here?"

"Yes, sir," she said. "We found them in back of the house when there was a snowfall. And the bark had been peeled off the tree a bit round there from the bottom way up almost to the top of the tree."

Once again I had hit upon the right question. Now I tried to clarify: "In other words, you think that this thing might have eaten the bark, is that it?"

"Nah, I just don't know what ate it, but something did."

Well, at least she seemed honest! I turned my attention back to the sheriff with this new information.

Final Interview with the Sheriff

"Did you see these footprints, too?" I asked.

"Yes, sir ... yes, sir," he said. "My wife called me to the back door one morning after she had gone out in the yard. And she told me to come look at some footprints she had found. And I went out and looked at them.

"I have never seen any footprints that quite resemble these. I would describe them as being large; and if I had to so, I would say they looked something similar to a bullfrog's foot. I hope that don't sound too weird. It was just a real long, wide foot. I'd estimate the track to be, oh, eight to ten inches wide and almost twice as long."

"Where did these tracks go?" I asked.

"They were in this area," he answered.

"Where we are standing right now?"

"Yes, sir," he confirmed. "They lead to the pine grove at the back of the house."

"Did you follow them beyond that pine grove?"

"No, sir," he said. "At that time, I didn't really want to find out what it was. I wasn't really eager to find out what it was."

"Okay, very good. Right now, I'm a little bit concerned about my wife," I confessed. "Lorraine and Ralph went exploring that same pine grove ... I hope 'Bigfoot' hasn't got the two of them." I picked up the bullhorn Ralph left me and bellowed for Lorraine.

"I have my gun," the sheriff offered. "Now I always have my gun with me. I have had several people ask me why, and I never did really explain why, because I figure they wouldn't believe me. Since I saw this thing, I know it exists around here, and I am cautious of it. I feel that I should be armed," he explained. "I could have shot this thing several different times, but I didn't, because I didn't want to wound it. If I did, it might hurt some people around the area," he said matching his neighbor's concern.

"Sir?" the sheriff suddenly asked me. "Would it be all right to ask my neighbor something just to prove a point here more or less?"

"Sure," I said. Meanwhile, his neighbor looked just as puzzled as I was.

The sheriff turned to his neighbor and said, "Did I ever tell you anything about this creature that we're speaking of here before the incident you had with your son?"

"No, you had not," the neighbor admitted. "You did not say anything about it. I was the one to come up to your house and ask you if you had seen what happened. You said no. So I described it to you. You didn't say anything about it, 'til I went up there and spoke about it to you."

The sheriff turned back to me and said, "I just thought that was important. This is the real thing. I mean what I've told you. I've been expecting somebody to ask to check this ol' boy to see if his mind is all right! I would give anyone permission if they would like to check this thing out here for my own benefit," he said, pointing to his head.

I laughed and said to everyone around me, "I've interviewed thousands of people, and I can say this: you are all very sincere in what you are saying."

"Yes, sir. Yes, sir, we are." He nodded his head with a serious expression on his face that reminded me of the troubled countenance of Abe Lincoln—another humble but honest man.

Just as I was thinking this, I heard Lorraine's voice as she and Ralph came around the neighbor's house. She looked animated but none the worse for wear. "Why did you call me like that?" she demanded. "You scared him off!"

I had seldom seen Lorraine so upset. "Did you see him in person or in your mind?" I asked.

"In my mind, but physically he was nearby," she answered, calming down a bit. Disappointment and frustration still clouded her face.

Lorraine Warren's Impressions

I introduced the sheriff's wife and neighbors to Lorraine and Ralph, and tried to explain what she had been doing. Everyone stepped a little closer as I began to question Lorraine. "What did you pick up psychically through your extra senses?"

"Ed, I went where this grass is growing, I guess that was a cornfield. I'm not a farmer, so I'm not sure, but that grass is growing tall. To protect my skirt, I spread out my shawl before I sat down on the ground. I went into like another awareness while concentrating on the creature. I sat in different places and finally felt the animal very close to me.

"I told it psychically that it had nothing to fear from me, and that I wanted to know and understand it."

"Do you mean you were with the creature there in the woods?" I asked, pointing to the same pine grove where I was told strange footprints once led.

"Oh yeah, I was there and it was there. It had to come, you know," she said.

"Did you will it to come to you?" I asked, trying to explain how Lorraine's sixth sense worked to everyone present.

"Yes, and when I did, I felt it; and it did seem to feel us," she confirmed. "There are two of them—just two. There is one that is wandering, but there are two of them."

"So, in other words, there was only one in the area at this time?" I clarified.

"Yes," she said. "There is a mark on the lip of this ... I hesitate to call it an 'animal.' It is so humanized. He was tall with big thighs like a man who works out. He was covered with hair, but the hair on his arms was longer than any place else. He had a birthmark or old injury. His foot felt pain. I saw blood. When he stood up, I smelled a pungent odor. Then he moved from the grassy area to the woods where he lived. I saw a deep gully, and where the gully got narrow, I saw caves.

"His eyes were dark, intelligent, and trusting. This creature had the ability to communicate thoughts. Animals can only communicate emotions.

"His one foot had been badly bitten, and there had been fresh gunfire. People have fired at it. I could smell the gunpowder telepathically. I also saw a man chasing him into the woods with boards. This creature is staying its distance because it is afraid to trespass."

It sounded to me as if Lorraine might have been describing the shooting incident at the more distant neighbor's, when the creature was chased into the woods, as described earlier by the sheriff. Yet, Lorraine was nowhere near us when I was told these stories.

"Is it a dangerous creature?" I asked her.

"No, no way is it dangerous," she quickly answered. "It doesn't mean to harm anybody. It is more apt to seek compassion and acceptance than try to hurt or harm anyone. It finds it is easier to reach out to children. And it is not carnivorous. It prefers vegetation. That's why its droppings disintegrate and are hard to find. I also saw it walking in the woods where it beds down, and where it suns itself—where it stays during the day."

"Is it nocturnal?" I asked.

"Yes, it is a nocturnal type of animal," she answered. "It does a lot of its traveling at night."

"What is your psychic impression of this creature? Is it of this world?" I asked.

I think it is more physical than spiritual, however, I think it resides and periodically crosses over from a different physical plane. They are just as surprised by us as we are of them."

"Fascinating," I said, and meant it. This was considerably different from the paranormal phenomena we tend to explore. Multiple physical dimensions are a whole other area of study. I was just beginning to get comfortable with ghosts and goblins. I wasn't sure this old dog could learn many more new tricks.

Meanwhile, the morning light had given way to a blazing noon sun. I didn't see any window air conditioners hanging out of the front windows of these houses, and Ralph, the professor who introduced us to this case and these delightful people, was suddenly looking anxious to leave.

Interview with Ralph

"Could you tell us what your impressions were while you were with Lorraine?" I asked.

"I felt there is definitely something there," he answered. "Way down close to the water there, we could hear ...it was a shush (thump), shush (thump), like when a foot hits the earth. It sounded much different from a bird or any kind of animal. We heard some walking, and we thought we saw a glimpse of something; but we couldn't tell you what it was."

Ralph was describing—in his words—the same heavy footsteps that the neighbor's wife described in her words. "Do you believe this could be a relative or actually one of the 'Bigfoot' or 'Sasquatch' creatures we've heard about?" I asked.

"I believe it is," he said. "Now I really believe it is." He practically twitched and nervously played with his car keys. He obviously heard something that made him too uncomfortable to linger about discussing possibilities. He looked like a man who would prefer to discuss the case a few miles away with a stiff drink in front of him. It is one thing to speculate about the paranormal and another to face it up close and personal.

I wrapped up my taped interview with one more question: "I understand that you've lived in this area most of your life—in fact all of your life. Have you ever heard about similar sightings?"

"Oh, yes," he admitted. "I'd say there have been documented sightings reported over at least the last fifteen years."

His matter-of-fact tone, and that of the other people I interviewed, reminded me why science needed to look closer. In reality, local people are more apt to be familiar with their local creatures, no matter how bizarre and unusual they appear to the rest of the world. This was the case with the "discovery" of the giant panda and squid, as well as the gorilla and platypus. As strange and startling as the sightings were, the local folks here in Tennessee only brought it to the attention of the media when they thought it was a threat.

Nonetheless, this abnormal creature was not posing for photographs, our driver was looking like he was ready to bolt, and my stomach was beginning to make sounds as if it belonged to Bigfoot. We thanked everyone and bid our good-byes, while Ralph cranked up the air conditioning in the car. As soon a Lorraine and I jumped in the car, Ralph took off in a cloud of dust. I was eager to get back to civilization and lunch.

Historical Perspective

Just five miles from the Vermont border, the tiny town of Whitehall in New York State made the news with a similar sighting. Teenagers were the first to report a huge, hairy creature seen striding upright along the roadway. When the police came to investigate, they also saw the creature from a distance. There were at least nine eyewitness accounts—many of them "reluctant" law enforcement officials. According to the August 30 issue of the Glens Falls, New York *Post Star:*

> "Although descriptions vary somewhat, the creature has been widely described by both police officials and civilians as between seven and eight feet tall, very hairy, having pink or red eyes, being afraid of light, and as weighing between 300-400 pounds. It reportedly makes a sound that has been described as a loud pig squeal, or a woman's scream, or combination. The creature walks upright, rather than all fours,

which has resulted in the eyewitnesses ruling out the possibility of a bear."

In the same article cited above, Whitehall Police Sergeant Wilfred Gosselin said: "Footprints much wider and three times the length of a man's were found in the area. These footprints did not have claws."[27]

While Whitehall town was debating the legitimacy of the sighting, Clifford Sparks, owner of the Skene Valley Country Club in Whitehall, came forward to report that he had seen the creature the year before. According to him, at about 11:30 one night in May 1975, he was connecting water hoses on the golf course when a large silhouette caught his eye. He described it as a large, seven-foot giant moving with a "sloth-like" motion. In his words:

> "I'd say he was about seven foot, and he just had long ape-like arms. He was hairy, but I didn't notice any flowing hair like a human. The thing that got me the most was the red eyes and the flared nostrils like pig nostrils. You just didn't seem to really realize what was happening at the moment you saw him. You were shocked!"[28]

The Whitehall incident was not the first encounter on the East Coast. In October 18, 1879, the front page of the *New York Times* declared: "A Wild Man of the Mountains, Two Young Vermont Hunters Terribly Scared." It described an incident between the pair and a five-foot-tall, red-haired man-like creature. One of the hunters fired on the "wild-eyed" wild man, who began screaming. The men dropped their weapons and fled the area, fearing for their lives.

The late Dr. Warren L. Cook, former professor of history and anthropology at Castleton State College, Vermont, had researched the New York and Vermont "Bigfoot" encounters quite extensively. Dr. Cook felt it was likely that these creatures regularly migrated. He said: "It stands to reason that the creatures would tend to follow the same paths year after year. Those paths can be presumed to be thousands of years old."[29]

The book *Monsters of the Northwoods* written by Paul and Robert Bartholomew, William Brann, and Bruce Hallenbeck (North Country Books, Inc., Utica NY, 1992) documented 140 "Sasquatch" sightings in New York and Vermont alone. They trace reports back to the Algonquin Indians' "Windigo" and the Iroquois "Stone Giants."

Around the world, there seems to be a chain of sightings that trace back hundreds of years and continue to this day. Respectable and credible witnesses have observed these gentle beings on virtually every continent. Footprints and handprints have been documented and preserved in plaster. Hair samples have been collected from sites worldwide. Even audio recordings have been made of the shrieks these creatures make. Yet these samples have consistent characteristics that still defy classification.

Possible Conclusions

The folks in Tennessee that Lorraine and I met were not well-read, traveled, or educated. Yet, they described in their own words a creature that matched the physical, sound, footprint, and light sensitivity descriptions of the creature described by others on the East Coast, in California, and in many places around the world.

Lorraine's psychic impression, which has always proven reliable, is an interesting one. Rather than seeing a spirit of a creature that existed prior to man, she seemed to think the creature actually existed and crossed back and forth from another dimension. While science continues to explore multi-dimension and universe theories, the truth about "Bigfoot" remains an intriguing and recurring mystery.

Perhaps the Loch Ness Monster sightings have a similar explanation.

Case Study #9
Scottish Spirits

All the names in this true story have been changed to protect the privacy of the individuals involved. Ed Warren describes the case.

Background

Lorraine and I fell in love with Scotland the first time we saw it. It is the most undeveloped civilized country we know. It is like going back into time, without giving up the conveniences. Every spring we tried to take a group of investigators with us to experience the rugged beauty and tour the country's many haunted castles and sites.

In May, acres of brilliant yellow rape brighten up the horizon with broad bands of gold. Sheep and sweet white lambs—some with black faces and feet—dot the bright green fields. Large Highland cattle with long, brown hair lumber alongside our car on winding roads. It takes us hours to go short distances because of our constantly stopping to appreciate and photograph spectacular views. There are few road signs and no strip malls, shopping centers, or housing developments. Instead, our eyes and cameras capture craggy mountains with waterfalls ... breathtaking cliffs at the ocean's edge ... ageless, tiny towns ... castle ruins ... and farms with Shetland ponies—their manes and tails blowing in the relentless wind.

This particular year—2000—Lorraine and I were invited to investigate a hotel in the northern Scottish

Highlands by the River Spey. We learned later that the hotel began life as a nineteenth-century hunters' lodge and was converted into a hotel after World War I. An old ferry used to cross the river—the Boat of Garten near Inverness. A bridge replaced the ferry by 1899, and that bridge was replaced in 1974.

This year's group of researchers ranged from ages twenty to fifty-something and included students, scientists, and writers. We traveled together in two cars and agreed to meet photographers and reporters from an American magazine at the hotel at a prearranged date.

We added this detour to our scheduled trip in response to a faxed request we received from the hotel manager. The new owners were concerned that unexplained disturbances were causing both staff and guests to be uncomfortable. According to what they told us, pictures and furniture moved mysteriously ... there were strange reflected images ... and heavy fire doors had swung by themselves. One guestroom had so much strange activity that they reportedly were forced to remove the door and use the room only for storage.

It was a long drive from Edinburgh the day we arrived at the hotel. A bridge repair detour took us out of our way on roads that were already unfamiliar to us. By the time we reached our destination, I was famished and the rest of the group was calling me cranky.

It was dusk as we pulled up to this spooky, stone hotel. It seemed to dissolve into the gloomy gray light as if it was a ghost itself. Its many black windows looked like vacant eyes. Maybe once I had something to eat I might feel differently about it. I sent Lorraine inside to make sure they were still serving dinner while I supervised the unloading of the luggage.

Ghost Tracks

I found out later that Lorraine almost fell flat on her face when she entered the hotel's lobby. There was a step down she hadn't anticipated. Once at the front desk, she announced our arrival, inquired about dinner, and asked for the manager or hotel owner. That is when we learned that the owners were away on vacation and the manager was not working that night. In fact, the manager was not expected to be there at all during our stay. Despite the flurry of faxes and phone calls that brought us thousands of miles to be there that night, there was no one to greet us.

In all our years of investigating around the world, we have never had such a strange welcome. Fortunately, the literary editor and two photographers from the American magazine were there as planned. They greeted us enthusiastically and requested we join them at their table in the dining room. I didn't have to be asked twice, and raced to the table as fast as my stiff, aging knees would allow. Others in our group headed for the bar to investigate Scotland's most famous spirit—scotch whiskey.

While Lorraine and I ate, the magazine journalists interviewed us. As I finished dessert and reached over to steal some of Lorraine's, I wondered aloud whom I would be able to interview regarding these alleged hauntings. We called over the hotel's night manager and discovered that even the staff who had witnessed the events were not present. He agreed to call the off-duty bartender and cook who lived nearby and ask them to come to recount their experiences.

After dinner, we reconnected with our researchers, who fortunately had not drunk on empty stomachs. They accumulated and tested their equipment while we waited for the hotel employees who were going to tell us about the strange events. The magazine writer and photographers hovered nearby. There didn't seem to be any other guests in the eerie hotel.

Finally, the hotel night manager introduced us to two young men. Michael, the bartender, was of average height, had jet-black hair, and was thin and wiry. It looked like he hadn't shaved on his day off. Raymond, the assistant chef, was taller, blonde, and lanky. They seemed very comfortable with one another.

I called the investigation to order and announced the plan. "I'm going to interview these two young gentlemen, while Lorraine explores the rest of the hotel to see what she can perceive through her psychic senses. Some of you may stay with me and the rest can go with Lorraine."

Although the evening meal had restored my sweet personality and I hadn't eaten onions or garlic for dinner, I was left with only the two confused hotel employees and one researcher while everyone else clamored after Lorraine. I would actually get more attention if I were invisible, I thought to myself. Abandoned by the multitudes, my little group and I found and settled into a tiny lounge below the dining room. The researcher started the tape recorder, and I began my interview with the hotel bartender. A glance at my watch revealed that it was just past 9 p.m.—the start of the "psychic hours."

Interview with Michael the Bartender

Michael, looking uncomfortable in his own skin, sat on the coach in front of me. I began by asking how long he lived in the area.

"About fifteen years," he said in a pleasing Scottish brogue.

"How long have you worked here?" I asked.

"About a year ... just under a year, we'll take a week or two," he answered, relaxing a little.

"I understand you experienced some unusual things here at this hotel. Could you tell me about that, please?"

"There was just one night ... during the winter last year. At New Year's, there's a lot of people about. Otherwise, it's just myself and one of the chefs, Raymond," Michael said, nodding his head in his tall friend's direction. "We were here alone at nights a lot in the winter. It's my job to go around and lock up the hotel and check all the fire exits and close them.

"Well, this particular night, I went up to the first floor, was just starting to walk along the corridor, when I came to some swing-doors—the kind you push to go through. I was just about to press the doors to go through and looked through their glass windows when I saw the next set of doors begin to swing by themselves! You know they went back and forward—just flapping—as if somebody had run through them. But there was no one there.

"I just turned around and kind of ran back. I came back down to the bar. There was a couple of local guys still there. I just couldn't speak or anything. And they were like: 'What's wrong with you, what happened?'"

I bent towards Michael with increased interest and asked, "You were terrified?"

"Yeah," Mike admitted. "Everybody said I looked white and like I'd seen a ghost. I said, 'Something really strange just happened.' And they said, 'Well, what did you see?' I didn't actually see anything, you know, it was just the doors flapping by themselves.

Cheryl A. Wicks

"They were saying things like when I pushed the doors, I must have caused a draft for the other ones to flap. So we all went back up together. We tried every feasible way to get the doors to do the same thing; but we couldn't."

"Those doors are hard to open," I observed. I had to go through doors like them when I went to my room after dinner, so I knew.

"Yeah they are," Michael agreed. "You have to push them. It was literally like someone had pushed them and ran through, with the doors flapping after they had gone through."

Michael straightened up on the coach, leaned forward, and looked me in the eye. "You know, I have never believed in ghosts or ghouls, or whatever. I even brought my wife with me to back me up that I have never ever experienced or believed in anything like this before. This was the first time, and everyone in the bar said that I had been white."

Later I found out the magazine people had separately interviewed the assistant chef Raymond who helped Michael close the hotel that creepy night. Raymond said of Michael, "He was as white as a sheet and shaking. He doesn't go for all that spook sort of thing. So when he said what had happened, of course, I believed him."[30]

Mike continued his story. "With three or four people with me, I felt a little bit more at ease, and they all helped me lock up the hotel. They tried every conceivable way to convince me that it was a draft or the air or something, but we couldn't make the doors move at all by themselves."

"It wasn't the wind or some other draft that caused those doors to swing by themselves like that?" I pondered.

"No, all the doors and windows were already closed," he confirmed. "It was cold outside. Well, after that, I told my boss that I wasn't willing to walk around the hotel alone at night. I was only willing to lock up when people were around ... before it got dark or anything ... and only at this time of year when I know there are people in the guestrooms."

I probed further. "Have you ever felt a presence in the hotel ... that something is watching you?"

"The thing was, the hotel was being re-renovated at the time," Michael explained. "The walls were being knocked down and such like. And I don't know, but there was just ... there was an uneasy feeling. One of the local electricians working in the hotel at the time commented that he felt something was watching him as he was doing the electric work.

"There was an electrician working up there when he felt something. He'd be doing something and he'd turn around, thinking somebody was standing there watching him. Afterwards, he wouldn't come, because he said every time he was up here, there was somebody watching.

"After I told these few locals in the bar that night, everybody in the whole village sort of knew that I had this experience. There was a bit of 'mick-taking,' as it were. But when I mentioned it, this electrician said, 'Well, when I was working up there, I felt as if somebody was watching me.' Also, when I mentioned my experience to Raymond, he said he had a similar experience in the same place. You need to ask him. He just said to me that he had a similar experience of something strange."

"Did this coincidence scare you?" I asked.

"Yeah, well you know, we were obviously a bit freaked out about it. We were the only two here those nights ... and he actually stays at the hotel. So it was a wee bit concerning, if you know what I mean. Especially because it happened in exactly the same area."

"Exactly what area is this?" I asked.

"Raymond and I both had this experience on the second floor, in between the two sets of swinging doors where the spiral staircase comes up. Whereas the electrician had been working exactly on top of the same staircase on the third floor."

The investigator taping the interview pointed out that particular spot was directly en route to my room. I reminded the investigator that her and her husband's room was just upstairs and off the same corridor where the electrician felt watched.

"How old is this hotel?" I asked while contemplating alternative sleeping arrangements.

"I think it's probably near 150 years old," Mike estimated. "I think it was built for hunting, shooting, and fishing."

"Has anyone besides the electrician and the chef Raymond ever told you about any strange experiences here?" I asked.

"No."

"You mentioned renovations? Sometimes they can disturb otherwise dormant spirits. What changes were taking place?"

"They were knocking down walls. The renovations were actually in the second part of the hotel. I'll show you when we go up, 'cause it is clearer to say. This main area is the oldest part, and all the other bits have been added onto the hotel over the years. That's why I couldn't actually say how old the hotel is. It probably started as a small house ... or a very, very small hotel—nothing like the size it is now."

"In other words, the area where you, the chef, and the electrician felt something unnatural happened was the oldest part of the hotel?"

"Yes," he confirmed.

"This is all very interesting. You said your wife came with you tonight. May I talk with her?"

"Yeah, sure," he said. "I've got my little girl with me as well. If she can come through as well, it's not a problem. She's one and a half."

"Oh sure, of course," I said.

Interview with Bartender's Wife

While Michael scrambled out of the room to find his wife and daughter, the researcher and I changed the tape in the recorder and labeled the one we had removed. Raymond remained stiff and silent in a corner chair, waiting for his turn in front of the microphone. A minute or two later, Michael came back with a pretty, petite young woman with dark hair. Their daughter was a miniature of the mother. They both clung to the father.

I introduced myself, joked around with the little girl, and got everyone comfortable on the couch. After explaining what I was doing, I nodded to my assistant, who started the recorder.

"When your husband came home and told you what happened here at the hotel with the doors, what did you think?" I asked.

The woman's Scottish accent was even thicker than her husband's was. "At first I laughed, because I thought 'e don't believe in ghosts at t'all. In fact, 'e avoided the subject for years. But 'e came home so freaked out about it."

"Did you believe what he told you?"

"Yeah," she said, "'e was in such a state that ... yeah."

"What did he tell you he saw?" I asked, looking for consistency.

"Well, 'e just told me about d'e doors flapping ...and d'here was nobody d'here. 'E couldn't understand why d'e doors did d'hat. 'E said 'e just saw d'he doors flapping and ran."

The baby started to wail, so I released the family to the hall outside to wait for Lorraine. I asked Raymond to move to the couch so I could interview him regarding his strange encounter in the hotel. He nodded, unfolded his tall frame, and planted himself in the recently vacated couch. He wrapped his long arms around himself and rocked nervously. When I asked him his age, he admitted to be twenty years old.

Interview with Assistant Chef

"How long have you worked in the hotel?" I asked, trying to encourage him to relax.

"I'm from South Africa," he announced in an accent that sounded British. "I've been at the hotel here two years."

"I asked the other young man if he knew how old this hotel was. He wasn't quite sure. Do you know?"

"Uh, not off hand," Raymond stammered. "There's actually an old picture in the cocktail bar. I think it has a date—like eighteen-something. The hotel is quite old, I would say."

Ghost Tracks

Later, I had an opportunity to study the picture he referenced. The picture was larger than poster size and dated 1899. This is when the first bridge was installed to replace the ferry. Since the hotel building was in the picture, it was obviously built earlier in the 1800s.

Meanwhile, I continued with the interview. "What unnatural experience did you have at this hotel?" I asked the handsome young man in front of me.

He glanced down at his fidgeting hands and began: "Well, just that I'd finished my shift one night ... I had been downstairs in the laundry room next to the kitchen. As I was coming up the stairs ..."

He seemed to choke up. It was as if he was still frightened. "How long ago was that?" I asked, hoping to get him to relax a little.

He looked up and I saw his green eyes, as he said, "This was quite awhile ago ... about a year. It would have been when the hotel was being renovated."

"And what time was it when you had this experience?" I coaxed.

"I think it would have been around Christmastime," Raymond answered.

"No, I mean the time of day or night?" I clarified.

"Oh," he said, finally smiling a little. "The time of day ... it was the evening ... about ten or eleven, I'd say."

The psychic hours—when more paranormal activity is apt to occur—are considered to be between 9 p.m. and 6 a.m. It seems to be easier for spirits to manifest themselves in the dark and for us to notice them. Demonic entities are also apt to avoid God's light.

"So what were you doing at the time? Where were you going, and what were you about to do?" I asked.

"Well, I was just going upstairs, from the first floor, past the second floor, up to the third floor where the staff's rooms are. I was going to my room. I was in Room 3 during the renovations," he explained. He sat up taller, leaned forward, and began to speak faster.

"I was going to the double doors. There are two sets of these doors. One set is at the top of the flight of stairs leading up from kitchen. The other set of doors is farther on down the corridor on the same floor.

"From the direction I was coming, you have to pull the doors. I got to the top of the first flight of stairs, and I went to pull open the doors. What scared me was the fact I had just seen a reflection in the door's window glass. What got to me was there was light on the other side of the door, and it was dark where I was. I wouldn't have thought I could have seen a reflection."

I agreed and encouraged him to describe what he saw.

"It just seemed like a gray shadow. I didn't really want to investigate, to say the least. I just didn't like it. It was quite disturbing," he admitted.

"Could you make out any features in this image?" I asked.

"It seemed ... seemed to be like a face, but I don't want to say, 'cause I'm not too sure what it was, you know. It seemed like a long drawn face, you know. Like it was a gray ... a grayish image ... and it was like really drawn out."

"But was it a human face or ... something you couldn't quite make out?" I pressed.

Raymond offered: "It could have been human. I honestly ... no, I'm not sure."

"Okay. So, after you saw this thing, what did you do then?"

"What did I ...? I just ... I went straight to my room. Yeah, I didn't stay there in the hall or anything," stammered Raymond.

After you went to your room, did you think that you had seen something unnatural?"

"Yeah. Yeah, definitely!"

"It seems to me that what you saw really scared you. Is that correct?" I asked.

"I've had a fairly religious upbringing," Raymond volunteered. "I've seen and heard of a lot of things, you know. But this was unique due to the fact that you wouldn't expect a reflection to suddenly appear where there isn't anybody. And it looked human like! It just gave me a shock, basically."

"I can understand that," I said, trying to comfort him as if he was my own son. "What you could have seen is what we call 'crystallomancy.' A spirit can reflect its image onto a shiny surface or a mirror, a glass. You see this reflected image rather than the spirit itself. The fact that you were in the dark and the corridor was lit from the other side, tells me that you weren't looking at your own reflection. What you were seeing was probably unnatural. In other words, what you saw really happened, even if it is not what is considered normal."

I don't know if this made him feel better or worse. Before we could discuss it further, excited voices were heard out in the hall. My wife and her entourage of researchers, reporters, and photographers had gathered with the bartender and his family. I cracked open the door and they all burst into the room, babbling at once. I called the chaos to order and asked Lorraine what happened.

Cheryl A. Wicks

Lorraine's Initial Psychic Impressions

The excitement seemed to be centered around the unused guestroom on the second floor. This is the same room where the door had been removed because no one was able to stay in the room. It had been used only for storage for over a year.

"Okay, Ed, what I felt was, a man was killed upstairs in that room. There was a great deal of animosity between these men before that night," blurted Lorraine.

"How long ago would you say this happened?" I asked.

"There are two different periods of time that something goes on here. There is something in the 1920s and then there is something again more current. I believe that the haunting that occurs as a result of someone being killed was in the twenties."

Lorraine explained that she felt the "other" haunting was the result of an accidental death that happened more recently than the 1920s. Since that haunting seemed less active and frightening, she concentrated on the phenomenon surrounding the earlier event and apparent murder.

"Do you want me to communicate with this spirit? I won't do it without you." Lorraine said. She felt vulnerable while she was in a light trance and always wanted to make sure I was there to protect her as best I could. We both knew that things could turn bad if one was not alert and careful ... not to mention experienced.

I looked around me at all the eager faces and knew if I said "No, let's go to bed" that I was apt to be the next ghost haunting this place. Instead I said: "Yeah, of course."

"But I want to ask ..." Lorraine said, stopping everyone in their tracks from stampeding the door. "What did you find out from the interviews?"

I summarized what the bartender and chef claimed they had witnessed and where it happened. My researcher reminded me of the electrician's apparent experience in the same general area.

Lorraine interjected: "I didn't know any of this until just now, but when you told me about the reflection, I thought: Oh my God, that's where it happened to me!"

She went on to explain that while she was coming up the back staircase from the kitchen on the ground floor and approached the top of the stairs, a researcher opened the double doors for her; and she saw a dark shadow on the next set of doors. The magazine reporters and investigators were right behind her at the time. But by the time they rushed to the same spot, the image was gone.

She also had a psychic impression of a man running through the doors and going downstairs via a route that was no longer in existence in the hotel. This was the entity she wanted to try to reach.

Between the two sets of swinging doors in this haunted corridor is a spiral staircase that leads up to the third floor. It is at the top of these stairs where the electrician was working when he reportedly felt watched. The bartender was approaching the area from the front of the hotel when he saw the doors that the chef and Lorraine approached from the back of the hotel swing wildly by themselves. The chef had seen a gray image on the same doors that swung mysteriously. Lorraine saw a black shadow on the doors the bartender had been looking through.

Only a few feet away, between these two sets of fire doors, was the guestroom that could not be used. That is where we decided to try to communicate with our mischievous spirit.

Haunted Guest Room

We all gathered in this small room that was just big enough for a double bed and a couple of dressers. Stacked mattresses and mirrors leaned against the outside wall along with nicked and scratched wooden headboards. Extra lamps with cords wrapped around their bases rested on top of discarded dressers pushed into corners. A coffee table and eclectic assortment of chairs were scattered about the room. There were two tall windows—one opening to the back and one opening to the side of the hotel. Although these windows were cracked to let in the cool evening air, the room's atmosphere smelled stale and felt stuffy and heavy. Outside the windows, the night was so pitch black it was as if nothing existed beyond the warped glass panes.

Just after dinner, two of our researches had videotaped the halls, common rooms, and this particular room before they followed Lorraine around the hotel. It was in this room that their digital camera picked up white flashes of light moving like caffeinated fireflies flitting from one corner of the room to the other. We could see this on their camera's review screen.

Lorraine and I have seen these energy "globules" in all sizes and shapes in haunted graveyards, houses, and buildings all over the world. They usually are an indication that psychic energy is present. Sometimes they are visible to the naked eye, but often they only appear on pictures taken by still and video cameras. Our researchers had been in the room by themselves without any flash equipment when they scanned the room. Based on what their digital video camera was telling us, there were more than dust bunnies in this room with us.

Lorraine stood in the center of the room and recounted for me: "Earlier, I felt that two men had a violent confrontation in this area. Right here is where somebody was murdered," Lorraine said, pointing to where a bed might have been, in front of the side window.

At that point, the magazine photographer standing in the doorway spoke up. "Lorraine, I didn't tell you—but I just told Ed ... When I came up here and was looking for pictures to take, I walked all over this floor, wandered into here, set up my camera, and took my first picture of that exact spot. I felt some energy right by that window. That's where my picture was."

"You did?!" Lorraine responded. "Well, that is definitely the area where it took place ... definitely the area," she confirmed. She went on to explain, "There had been a great deal of animosity between the men. After the murder, the murderer ran to the stairs. I went that way, but I couldn't find the stairs he used." She led us out of the room to the corridor between the two sets of swinging doors, and continued. "This is just an extension of the hallway."

"This is the new section of the hotel here," the bartender Michael pointed out. "This is where the renovation was. This used to be the outside wall of the old hotel," he explained, indicating where additional guestrooms now existed. "If you can imagine, it was just like a small block."

"Then, that's why I was confused about the stairwells, Ed. What I was seeing clairvoyantly through the eyes of the murderer was different than what exists today," Lorraine eagerly explained.

That could also explain why there have been so many disturbances since the hotel renovation. We have found that renovations where a tragic event once occurred can often trigger paranormal phenomena. Sometimes the entity seems disturbed or confused by the changes.

All of a sudden, Michael stopped, stiffened, and turned pale. "Like I don't believe ... well I try not to believe in this, but up here and down the landing I can feel something, you know."

Moving again back towards the storage bedroom, Michael relaxed and continued his hotel tour. "The existing main building was probably only about four or five rooms. It started off as a lodge."

"Ah!" Lorraine said. "There's where I think the source of this haunting started. That's why I think I had this idea that these men knew each other ... that they had seen each other here many times ... that this was a men's club or a lodge. That was the impression I had. These two men weren't strangers to each other. And the bad feelings between them were something they had carried for a period of time," she explained.

Michael pointed to the nearby fire doors and said, "When I saw something, it was like ... as if somebody had just ... it was like somebody must have just ran through the doors."

"That's exactly what he did. He ran through the doors," Lorraine confirmed. She based this on the psychic impression she had before hearing the bartender's story. "When I was downstairs, somebody opened those doors, and as I looked up the stairway, I saw something dark right by these other doors," she said, indicating the next set of swinging doors down the hall. "So, something was right there just moments ago! The stairway was confusing to me. I saw telepathically from the angle he ran, and the walls were changed and different then."

Michael repeated for Lorraine's benefit, "My wife can tell you I never believed in any of this sort of thing before. When I went home and told her, she believed me, because she knows I wouldn't just come out with something like that."

"Right, because you weren't open to it or prone to it. That makes sense. It happened spontaneously. Let's go back to that room and try to communicate with whoever, or whatever, it is," Lorraine suggested.

As Michael started towards the room, he said, "It was like a flashing impression. To me it was not friendly."

"No, it is not," Lorraine confirmed. "It is anything but friendly ... anything but. Whatever his intention is, it is very negative ... it seems very evil."

It was getting past my bedtime. Digesting the large, late dinner I had was taking all my energy. I waved everyone inside the open guestroom and pleaded, "Let's settle down and try to communicate in here. Get ready to douse the lights."

Our researchers gathered around with their video equipment, cameras, and recorders. I sat Lorraine down in the most comfortable chair I could find, by a discarded coffee table, and made sure the tape recorders were as close to her as possible. I then situated myself by the door, not too far from Lorraine.

One magazine photographer stayed in the room; the other stayed just outside the doorway with the reporter. We coaxed the bartender Michael to come into the room with us, but his family and Ronald the chef insisted on staying outside. Raymond actually began to tremble at the idea of going into the room.

Cheryl A. Wicks

A Psychic Experience

"Michael is going to sit with me, Ed," Lorraine announced.

"Yeah, that's good," I agreed. Often, if a paranormal phenomenon has made itself known to someone, that someone may be the catalyst to attract it back.

As we were setting up another chair next to the coffee table, Lorraine said, "I just sensed something very, very negative just now. Ed, there are numerous experiences here."

Michael paled and said, "I felt it, too. It felt like a tingling."

"Yes, and it's like a pressure—a heavy pressure. It doesn't want us to be here," Lorraine added.

Michael reluctantly sat down beside Lorraine while everyone else found and settled into a spot around the room. The magazine cameraman asked if his video camera light would be too bright.

"Yeah, honey, we can't have light, dear," Lorraine explained. "I'm sorry. I wish I could, but I can't."

We weren't trying to create a spooky atmosphere or cover up any magical sleight of hand. The dark keeps us from being distracted and makes it easier for spirits to manifest and communicate clearly. We even convinced our more timid members of the group staying out in the hall to turn off the lights.

Lorraine began by reassuring the off-duty hotel bartender, who was now sitting next to her and looking uncomfortable. "All right, Michael, I'm not going to let anything happen to you, honey. Believe me, I won't let anything happen to you. Do you believe in God?"

"I used to go to church when I was young, but ..."

"Did you go to the Church of Scotland?" Lorraine asked.

"...and the Roman Catholic Church," Michael answered.

"Have you been baptized?" asked Lorraine.

"No. I was never christened," Michael responded.

Lorraine was trying to determine if he had a belief system or other protection against possible evil entities. We never really knew who or what would come when invited. This is why we always strongly advise against inexperienced people doing this on their own or by playing with Ouija boards and the like.

Lorraine questioned Michael further. "After the experience you had at this hotel, can you believe in the possibility of a spiritual world?"

"There has to be hard evidence for me. I need somebody to say there's proof. Everyone has a belief in something; but when people say, 'Do you believe in God?' ... I don't believe in Jesus and the Bible and all that, is what I'm saying ..." Michael explained.

"Okay, but you believe that there is a Supreme Being?" Lorraine asked.

"Yeah. In a way, yeah. But, I never had a reason to believe in God, really," Michael admitted. "My wife is a strong believer in God and I got married in a church. And I'll do anything for my wife, but she is probably against my being here just now because she knows what my belief is ... deep down, if you know what I mean. So she doesn't really want me to be here. So, I'm saying to you ... as long as you give me your word..."

"I'll protect you. Nothing is going to happen to you, dear," Lorraine reassured him. Then she turned to me and repeated what she just learned to make sure I knew he might need some extra protection. "Ed, Michael doesn't believe in God. He finds it difficult and he is worried and very nervous. So he wants me to take care of him. When I pray and I ask for protection, I'll ask for it for him, honey."

She was asking me to do the same. Also, as the demonologist of the group, I was there as the "policeman" watching for demonic intruders. It helped to know who was apt to be most vulnerable. While my primary concern was always Lorraine, we both knew those who lack faith were more apt to be targeted. Yet, he wasn't in any real danger as long as we knew this.

We quieted the murmurs outside in the hall and Lorraine started the session by crossing herself and reciting the Catholic St. Michael prayer ...

> "In the name of the Father, the Son and Holy Ghost, amen. St. Michael the Archangel defend us in battle. Be our protection against the wickedness and snares of the devil. May God rebuke him, we humbly pray. And you, oh Prince of the heavenly host, through the power of Christ, cast into hell Satan and all evil spirits who wander the world seeking the ruin of souls. Amen."

She added, "Watch us all—particularly Michael, because he finds it hard to believe and he's very, very fearful. Make sure he is protected—and his wife and child are protected—when we try to help the spirit that is here. We want to understand why it is here and what we can do to help it to accept its death and move on."

After asking for protection and clarifying our motive, Lorraine began to call the troubled spirit to her.

"Whoever you are and whatever your intent ... so negative, so evil that you just continued to pursue it until you found that man. You ran through these halls. You opened doors. You just went absolutely wild to find that man that you hated so badly. And when you finally found him, you killed him so violently, and like a coward you ran and left here. But everybody knew who you were.

"Why do you remain? Why do you continue to remain here? Are you finding it difficult to accept your death because of what you did? The spirit of the man you killed is no longer here. He has found his peace through his faith. And I hope and pray that I can help you, too, so you no longer bother the people who live here and work here.

"I know the staff people who work here say you still, in a way, try to bother them. And it seems mostly men that you go after. I don't know what your problem is ... besides from being a very violent, evil person. But I hope and pray to God that you don't have the mark of the demonic or demon in you in carrying out your deeds."

It suddenly occurred to me that given his past experience, Michael might be more successful in inviting the spirit to us. I interrupted and said, "Michael, tell the spirit that we want it to come back now ... so that we can communicate with it. It came to you once and frightened you. Now we want it to come back so we can try to understand why it did that." A mere thought along these lines would do.

Suddenly Lorraine said, "Look at his eyes ... look at him!"

Michael mumbled, "I'm getting this feeling ...."

"What are you getting?" Lorraine asked.

"I don't know. I ... I got a couple of glimpses of things. I don't know. Can you see things in your mind?" Michael asked, surprised.

"Yes, that's why we're here," Lorraine said in a comforting voice.

"Do you see a chef?" Michael asked in a voice completely void of his Scottish accent.

"A chef ... you mean the man that's wearing clothes like the kitchen help?" Lorraine countered. It seemed they were both seeing the same thing telepathically.

"Kitchen whites," Michael confirmed.

"Yes ..." Lorraine said dreamily. "That's the connection. He's coming through you," she observed.

Michael continued in his newfound voice. "I see a chef and a ... there's like ... and is it like a young housemaid or is it like a daughter ... of somebody who owns the hotel or something? I don't know. I just got the picture. I don't know. It is just like a shape of a young girl ... a schoolgirl."

"Yes, a school-age girl," Lorraine agreed.

"I don't ... Something just flashed in my eyes."

Someone who should have known better had just taken a flash picture. "No flashes, please," I growled. Once a clairvoyant trance is broken, it may be hard to restore.

"I don't like that it's speaking through me, Lorraine. I don't know. Can I have a whiskey before I go on?" Michael said, breaking out of his trance. His soft Scottish brogue had returned.

"Do you see him, Lorraine?" I asked trying to keep things on track.

Even Lorraine was losing focus. "As I sat on the stairway earlier, I could see kitchen help, Ed. That is what I could see. I wondered then if it didn't have to do with the something tragic that happened."

"It looked like a chef or a cook or something like that," Michael clarified. "I imagined it was a chef here in the hotel."

Lorraine added, "I wonder if ... maybe it was a tool from the kitchen that the person used. He may have used something from the kitchen, Ed, to kill that man. And the young girl ... I don't think the young girl was witness to it, but I think one man knew that the other man had done something to that child."

"Can you see the man, Lorraine?" I asked in another attempt to get both her and Michael back to the telepathic pictures inside their minds.

"The man appears to be dark-haired," Lorraine answered, looking inward again.

"Yeah," Michael said softly, dropping his accent again.

"You see that, too?" she asked.

"Yeah ..." Michael said, drifting away.

"And it's not ..." Lorraine started.

Michael finished. "It's not long hair, it's just shoulder length." The bartender seemed to be reading Lorraine's mind as well as sharing the same telepathic view.

"That's right," Lorraine confirmed. "He looks well-groomed enough, as far as that part of it goes. I'd say, he's medium height, and the clothes that he's wearing are white. But he is, has ..."

"Stubble," Michael finished for her.

"Yeah, he's not clean-shaven, but what do you call it, honey, he has a very evil intent on his face. His face don't ... his face looks crazed, honey," Lorraine said, speaking to Michael.

"How old is he?" I asked them both.

"Thirty," Michael answered.

"I'd say he's about thirty," Lorraine said at the same time. "Oh see, that was in unison! So, we are both looking at the same person, Ed," Lorraine added almost with glee.

"Lorraine, how is he dressed?" I asked, trying to get her focused again.

"He's dressed all in white. And the shoes he's got on are kind of messy looking. They are very messy. I don't know, he stepped in dirt, I don't know. And he's got on ..."

"Some dark clothes underneath," Michael offered.

"No, I don't see that; but I see one of those big long aprons that goes over his head and has a bib to it. He has on that big long apron ... and he has the weapon in his hand," Lorraine added.

"What is the weapon?" I asked.

"It's ..." Lorraine began.

"... A knife," said Michael, "and it goes along like that and has pointy tips on it." He drew an outline with his hand and arm in the air, and then dropped them back to his side.

"Yeah, it is like that, Ed, yes." Lorraine said this without glancing at Michael.

"Is that what he killed that man with?" I asked.

"Yes, right there," Lorraine said twisting her body in the chair and pointing in front of the dark window that faced the side street. "Right over here."

"Can you call this man to you?" I asked Lorraine.

"I believe ... I believe his name is Gus, Ed," Lorraine offered. She then began to try to communicate with this individual. "Gus, if we could, we only want to help you to leave this place. You are frightening a lot of people. You are choosing certain people that either resemble or are otherwise familiar to you. Are you trying to reach out, or are you trying to replay that night? Are you going in this room and doing the things you're doing in the hall because you're looking for him? He's no longer here."

Michael interjected, "He doesn't want to speak to you. He doesn't speak to women."

"He doesn't," she admitted. "Then speak to him," she said to Michael. And to the wayward spirit she said, "Then you speak to him, Gus."

"He doesn't want to speak," Michael said.

"Yes, he has to speak, otherwise he is gonna stay here," Lorraine explained. "Why doesn't he like to speak to women?"

"He was concerned about the daughter of the owner of the hotel," Michael offered.

"Yes, all right, what about this daughter?" Lorraine asked.

"This other man hurt the daughter," Michael explained.

"That's what I felt he was so angry about," Lorraine confirmed.

"And now he's moving away," Michael told us.

"Tell Gus, Michael, that we want to help him ... that everything ... that a lot of time has passed," Lorraine pressed.

"He's okay ... he's moving on ... he's all right," Michael reassured her.

Lorraine persisted. "He has to leave here. He has to go to the light ... he has to go towards some loved ones that he knew during life, who have gone on. He has to go with them in spirit and leave here. Time has gone on. Everything he feels ..."

Michael explained, "He's feeling pressured by everybody here, though."

"By all these people?" Lorraine questioned.

"Just the clicking noise, he doesn't feel relaxed," Michael clarified.

"All right, don't shoot pictures. Don't make clicking sounds," Lorraine admonished everyone in the room.

"It's not people, it's just any kind of sound that is unusual ..." Michael repeated.

"It makes him jumpy," she stated calmly. "Because he still feels people are after him."

"The hotel owner is after him ... it was the hotel owner's daughter," Michael clarified.

"Yes, all right," Lorraine agreed.

"He's going away," Michael said.

"He's leaving us now?" Lorraine asked.

"I believe so. Yeah. He's drifting away," Michael confirmed.

The spirit was not just leaving Michael and Lorraine, he was leaving this world. I have sat through enough of these sessions to recognize the difference.

"You can feel it," Lorraine murmured, relaxing in her chair.

"Yeah, he's gone," Michael said.

"I can feel the energy lifting, too. Anybody else feel it? It's gone, honey," Lorraine said, opening her eyes wide.

"Is it gone for good or just gone?" I asked to confirm my own impressions.

"I hope it's gone for good, but I don't know," Lorraine admitted.

"It's just like he was going more into the distance," Michael explained.

"Yeah, and all that tight feeling in my throat and all has left. I had my arm next to Michael's arm, and I no longer feel tension from him either," Lorraine added.

"Maybe you helped him to pass over then," I suggested, referring to Gus.

"Could be," Michael said. And this was from a guy who just moments ago claimed he didn't believe in another side.

Michael suddenly commented in his original Scottish brogue, "That was the strangest thing ... strange pictures in my head, there."

"That is what it is like to see psychically," Lorraine explained.

"It was like a cartoon thing," he revealed.

"It is like a cartoon thing, that's right," Lorraine agreed.

"But unlike a cartoon, it was like it was right there," Michael clarified.

"Like they are right there," Lorraine confirmed. "Yes, they are right there."

"But it was coming out of my head," Michael said, shaking his head. "When I first came in here, I didn't get a picture of him. All I got was a picture of the young lassie. But she wasn't like in a housemaid's outfit or anything. She was the daughter of the owner of the hotel or something; because everybody ... like everybody had to respect her. I don't know. I just had a feeling that it was the hotel owner's daughter.

"Maybe you should try to speak to Raymond and have him try to do this as well," Michael suggested. "I'm saying that he's more of a religious guy. Maybe that will help. It's like I say, I never had to believe in anything, but there's something very weird going on here."

"Oh yeah, that's an understatement," Lorraine laughed. More quietly, she said, "Raymond is afraid." She then leaned over in her chair and called out into the hall, "Raymond, it's all over with, hon. We're finished."

The lights came on, and I thanked Michael for his cooperation. The magazine photographers wanted to take pictures of Lorraine and me in the room. After getting his picture taken, Michael rejoined his family and his friend Raymond in the corridor.

The hotel didn't strike me as the kind of joint where I'd find a chocolate mint on my pillow, but I was eager to get back to my room and bed. However, as we tried to leave the disheveled guestroom and satisfied photographer behind, Michael accosted us in the hall.

Reluctant Psychic

"I'd like to know really ... I'd like to know what you did to me there," he said confronting us and looking agitated.

"Oh, I didn't do anything to you, honey," Lorraine reassured him.

"But Raymond and his girlfriend Dee were watching from the doorway and said that I looked strange ... that I was not my normal self. That's why Raymond was afraid to come in and be with me."

"Ed, you've got to explain to him that I didn't do anything to Michael," Lorraine pleaded.

"You just envisioned a Christ light," I soothed them both, putting an arm around Lorraine.

"Yeah, that's all I did," Lorraine said, looking over at Michael. "I prayed for you. I just envisioned you in a Christ light. I prayed for you and gave protection to your family. But I didn't do anything else to you."

"As long as my wife and daughter are okay and not touched by this in any way," Michael said calming down.

"No, no they won't be touched by this in any way," Lorraine confirmed.

Trying to lighten the mood, I offered, "Personally, I like to envision myself in a room full of jelly donuts."

Both Lorraine and Michael laughed. Then changing the subject and referencing the ghost, Gus, Michael said, "Well, he definitely didn't want to speak to women. Sorry."

"You didn't offend me!" Lorraine quickly corrected.

I added in the way of explanation, "This Gus guy was apparently afraid of women, and doesn't know how to communicate with them. That's why he was coming through you, Michael."

Lorraine offered, "He was intimidated by them, maybe."

"He didn't say ... he didn't say anything," Michael recounted.

"You were given impressions instead of words," I surmised.

Mike repeated, "Yeah, it was ... it was like a cartoon or something.

"That's what we call 'clair-vision,'" I offered. "'Clair-audio' is when you hear things telepathically. People can even smell or feel things. You were seeing them in what is known as your mind's eye."

"He's never experienced anything like that," Lorraine observed. After all these decades, she was probably remembering how strange and frightening it was when she first discovered her clairvoyant abilities.

While we were having this conversation, the magazine people were taking notes and hanging about like bats in the gloomy corners of the carpeted corridor. One photographer asked Michael, "Did the flash bother you in there?"

"No, it was the noise ... actually," Michael clarified. "Click ... and he was running off into the hills. That's what it felt like ... that he was going down a valley; and he just moved farther into the distance. There is nothing here now. There's nothing here."

"No, I don't feel anything. I don't feel it anymore, either," Lorraine confirmed.

"But I felt it downstairs in the kitchen when I was coming up," Michael recounted.

"Well, I did, too," concurred Lorraine. "But you realize that that's where Gus ran after he murdered."

Michael's face brightened. "That's right, that's the way he would have been running when I saw the doors flap that night."

"Yes, he was reliving that moment, probably the most terrible moment in his life," Lorraine explained. "Do you know how long ago the renovation took place?"

"All I know is that this hotel changed hands eight months ago, roughly August of last year. Since then, they have been renovating the hotel," Michael answered.

"And that's what triggered these paranormal events," explained Lorraine.

"It is true ... in those spots, you can feel something, but in the new section, you don't ... there's nothing. You don't feel any queasiness or butterflies or anything like that. But when you stand up at that top floor ... and you stand here, and you stand in that kitchen area ..." Michael said, shaking his head in amazement.

Lorraine agreed. "All those places are all right in line. They are all in the old part of the building where the tragedy happened ... and you are able to tell that!"

"It was the strangest thing," Michael reminisced. "I would close the pub down, which would be eleven o'clock at night. I would give everybody their last drink, pull the shutters down, say, 'Right, I'll be back in five minutes,' and just go up and lock up the hotel.

"So I'd go up to check the fire exits and everything. And I walked up this one night, and I came right back down. I never said anything to anybody in the bar. And they were like, 'What happened? What's gone on? Was there a fight, has somebody been stabbed or whatever? What's happened?'

"I said: 'I just had a really weird experience. Will you all come up the stairs?' Three or four guys did. I can give you their names. If I had been here earlier on, you could have spoken to them. I could have got hold of them for you, as well. They all came up, but they never felt anything.

"I think if there is more than one person, there never seems to be that experience, if you know what I mean. I've taken my wife and everyone up. I thought: Let's take the dog up, 'cause if you take the dog up, dogs can sense these things. And dogs are able to tell."

"That's right, they can," Lorraine agreed.

"But we never actually ever did that 'cause, you know, the dog's kind of like a lapdog, if you know what I mean. But when Raymond heard, he came to me and he said: 'Oh no, Michael, I saw something in the door window in the same spot.' He was kind of upset."

We all nodded while Lorraine and I tried to make our way through the same doors to our room. But Michael still had something to say.

"I promise you this ... I am not lying."

"We believe you," Lorraine said. Actually, she believed her own extrasensory perception and her impressions did not conflict with Michael's.

"Well, most people aren't so sure, you know," Mike reflected, looking tired. "You know what I'm saying ... I'm not just winding these stories up, or anything like that. You know that. Honest to God, I wouldn't do that."

"Yes, and thank you for coming back to the hotel to meet with us on your night off," Lorraine said.

"It's okay. When the hotel manager called my wife and said you people were in the hotel and wanted to speak to me, I came straight over; but I feel ... although I've had a couple of drinks ... I don't want you to get me wrong. I'm not drunk, or anything like that. It's the first day of my holidays today. I'm on a week's holiday."

"That's all right. It wasn't a problem," I reassured him while continuing to push Lorraine towards our room.

"You know, when I was in that room with you," he said, "I was looking out into the hall, most of the time. I preferred to look where I can get away ... where I could escape."

"Michael," I laughed, "you're never going to make it as one of our investigators."

He laughed, too, and admitted, "I'll tell you one thing, I drink a lot more now since I started working here!" Then he added: "My parents left it up to me to decide whether I believed in ... God and everything. They didn't christen me or anything. They said it was up to me to do it. My wife is strongly ... not strongly; but she believes. And she believes what I say. I didn't want you to think I'm some idiot, if you know what I mean."

"We believe you, dear," Lorraine reassured him, looking over her shoulder.

Ghost Tracks

We said our good nights to everyone and finally made our way to our room and bed. However, all of our researchers planned to stay up to photograph, video- and audiotape the hotel throughout the "psychic hours." We agreed to convene in the lobby sometime before noon the next day to review any experiences or discoveries.

Later that Evening and the Next Morning

A couple of researchers took a tape recorder down to the lobby, the kitchen, the back stairs, the corridor between the two sets of swinging doors, and the guestroom—now a storage room—where Lorraine had sat with Michael. They kept asking questions ... allowing time for a possible answer they couldn't hear with their ears. In some cases when the tape is replayed, a voice can be heard answering the questions. However, this did not happen in this investigation.

Another pair of researchers videotaped the hotel hoping to capture more "ghost globules." Aside from what they had filmed earlier in the abandoned guestroom, nothing was observed. Still other researchers used light meters and galvanometers—registering unexplained energy flow—to monitor any anomalies. Nothing unusual appeared.

When Michael, Raymond and his girlfriend, and one or two other locals learned that our group was in Scotland to investigate multiple haunted sites, they took some of our other researchers on a wild ghost hunt. First, they explored a graveyard where witchcraft had reportedly been practiced. Then they were taken to a secluded site that seemed to have been a former slaughterhouse. Both places made our researchers uncomfortable, and they insisted on coming back to the hotel.

Once back to the deathlike silence of the now dark and gloomy hotel, they bid their new friends good-bye and went to bed. Because nothing seemed to be happening at the hotel, the other researchers also retired after the long, exhausting day of traveling. By 4 a.m., the only creatures stirring outside our rooms were shifting shadows. Or so we thought.

The next day was bright and sunny and full of disturbing surprises. A tire on our van had been slashed. When the bar was unlocked for cleaning, all the pictures had been rearranged. Tables and chairs from the dining room as well as mattresses from some unoccupied guestrooms were stacked on top of one another in the center of the room. There were also scattered piles of dirt as if poured through a funnel.

When the head housekeeper unlocked her utility room, she found a dusting of powdered soap covering everything evenly like some bizarre snowfall. Curse words were written in the powder covering a small table in the room. No one but the housekeeper had a key to the utility room, and there was no evidence of lock tampering.

The staff was visibly upset. Many were angry. Some blamed Michael and Raymond. Others didn't know what to think. Lorraine and I were not too sure ourselves.

The stacked furniture and funneled dirt were all too familiar to us. Also, it is hard to believe that no one would have heard someone move that much furniture around from one floor to the other. Most of our researchers didn't retire to their rooms until the wee hours, but still stayed

Ghost Tracks

up to write notes, check what they captured with their equipment, and discuss the case. Meanwhile, Lorraine and I are early risers ... as is the morning hotel staff. Also, if this was staged, how would these people know how to do it and what to do?

Lorraine and I, as well as other credible people around the world, have witnessed the silent, swift movement of furniture. The explanation we offer is teleportation. The poltergeists associated with this phenomenon aren't labeled "mischievous ghosts" for nothing. On some of our most horrific cases, Lorraine and I have seen large objects dematerialize and materialize elsewhere before our eyes ... furniture move, dance, and fly by itself. All of this is done silently. One minute it is there, the next minute you are tripping over it somewhere else. Unfortunately, such activity usually occurs where there is an evil infestation.

Before we could tell one late-rising investigator what had happened, she reported that her favorite pen went missing from her room the morning after she used it to make notes at night. She commanded that it be returned in the name of Jesus Christ, and found it outside her guestroom door. It was lying on the floor in the very spot where the electrician had said he felt watched.

Lorraine and I felt we would need to spend much more time to determine if this phenomenon was ghostly, demonic, or simply the work of a roguish, undersupervised staff. It could also be a little of everything. After all, bad behavior attracts bad spirits, and bad spirits inspire bad behavior. It is also common for the demonic to isolate victims and make them appear to be guilty or crazy. Yet, we have also uncovered frauds, whereby someone desperate for attention or greedy for the money they think it will attract is eager to try to fool or frighten people.

However, without the on-site support of the hotel owners or senior managers, Lorraine and I decided not to pursue the matter further at that time. We already had a full schedule planned for our limited time in Scotland. Before we made changes in our itinerary, we felt those who asked for our help should at least have the courtesy to meet with us.

Epilogue

By the time we had returned to the States, the owners and manager had returned to the hotel. When we followed up, they claimed that all disturbances had stopped. We may never know if they stopped as a result of disciplining employees, our success in coaxing a wayward spirit home, or because we ourselves were not there to trigger a psychic response.

Evil is intelligent and can communicate from continent to continent. Rather than lay dormant, as it tends to do when approached by doubtful investigators and clergy, it has been known to challenge us, being familiar with our work.

Evil is also attracted to tormented souls. By releasing this spirit, we may have disturbed something. Also, Michael had been vulnerable, but we protected him. This could have been another cause for ruffled raven feathers. The damage we found the morning after could have been triggered by our intervention in both cases. If so, however, it is not surprising that such phenomena would resume dormancy, without further encouragement or invitation.

There is also the possibility that the new hotel owners wanted to attract attention and business to their hotel.

Inviting the magazine crew and us to their establishment might have satisfied this need.

These ambiguities are what make this research so difficult. We are dealing with the psychology of the victims as well as paranormal entities. And they are all intertwined. Selfish or destructive motives attract and feed negative energy. Negative energy feeds selfish and destructive motives and actions.

Yet, both Raymond and Michael seemed genuinely frightened by their experiences. Lorraine also saw telepathically the same things Michael described that strange evening. In addition, the young men and Lorraine felt and saw similar things in the same section of the hotel. And the ghost globules captured on video, taped by independent investigators confirmed the presence of spiritual energy.

We were never able to uncover any reports of a murder in the hotel, but local historic records were sketchy in this remote village. Lorraine also points out that an unreported or unpunished crime could itself be a reason for a haunting ... the renovation, the trigger.

This case also illustrates how paranormal energies and entities seem to always be around us, everywhere. Our behavior, attitude, motive, and beliefs—and those of the people around us—play a big part in what we attract and what we might unintentionally release.

SECTION V

Paranormal Research: Snake Oil or Science?

*"There are two ways to be fooled.
One is to believe what isn't true,
the other is to refuse to believe what is true."*
Soren Kierkegaard

Ed and Lorraine Warren welcomed the eclectic group of psychic research students. They had learned about ghosts, evil infestation and possession, and how the Warrens went about investigating reports of paranormal events at the request of clients around the world. Yet, all this information barely scratched the surface of everything the Warrens had experienced and learned over fifty-some years doing this work.

Now it was time to encourage the students to do their own research in the library as well as the field. The best way they found to do this is to pique their interest in what science has found and is finding with the help of modern technology.

Lorraine opened the evening's lecture. "Through my clairvoyant skills and decades of field research, Ed and I have found very little discrepancy, if any, with what we find in the Bible or what many religions teach us. Historically, science has always had a love/hate relationship with the mysterious and any discoveries that challenge a preconceived understanding. Science has often been at odds with the world's religions. Religion has often been at odds with science. Yet, both hold truths and can learn from one another."

Historic Summary

Lorraine settled on her tall stool and began, "In 1848, the Fox sisters of Hydesville, New York claimed they were communicating with the dead through a series of rappings. Soon mediums and mystics proliferated and séances became the rage in both Europe and America. These so-called spirit communications ran from rappings and ghostly mutterings to the more entertaining movement of objects or materialization of apparitions. Private client lists and public audiences expanded in response. By 1855, spiritualism claimed two million followers in the U.S. and Europe.[31]

"Spiritualism has always played a significant part of humankind's history. It is about man's relationship and interaction with a non-physical world—the bizarre, frightening, and miraculous. Throughout the ages, religion offered its interpretation, and everyone from psychics to witch doctors has offered theirs.

"Organized psychic research began in the late 1800s in an effort to prove or disprove paranormal activity associated with spiritualism. In 1882, the Society of Psychical Research in London was founded ... followed by the American Society for Psychical Research in 1885 and the French Institute Metapsychique International in 1919.[32] The Committee for the Scientific Investigation of Claims of the Paranormal (CSICOP) was founded as recently as 1976."[33]

Ed added, "Science first approached paranormal claims assuming they were delusional. Parapsychology began as an obscure subdivision of psychology. Those who first pursued this field of study were often considered in need of therapy themselves. Despite the field's shaky reputation, Sigmund Freud at age 65 wrote American researcher Herewood Carrington: "If I had to start my life over again, I would rather be a parapsychologist than a psychoanalyst." Later, to his biographer E. Jones, Freud declared he wouldn't hesitate to bring about the hostility of the professional world to pursue this "unpopular point of view." Freud's curiosity and interest in this field reportedly came from his encounters with psychic phenomena and ESP, including a very convincing case of telepathy."[34]

Lorraine continued, "Parapsychology is now a respected member of the American Association for the Advancement of Science with its thousands of respected and notable scientists. As of 1969, American science has been dealing seriously with the subject of haunted houses, clairvoyance, telepathy, and telekinesis. Today, more and more universities and colleges are devoting departments and special projects to the field. It is also a field beginning to attract the attention of brilliant minds from physics and engineering.

"From the earliest days of psychical research, most of the manifestations studied were found to be clever magic tricks. Raps, table tilting, object moving, materializations, ghostly music, spirit lights, and strange scents would conveniently occur in environments controlled by the medium during séances or fortune telling sessions. Those who claimed to materialize spirits were caught impersonating the spirits themselves. Most psychic readers seem to be more adept at reading people than cards or communicating with the dead. Yet, there are problems with these studies, and there have been exceptions.

"I and other credible clairvoyants will tell you that ghosts do not perform on demand. Arthur Ford, a medium who *never* was proved to be a hoax, explained that no medium could perform 100% of the time. He felt that rather than admit an off day, most mediums would cheat. An eminent British physicist and chemist, Sir William Crookes, found that some mediums would resort to tricks if given the chance or pressured. However, they could produce apparently genuine phenomena if well controlled. He felt that although fraud was rampant, it could not account for all the activity."[35]

Ed began to stroll around the room as he offered, "What makes psychic research a frustrating conundrum for skeptics and believers alike is that it is not easily controlled. Paranormal entities seem to react to certain situations and people that are not easily duplicated. Sensitives—clairvoyants and children—who are more apt to experience the preternatural are also less likely to be believed. The phenomenon is not likely to perform on demand. In fact, when it does, it is very probable that all or most of it is staged.

"Yet it has also been demonstrated that with experience and training, psychics can better access and understand the metaphysical information that seems to be present or deliberately communicated. One of the most celebrated mental mediums was Leonora Evelina Simonds Piper. Mrs. Piper was the subject of study of psychic researchers on both sides of the Atlantic. She is credited with providing some of the first good evidence of survival after death."

Ghost Tracks

Lorraine explained, "Mrs. Piper was born in 1859 in Nashua, New Hampshire. When she was eight years old, she felt a sudden sharp blow to her right ear, accompanied by a hissing sound. This was followed by the words, 'Aunt Sara, not dead, but with you still.' Her mother made a note of the day and the time this occurred. Later they learned that Aunt Sara had in fact died at that moment.[36]

"Mrs. Piper's mediumship began in earnest in 1884 after Leonora's father-in-law brought her to a blind clairvoyant famous for his psychic diagnoses and cures. She lost consciousness and seemed to fall into a trance herself. Shortly thereafter, she became comfortable with her own abilities and began to give private sittings in her home.[37]

"William James, involved in the establishment of the American Society of Psychical Research (ASPR), went to Mrs. Piper in 1885, looking to prove fraud. The detailed knowledge she revealed stumped him. After two years of studies and controlled sittings, Mr. James was unable to find fraud.[38]

"When Richard Hodgson arrived from Europe to take charge of ASPR, he also took over the investigation into Mrs. Piper. In Europe, he had become the scourge of English physical mediums and had learned a great deal about conjuring. He, too, approached the case assuming her to be a fraud. He kept detailed records of all Mrs. Piper's sittings, hired private detectives to follow her, and screened her mail. She never behaved suspiciously, but continued to make remarkably accurate statements about people she never met or heard about.[39]

"Mrs. Piper's talent was considered so extraordinary that between 1889 and 1890 she was sent to England for sittings under close supervision of English psychical researchers. In England, as in the States, anonymous sitters went to her, or proxy sitters would attend in place of the person for whom the séance was intended. There was also a series of "linkage experiments," whereby a series of persons were interposed between the interested party and the sitter. None of the intervening people or sitters even knew the name of the subject individual.[40]

"Yet, Mrs. Piper continued to perform with astonishing success. Hodgson published a cautious report on his work with Mrs. Piper in 1892. By 1898, however, he admitted his conversion to the "survival hypothesis" as a result of his study of this medium. After giving much of her life in the service of science, Mrs. Piper died at the age of 91 in 1950. Thanks to her and Hodgson's work, many researchers who had previously doubted the possibility of survival after death became convinced of its actuality."[41]

Ed spoke up. "Clairvoyants like Lorraine can see what others often cannot see with clarity. After describing what she sees to a sketch artist, pictures have been matched to a long-deceased person who was completely unknown to Lorraine. During one psychic investigation, Lorraine described kneeling nuns in pews and a standing monk turning the pages of a large book in a haunted monastery. Although nothing was visible, researchers took pictures where Lorraine indicated the activity was. When the pictures were developed, there were ethereal images of the monk and the nuns just as she described, just where she said they were.

"Thousands of people have taken pictures with ghostly orbs and wisps where there was no flash, smoke, or particles in the air. In one series of photographs in the Warrens' archives, the orb elongates, forms a human shape, and then develops the clear features of an eighteenth century woman. Black shadows moving independently have been captured on film and video. Infrared photos pick up glowing eyes and silhouettes where nothing appeared to the physical eye. Digital cameras pick up streaks of light and orbs at the same time researchers are looking at the same sight and seeing nothing with their eyes. Mysterious images of people who were not physically present appear in routine home photographs or on reflected surfaces."

Lorraine added, "While modern technology has improved our ability to gather proof, it has also made it easier to enhance or doctor images. Yet, a huge archive of untouched pictures remains unexplained. Skeptics believe these images may actually be created by the mind. In other words, if you think it enough, something may actually appear on film ... or objects may move. There is also some evidence to support that mental or emotional disorders—temporary or otherwise—can lead to paranormal manifestations."

"However," Ed commented, "psychiatrists and psychologists who study mediums agree that there is a clear difference between mediumship and schizophrenia. Schizophrenics have no control over their mysterious voices, visions, and personalities. These manifestations occur spontaneously, often without warning, and are hard to stop. Victims become disoriented by their experience and cannot function normally. Mediums, however, can control their psychic gift, can use it productively, and can carry on normal lives.[42]

"The same distinctions have been made between trance mediumship and multiple personality cases. The latter have little control over when they will switch from one personality to another. Mediums, however, go into a trance at will. Moreover, multiple personality disorders are typically based on a traumatic childhood while mediumship often develops in adulthood."[43]

Lorraine stood up and stretched her legs before continuing. "The workings of the mind are mysterious enough without adding the supernatural. This is why science is more comfortable with controlled exploration. Professor Joseph B. Rhine of Duke University was one of the first to start measuring what he labeled the 'psi' factor in man. About the same time psychiatrist Dr. George Sjolund established special labs to test this extrasensory perception (ESP) in Baltimore, Maryland. In 1970, Dr. Sjolund concluded: "All the evidence does indicate that ESP exists."[44]

"The book *Psychic Discoveries behind the Iron Curtain* written by Sheila Oastrander and Lynn Schroeder was reviewed by Dr. Thelma S. Moss, assistant professor of medical psychology at the UCLA School of Medicine. She commented, '...in 1970, Soviet materialistic science has pulled off a coup in the field of occult phenomena equal to that of Sputnik rising into space in 1957.'[45]

"After reviewing the same book for the *Los Angeles Times,* writer Nat Freedland observed, 'Scientists in Eastern Europe have been succeeding with astonishingly far-reaching parapsychology experiments for years. Instead of piddling around endlessly with decks of cards and dice like Dr. J.B. Rhine of Duke University, Soviet scientists put one telepathically talented experimenter in Moscow and another in Siberia twelve hundred miles away.'"[46]

Ed added, "Not to be outdone by the Russians, the Americans have since done more than 'piddle around' with lab cards. The *Los Angeles Times* reported on February 11, 1971 that *Apollo 14* astronaut Edgar D. Mitchell took aboard ESP cards. As an experiment, he successfully sent mental messages from space to engineer Olaf Olsen in Chicago. This proved beyond any doubt that telepathy works even from the outer reaches of space.[47] The study initially was made to explore the possibility of emergency communication, but the potential benefits are more far-reaching.

"The Remote Viewing Institute, headed by retired army Major Ed Dames, focuses on the development of extrasensory skills for intelligence gathering. With little more than a person's name, trained gifted people are able to accurately describe the individual's surroundings. They have been successful in locating kidnap victims this way. The utilization of remote viewers by the military are also highlighted in Dr. Russell Targ's book *Future War*. Although it is not apt to be part of this country's State of the Union Address anytime soon, ESP does seem to be an important part of our military research."

Lorraine resumed, "Nonetheless, the metaphysical and paranormal remains a largely unexplored frontier. The potential benefits to national security, law enforcement, mental and physical health, and even business are enormous. Not so long ago, clairvoyance was diagnosed as witchcraft or mental illness. Now it is being validated and enhanced in labs.

"Today, doctors and medical schools acknowledge the healing benefit of prayer, laughter, and positive attitudes. In every single drug trial, placebos always work for a certain percentage of people. Perhaps there is more than just 'mind over matter' at work here.

"*Nation's Business* carried an article as far back as 1971 entitled, 'Dollars May Flow from the Sixth Sense. Is there a Link between Business Success and Extrasensory Perception?' It concluded that '...the evidence we have obtained indicates that such research will be well worthwhile.' John Mihalasky, associate professor of management engineering at the Newark College of Engineering, found a correlation between superior management ability and ESP. Mihalasky maintained that most sound corporate decisions were not made based on logic but on intuitive skills."[48]

Ed addressed the group. "Someday, metaphysical evidence and testimony from validated clairvoyants may be just as reliable and credible as fingerprints and DNA. Law enforcers worldwide have reluctantly called on—or had thrust on them—the help of psychics in solving crimes or locating missing people. Dr. Maximilian Langsner solved difficult cases by staring at the suspect for thirty to sixty minutes. After doing so, the doctor was able to direct authorities to evidence that led to convictions.[49]

"Dr. Langsner was born in Vienna, studied under Freud, and traveled to India to research the 'inexplicable intuitive control of the mind.' He earned a doctorate in philosophy in India in 1926. He claimed he could read brainwaves. Modern science can also see 'alpha state' brainwaves, but has yet been unable to 'read' them beyond graphs and images."

Lorraine settled back on her tall stool and said, "Understanding the paranormal also would bring peace of mind to many. The idea that 'life' or consciousness in some form continues is comforting and reassuring to those who fear their own deaths or grieve for the loss of loved ones. We also may be less likely to kill others, or anguish over short-term frustrations and disappointments and impose our ways and judgments on others if we understood that there truly are infinite ways to be ... and an eternity of opportunity. Many religions already present this concept in one form or another.

"As far back as 1957, in an article entitled, 'A Crisis in Science,' *Life* magazine prophesied: 'The only "reality" is that which occupies space and has a mass—is irrelevant to an age that has proved that matter is interchangeable with energy. Set free of materialism, metaphysics could well become man's chief preoccupation of the next century and may even yield a worldwide consensus on the nature of life in the universe.'"[50]

Ed added, "Modern scientists acknowledge that there are many more than three dimensions. Einstein held that energy never disappears, only transforms. In 2001, nuclear physicists revealed the discovery of particles smaller than the proton and electron found in all atoms that continuously change between energy and matter. Could this be proof of our spiritual essence?"

Lorraine continued, "Gerald L. Schroeder, who earned his Ph.D. from the Massachusetts Institute of Technology, has written three books linking scientific discoveries to religious beliefs. His work has been reported in *Time, Newsweek, Scientific American*, and leading newspapers around the world. In his book, *The Hidden Face of God*, published in 2001, Dr. Schroeder points out that there is much more non-matter in our physical world than matter. In other words, there is more metaphysical than physical. He also suggests that rather than our minds being the creator of psychic phenomena, they are instead the antennae to the metaphysical reality that connects us all.

"Earlier, Albert Einstein wrote, 'A human being is part of the whole, called by us the *universe* —a part limited in time and space. He experiences himself, his thoughts and feelings, as something separated from the rest—a kind of optical delusion of his consciousness.'[51] (Regardless of how our ability to communicate and perceive things without physical substance or means is quickly moving from improbable to possible.)"

Psychic Research Observations

Ed handed Lorraine a tall glass of water and took over the speaking. "The keys to unlocking mystical mysteries are not apt to be labs and technical equipment, but the old standby for detectives and scientists alike—observation and interpretation. While study is ongoing and subject to individual interpretation, Lorraine and I and most field researchers of the paranormal agree on a number of consistencies and patterns. The first of these is…

"<u>Psychic Impressions</u> – Hans Holzer, Ph.D., professor of parapsychology at the New York Institute of Technology and author of several books, feels most ghostly sightings (85-90%) are only the replaying of a past emotional event. The Warrens concur that the most frequently reported 'phenomenon' is of a repeated image and sequence of events where a tragedy or suffering has occurred. Battlefields, hospitals, or sites where a murder or fatal accident has happened often reveal the same image to different people. Also, wherever there was repeated effort in life, there could be a psychic impression left after death. For example, there may be a recurring image of a man hanging up his hat as he comes home from work, or a woman in her garden. Sometimes these recurring events could be smells or sounds … children running up and down stairs, cigar or perfume odors.

"A theory is that such psychic phenomena are like a photograph that takes a picture with a flash of energy or makes an etching with repeated events. They require certain conditions for development; but when the right conditions exist, many different people report seeing and experiencing the same event at different times. There is nothing physically dangerous about a psychic impression.

"Next is... <u>Earthbound Spirits.</u> Many researchers clarify that a 'ghost' is an image of someone unknown while an 'apparition' is of someone you do know. Such images are only likely to be seen by 'sensitives' (clairvoyants, mediums, children, and animals) and people with whom the ghost feels an affinity. For example, the current property owner or visitor might look like the ghost's beloved son, daughter, or lover, or be mistaken as a former enemy. In other cases, they may share the same line of work, hobby, or circumstance.

"Most times, ghosts reveal themselves through disturbances, which are themselves a clue to who they are and why they are there. Renovations can disturb ghosts into activity. Genuine clairvoyants and mediums can describe and communicate with such entities to help identify them and encourage them to move on for the mutual benefit of all concerned. While earthbound spirits can move pictures, lamps, and play with electronics, they are not physically dangerous. Observers of this phenomenon might be startled or disturbed, but seldom terrified. Many co-exist with their ghosts."

Lorraine interrupted, "The primary reason some spirits remain 'earthbound' is because they have not accepted their death, probably because it came unexpectedly or because of a mental handicap they had in life. Some spirits remain to try to resolve unfinished business. While they might seek closure, the Warrens and other serious researchers are not aware of a ghost actually seeking revenge or justice. Instead, a ghost is apt to be suffering from their own sense of guilt or need to comfort others, including the one who wronged them. Other ghosts may stubbornly refuse to leave their house, place of business, or where they died. The emotional reasons people get stuck in life seem to apply to death as well. Earthbound spirits, however, seem to be less mobile in death than they were in life, and don't follow people from place to place."

Ed resumed. "<u>Transition and Crisis Spirits</u>—These apparitions are the second most commonly reported example of a ghostly sighting. They usually are images of someone you know. Sightings are reported of beloved pets as well as people.

"The most common is an image, voice, scent, or other manifestation of someone you know that has died a distance away from you. If they appear as visual images, they are apt to look as they did when they died. This is upsetting if their death was due to a violent accident or murder or the casualty of war. This is how many 'ghosts' earn a reputation for being frightening.

"A 'transition spirit' is apt to appear within forty-eight hours after the individual's death, could appear to more than one person at the same time and place, and is seldom seen again in that format. It is believed that these spirits are in the process of crossing over to the other side. They want to notify someone of their passing and to reassure that life continues. Observers of this phenomenon often feel a sense of peace despite the unhappy events that led to the sighting.

"'Crisis spirits' are those that appear to someone who is in an emotional or physical crisis. For example, the deceased husband who appears to encourage his wife driving in a dangerous snowstorm. Sometimes an image or other clues of a departed loved one may appear in happy moments or when family members are gathered. Still other visitations are reported when someone is severely sad or depressed. While those who experience this phenomenon may be startled initially, they also report feeling comforted and reassured."

Lorraine explained, "In both cases, dreams are a common vehicle for 'communication.' The entity has moved on, or is in the process of doing so. They are free to come back as needed or desired, anytime and anyplace; yet usually only one appearance is made. Often that is enough to enable both sides to 'let go.'"

Ed continued, "<u>Angels</u>—These entities have never been human, but serve as God's messengers according to most Christian doctrines. Other religions have identified similar entities. These spirits have physically materialized in crisis situations only to mysteriously disappear. Time and time again, such appearances are reported in hospitals, accident sites, and by hospice workers, and in all cultures and countries. One feels protected, relief, or peace when confronted with such an experience.

"Next we have the <u>Poltergeist</u>—This is German for mischievous or noisy ghost. The implication is that it is an earthbound or visiting spirit creating a disturbance. Property renovations have been known to trigger this type of phenomenon. Personality traits seem to stay with earthbound ghosts who might have been controlling, stubborn, bitter, or resentful while living. Others try to be helpful or playful and appear noisy or mischievous in the process.

"The formerly human spirits that come back from the other side have more power to move things and manifest things out of thin air. These entities can also follow someone. Earthbound ghosts—those spirits who have not crossed over—have weaker supernatural powers and are linked to a physical spot.

"The physical movement of household or office items and furniture with no apparent means of propulsion has been documented on film. Such activity has also been linked to the unconscious psychic abilities of emotionally disturbed adolescents. In some cases, therapy and maturity may resolve the problem. Otherwise, a legitimate clairvoyant experienced with psychic research could identify the spirit, determine what it is doing and why, and communicate with it so that peace is restored.

"Poltergeist activity can be frightening and dangerous. Physical blows, flying objects, or even slashes could hurt someone. Depending on the progression and level of violence, researchers like the Warrens fear the possible involvement of evil.

"And finally we have, Evil Entities—Satan, devils, demons, and all manner of inherently bad beings have been identified by virtually every religion practiced by mankind. Yet, evil spirits are also most apt to be either sensationalized or denied. The Warrens—as well as many others—observed distinct steps and manifestations that at first may appear to be benign paranormal activity, but can develop into something much worse and dangerous."

Lorraine reiterated, "Evil must be invited into one's life. This can happen directly through witchcraft and devil worship, or inadvertently through Ouija boards, tarot cards, inexperienced or ill-informed psychics, or destructive behavior including drugs, alcohol, violence, or association with evil worshipers. Evil entities were never human, and have inhuman powers. By nature, they are liars and manipulators. They will pretend to be something they are not to encourage people to either accept or welcome further involvement."

Ed resumed, "Once this happens, physical manifestations are apt to occur. These events are frightening and oppressive. They cause family members to turn against one another. Constant disturbances, voices, nightmares, and noise wear people down physically and emotionally. Once that happens, possession can occur. Unfortunately, possession may lead to the death of the individual and possibly others.

"Evil entities have the power to move large objects and transport large items—even people—from one place to another. They also can follow victims from one place to another or lay dormant indefinitely in an infested home or other inanimate object, waiting for someone vulnerable.

"Evil is also clever enough to play possum in the right circumstances. Yet, it is vulnerable to religious intervention and is forced to reveal itself and be cast out (exorcised) by the right hands. While many reported cases are in fact delusional or fraudulent, there are some that defy any other explanation to date."

Overall Summary

Once again, Lorraine stood up. "America is probably the most scientifically advanced nation in the world and has one of the best-educated populations. Yet, a May

Cheryl A. Wicks

2001 Gallup Poll of Americans eighteen or older revealed that over 56% believed in, or would consider, ghosts, haunted houses, evil possession, and communication with the dead. The percentage increased twelve percent since the same poll was taken in 1990. Based on the 2000 U.S. census, 56% represents over 117 million people ... an estimated 52 million with at least some college education. The cover story in the July 2001 issue of *Fortune* magazine read, 'Surprising Quest for Spiritual Renewal in the American Workplace.' This feature story and the poll both took place before September 11, 2001—before America's newfound vulnerability could be credited for a revival in spiritualism."

Ed commented, "Skeptics tell us we are only seeking refuge and guidance from a spiritual world, because our modern world seems impersonal and hostile. We also are still frustrated by the limitations of medicine, science, and technology.

"Perhaps our biggest fear of ghosts is that they don't exist. What could be more frightening than the idea that our lives and those we love are as temporary and expendable as tissue? If our existence continues in different forms, it is easier to believe our life has a purpose beyond meeting and exceeding physical needs. A growing body of evidence indicates this idea might be more than wishful thinking or religious doctrine."

Lorraine offered, "Ed—a recognized demonologist, and I—a validated clairvoyant, have been investigating and observing the preternatural for over fifty years. Mankind has been observing it since the dawn of human thought. Can thousands of years of human observation of paranormal phenomena be completely misguided?"

Ed answered, "Many credible skeptics say 'Yes.' However, in the past, many credible skeptics also insisted the world was flat, the sun revolved around the earth, and the platypus was a hoax. Prior to the nineteenth century, ESP was considered religious heresy. Early in the nineteenth century, meteorites were considered figments of our imagination. And long before Sir Isaac Newton discovered it, gravity existed and was observed.

"The skeptics have fears as well. Not so long ago, they feared the abyss beyond the flat edges of the world. They feared the earth not being the center of the universe. Persistent research led to discovery that changed our perspective of the world and its universe and our place in it. Today, many still fear the abyss of death. Research might eventually prove that instead of a sharp edge and end to life, it continues. This would change our perspective of life and our place in it.

"Science still doesn't know all the secrets of our universe, our physical world on earth, or even about our own bodies. Nor do Lorraine and I and other psychic researchers presume to know everything about the netherworld. They only offer theories based on their observations and the observations of others."

Lorraine points out, "Psychical research organizations have uncovered many frauds, but they also uncovered mysteries like Leonora Piper who left dedicated and persistent skeptics on two continents accepting the 'survival hypothesis'—existence after death. Meanwhile, work continues to this day on the serious study of ESP and all of its manifestations and potential applications.

"The late heart specialist and Nobel Laureate Dr. Alexis Carrel commented about psychic phenomena: 'The work of a scientist is to observe facts. What I have observed are facts troublesome to science, but they are facts.'[52] Another scientist, Dr. Gardner, observed: 'If there was one-tenth of the evidence in any other field of science that there is in parapsychology, it would be accepted beyond question.'[53]

"Joe Nickell, an acclaimed debunker and respected investigator for the Committee for the Scientific Investigation of Claims of the Paranormal admits, 'What we need is a kinder, gentler skepticism.' He clarifies, 'I'm not saying there's a fifty-fifty chance that there is a ghost in that haunted house. I think the chances are closer to 99.9 percent that there isn't. But let's go look. We might learn something interesting as hell.'[54]

"Ed and I thank you for taking a look. We hope you learned something interesting and that all your paranormal encounters are pleasant."

"The most beautiful thing we can experience is the mysterious. It is the source of all true art and all science. He to whom this emotion is a strange, who can no longer pause to wonder and stand rapt in awe, is as good as dead: his eyes are closed."
Albert Einstein

THE END

GLOSSARY

The words and definitions are only as they relate to the subject matter of this book

666 – alleged sign/number of the devil ... and insult to the Trinity

Angel – a never-human entity that can assume spiritual or human form

Apparition – spirit or ghost of someone recognized

Attraction – that which invites a haunting or evil into one's life

Brown scapular – two pieces of cloth joined by strings, worn on the chest and back under clothes, originally worn as part of a monk's habit. The wearer is "granted the peace of a happy death."

Clairvoyant – ability to see, hear, smell, or feel things not of the physical world

Crisis apparition – a ghost of someone known that appears to comfort or guide at a time of crisis. (Could also appear in times of celebration.)

Cryptozoology – science of hidden animals; investigates reports of unusual creatures

Crystallomancy – the reflection of a ghost or spirit in a shiny surface

Deep trance medium – clairvoyant that allows non-physical entities to speak through him or her

Demon – fallen angel that seeks destruction of God's creations, the ruin of souls, and control of free will

Demonologist – someone who studies evil and evil practices for its prevention and relief

Devil – lesser demons, fallen angels that seek destruction of God's creations, the ruin of souls, and control of free will

Divine – never-human entities that can assume spiritual or human form

Exorcism – religious rite to caste out evil

Ghost – non-physical representation

Ghost globules – orbs of energy frequently captured on film, but usually invisible to the human eye

Infestation – Evil residing in material objects or places

Intercession – a group confrontation encouraging someone to face a problem like addiction

Kirlian – a Russian-designed camera that can photograph auras of all living things

Levitation – suspension in air by no visible or physical means

Light trance medium – clairvoyant who can see and speak to and hear non-physical entities

Medium – someone who bridges the physical and non-physical worlds

Oppression – evil suppression of human free will and desire

Padre Pio – a pious, Italian Catholic priest, renowned healer, and exorcist, who died in 1968 and was beatified by the Church May 2, 1999

Parapsychology – the study of the paranormal

Placation – a group confrontation to stop someone from being angry

Poltergeist – a mischievous or noisy ghost (or something more demonic)

Possession – Evil residing within someone

Psychic – clairvoyant with the inappropriate but frequent connotation of fortune teller

Psychic impression – a recurring ghostly image of a person and event

Psychic paralysis – evil-induced deep sleep, immobility, or incapacity to speak

Psychosis – a serious personality disorder where contact with reality is impaired

Psychotherapy – treatment of a mental disorder through professional counseling

Religious demonologist – someone who has chosen the religious life and studies evil and its practices for its prevention and relief

Spirit – soul or ghostly image, but term used by many psychic researchers to differentiate between earthbound "ghosts" and crossed-over "spirits" that visit

Teleportation – the dematerialization and materialization of animate and inanimate material, moving it from one place to another

Transition apparition – a ghost of someone known that appears shortly after death

Endnotes

[1] Gerald L. Schroeder, *Hidden Face of God*, (New York: The Free Press, 2001), 184.

[2] Charles Dickens, *A Christmas Carol*, (Great Britain: The John C. Winston Company, 1938), 24.

[3] Sightings of the "White Lady" in Monroe, CT have been reported and documented for decades. Psychic photographs and a video of this mysterious specter are part of the Warrens' archives. The event with the fire truck happened in November 1992. The Warrens captured an interview with the truck drivers on video.

[4] Gerald L. Schroeder, *Hidden Face of God*, (New York: The Free Press, 2001), 294.

[5] Ibid.

[6] Ibid.

[7] Ibid.

[8] Rosemary Ellen Guiley, *The Encyclopedia of Ghosts and Spirits*, 2nd ed. (New York: Checkmark Books, Inc., 2000), 150.

[9] Ibid.

[10] Gerald L. Schroeder, *Hidden Face of God*, (New York: The Free Press, 2001), 153.

[11] Raymond Buckland, *The Witch Book*, (Canton, Visible Ink Press, 2002), 416.

[12] These papers resulted in a book, *Demon Possession*, John Warwick Montgomery (ed.), Minneapolis: Bethany Fellowship, 1976.

Gerald Brittle, *The Devil in Connecticut*, (New York, Bantam Books, 1983) 117-118.

[13] Rosemary Ellen Guiley, *The Encyclopedia of Ghosts and Spirits*, 2nd ed. (New York: Checkmark Books, Inc., 2000), 126.

[14] Ibid., 125.

[15] The rag doll "Annabelle" is now in the Warrens' occult museum behind protective glass. A priest, who challenged the power of the doll, met with a near-fatal car accident immediately following the incident. A young man who made the same challenge was not as lucky. He died in a motorcycle accident immediately following the incident. In both cases, the weather was clear and no other cars were involved. Yet, a mental image of the doll appeared just before the crashes, according to the priest and the boy's girlfriend, who survived the crash that killed him.

[16] Ford Fessenden, "Rampage Killers," *New York Times,* April 9, 2000, (National Section, Vol. CXLIX, No: 51,353): 1 & 28.

[17] Rob Waters, "The School that Stopped Bullies," *Reader's Digest,* (January 2003): 141-146.

[18] Aleksandr I. Solzhenitsyn, *The Cancer Ward,* (New York: Dell Publishing Co., Inc., 1968), 512-513.

[19] J.K. Rowling, *Harry Potter and the Chamber of Secrets* (New York: Scholastic Inc., 1999) 329.

[20] Rosemary Ellen Guiley, *The Encyclopedia of Ghosts and Spirits,* 2nd ed. (New York: Checkmark Books, Inc., 2000), 10.

[21] Ibid.

[22] She is referencing Padre "Pio," a pious Catholic priest and renowned exorcist from Italy who was beatified by the Church on May 2, 1999.

[23] Traced from actual drawings in the original letter. She allegedly made these drawings while her hand was controlled by another force. Note: The murderer in this true case turned out to be a dapper looking thin man who wore glasses and had the initials "R.P." She had no way of knowing it at the time, but evil would have known. Evil would have loved every minute of the crime and been eager to relive it. It may have even been involved, influencing or possessing the murderer.

[24] A scapular is two small pieces of cloth joined by strings, worn on the chest and back, under the clothes. It was originally worn as part of a monk's habit. Today it can also be a blessed

Roman Catholic religious medal, which can be substituted for the cloths.

[25] The "Promise" is that the wearer is "granted the peace of a happy death."

[26] Padre Pio was an Italian priest and renowned exorcist who was beatified in May 1999 ... the first step towards sainthood in the Roman Catholic Church.

[27] Excerpted from an article written by Paul B. Bartholomew, Whitehall, New York, "Bigfoot on the East Coast" for the *New England Journal for Psychic Research*, July/August 2000.

[28] From an interview with Clifford Sparks conducted by Paul Bartholomew at the Skene Valley Country Club on May 11, 1989.

[29] From an interview with Dr. Warren L. Cook conducted by Paul Bartholomew at Cook's Castleton, Vermont home on May 9, 1989.

[30] "How to Clean a Haunted Hotel" by Matthew Stadler, *NEST* Magazine, New York, NY, Spring 2001, pp. 139-149.

[31] Rosemary Ellen Guiley, *The Encyclopedia of Ghosts and Spirits*, 2nd ed. (New York: Checkmark Books, Inc., 2000), pp. 362-363.

[32] Ibid., 304

[33] Burkhard Bilger, "Waiting for Ghosts," *The New Yorker*, (12/23 & 30/02): 88.

[34] Hans Holzer, *Ghosts: True Encounters with the World Beyond*, (New York: Black Dog & Leventhal Publishers, Inc., 1997), 34.

[35] Rosemary Ellen Guiley, *The Encyclopedia of Ghosts and Spirits*, 2nd ed. (New York: Checkmark Books, Inc., 2000), 248.

[36] Ibid., 290.

[37] Ibid.

[38] Ibid.

[39] Ibid., 290-291.

[40] Ibid., 248-249, 291.

[41] Ibid., 291.

[42] Ibid., 248.

[43] Ibid.

[44] Hans Holzer, *Ghosts: True Encounters with the World Beyond*, (New York: Black Dog & Leventhal Publishers, Inc., 1997), 32.

[45] Ibid., 36.

NOTE: Dr. Moss is the professional who tested, validated, and measured Lorraine Warren's clairvoyance.

[46] Hans Holzer, *Ghosts: True Encounters with the World Beyond*, (New York: Black Dog & Leventhal Publishers, Inc., 1997), 36.

[47] Ibid., 33.

[48] Ibid., 32-33.

[49] Kurt Singer as told by Michael Gier, "A Murder Case," *Beyond Space and Time: An ESP Casebook*, ed. Martin Ebon (New York: The New American Library, Inc., 1967), 159-175.

[50] Hans Holzer, *Ghosts: True Encounters with the World Beyond*, (New York: Black Dog & Leventhal Publishers, Inc., 1997), 33.

[51] "Gleanings," *Newtown Bee*, (9/14/01): Sec. 1, p. 2.

[52] Hans Holzer, *Ghosts: True Encounters with the World Beyond*, (New York: Black Dog & Leventhal Publishers, Inc., 1997), 40.

[53] Ibid., 36.

[54] "Waiting for Ghosts," Burkhard Bilger, *The New Yorker*, (12/23 & 30/02), 98-99.

About the Authors

Cheryl Wicks, a published writer, is editor for the Warrens' *New England Society for Psychic Research (NESPR) Journal* and a former magazine publishing executive.

For more than fifty years, Lorraine Warren—a validated clairvoyant—and her husband Ed Warren—a respected demonologist—have been studying paranormal phenomena around the world. Their most famous case was Amityville, where they were the *only* psychic researchers invited to investigate the site shortly after the Lutz family fled the house in terror.

The Warrens are popular and respected lecturers and frequent guests on both television and radio. Their work has been the subject of hundreds of magazine and newspaper articles, two movies, and now ten books.

Printed in the United States
36923LVS00001B/39